Pro TypeScript

Application-Scale JavaScript Development

Steve Fenton

Apress®

Pro TypeScript: Application-Scale JavaScript Development

ISBN-13 (pbk): 978-1-4302-6791-1

ISBN-13 (electronic): 978-1-4302-6790-4

Publisher: Heinz Weinheimer
Lead Editor: Gwenan Spearing
Technical Reviewer: Mark Rendle and Basarat Ali Syed
Editorial Board: Steve Anglin, Mark Beckner, Ewan Buckingham, Gary Cornell, Louise Corrigan, Jim DeWolf,
    Jonathan Gennick, Jonathan Hassell, Robert Hutchinson, Michelle Lowman, James Markham,
    Matthew Moodie, Jeff Olson, Jeffrey Pepper, Douglas Pundick, Ben Renow-Clarke, Dominic Shakeshaft,
    Gwenan Spearing, Matt Wade, Steve Weiss
Coordinating Editor: Christine Ricketts
Copy Editor: Judy Ann Levine
Compositor: SPi Global
Indexer: SPi Global
Artist: SPi Global
Cover Designer: Anna Ishchenko

Distributed to the book trade worldwide by Springer Science+Business Media New York, 233 Spring Street, 6th Floor, New York, NY 10013. Phone 1-800-SPRINGER, fax (201) 348-4505, e-mail orders-ny@springer-sbm.com, or visit www.springeronline.com. Apress Media, LLC is a California LLC and the sole member (owner) is Springer Science + Business Media Finance Inc (SSBM Finance Inc). SSBM Finance Inc is a Delaware corporation.

For information on translations, please e-mail rights@apress.com, or visit www.apress.com.

Apress and friends of ED books may be purchased in bulk for academic, corporate, or promotional use. eBook versions and licenses are also available for most titles. For more information, reference our Special Bulk Sales–eBook Licensing web page at www.apress.com/bulk-sales.

Any source code or other supplementary materials referenced by the author in this text is available to readers at www.apress.com. For detailed information about how to locate your book's source code, go to www.apress.com/source-code/.

For Rebecca, Lily, Deborah, Victoria, and Mum

Contents at a Glance

Contents

About the Author

Steve Fenton has worked on large-scale JavaScript applications for over ten years, from online trading portals to cloud contact centers to health care decision support. He has been a vocal supporter of TypeScript since its release and wrote the first book on the TypeScript language in October 2012. As well as working full time in the health care industry, Steve has had an academic renaissance, first completing a national certificate in psychology and then enrolling in a distance learning course at Harvard. Steve currently lives in Basingstoke, United Kingdom with his wife Rebecca and daughter Lily. He can usually be found in his local coffee shop reading books on his two favorite topics: programming and psychology.

Acknowledgments

Many people helped me to write this book, both directly and indirectly. I am thankful to my team of reviewers, who patiently read my drafts, corrected my mistakes, and suggested improvements. If I introduced any errors after their reviews, I apologize sincerely. I am eternally grateful to Mark Jones, who has been my wingman on many projects; his constant support, encouragement, and friendship are priceless.

Martin Milsom and Dan Horrocks both contributed a keen eye for detail and a relentless enthusiasm that has helped me to maintain the momentum on this project. They both have a great future in software development.

Mark Rendle and Basarat Ali Syed applied their TypeScript expertise by reviewing the early chapters of this book. Their deep expert knowledge of the language and the related tools is an important part of this book and I appreciate the time they dedicated to it in their busy schedules, creating amazing software, speaking at conferences, writing books, and sharing their knowledge at user groups. Mark is the creator of the *zud.io* Azure Cloud Toolkit, which he wrote using TypeScript. Basarat is the author of *Beginning Node.js (Apress)*, due to be released shortly.

The Apress team has been both supportive and encouraging, happily directing my efforts throughout this project. My editor, Gwenan Spearing, has drastically improved my writing style; I believe this is my best work to date and I have her advice and guidance to thank for this. Christine Ricketts has helped me through the publishing process, showing me how to submit my drafts correctly and coordinating the project.

The open-source community has made a massive contribution to TypeScript, particularly the Definitely Typed project, creating hundreds of type definitions to make it easier for us all to use external libraries and frameworks within a TypeScript program. The team is expertly led by Boris Yankov, Diullei Gomes, and Basarat Ali Syed with notable contributions from Masahiro Wakame, Jason Jarrett, Bart van der Schoor, John Reilly, and Igor Oleinikov.

The TypeScript team has not only created a great language, they have also written a quality language specification and useful online articles to keep everyone updated on changes as they have been released. In particular, I'd like to thank Jonathan Turner for his articles, Luke Hoban for his videos, and Ryan Cavanaugh for answering my questions on specific details of the TypeScript language.

Introduction

Atwood's Law: any application that can be written in JavaScript will eventually be written in JavaScript.

—Jeff Atwood

TypeScript is a language created by Microsoft and released under an open-source Apache 2.0 License (2004). The language is focused on making the development of JavaScript programs scale to many thousands of lines of code. The language attacks the large-scale JavaScript programming problem by offering better design-time tooling, compile-time checking, and dynamic module loading at runtime.

As you might expect from a language created by Microsoft, there is excellent support for TypeScript within Visual Studio, but other development tools have also added support for the language, including WebStorm, Eclipse, Sublime Text, Vi, IntelliJ, and Emacs among others. The widespread support from these tools as well as the permissive open-source license makes TypeScript a viable option outside of the traditional Microsoft ecosystem.

The TypeScript language is a typed superset of JavaScript, which is compiled to plain JavaScript. This makes programs written in TypeScript highly portable as they can run on almost any machine—in web browsers, on web servers, and even in native applications on operating systems that expose a JavaScript API, such as WinJS on Windows 8 or the Web APIs on Firefox OS.

The language features found in TypeScript can be divided into three categories based on their relationship to JavaScript (see Figure 1). The first two sets are related to versions of the ECMA-262 ECMAScript Language Specification, which is the official specification for JavaScript. The ECMAScript 5 specification forms the basis of TypeScript and supplies the largest number of features in the language. The ECMAScript 6 specification adds modules for code organization and class-based object orientation, and TypeScript has included these since its release in October 2012. The third and final set of language features includes items that are not planned to become part of the ECMAScript standard, such as generics and type annotations. All of the TypeScript features can be converted into valid ECMAScript 5 and most of the features can be converted into the ancient ECMAScript 3 standard if required.

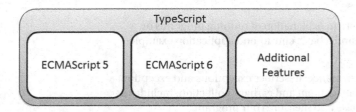

Figure 1. *TypeScript language feature sources*

Because TypeScript is such a close relative of JavaScript, you can consume the myriad existing libraries and frameworks written in JavaScript. Angular, Backbone, Bootstrap, Durandal, jQuery, Knockout, Modernizr, PhoneGap, Prototype, Raphael, Underscore, and many more are all usable in TypeScript programs. Correspondingly, once your TypeScript program has been compiled it can be consumed from any JavaScript code.

TypeScript's similarity to JavaScript is beneficial if you already have experience with JavaScript or other C-like languages. The similarity also aids the debugging process as the generated JavaScript correlates closely to the original TypeScript code.

If you still need to be convinced about using TypeScript or need help convincing others, I summarize the benefits of the language as well as the problems it can solve in the following. I also include an introduction to the components of TypeScript and some of the alternatives. If you would rather get started with the language straight away, you can skip straight to Chapter 1.

Who This Book Is For

This book is for programmers and architects working on large-scale JavaScript applications, either running in a browser, on a server, or on an operating system that exposes a JavaScript API. Previous experience with JavaScript or another C-like language is useful when reading this book, as well as a working knowledge of object orientation and design patterns.

Structure

This book is organized into nine chapters and four appendices.

Chapter 1: TypeScript Language Features: describes the language features in detail, from simple type annotations to important structural elements, with stand-alone examples of how to use each one.

Chapter 2: The Type System: explains the details of working within TypeScript's structural type system and describes the details on type erasure, type inference, and ambient declarations.

Chapter 3: Object Orientation in TypeScript: introduces the important elements of object orientation and contains examples of design patterns and SOLID principles in TypeScript. This chapter also introduces the concept of mixins with practical examples.

Chapter 4: Understanding the Runtime: describes the impact of scope, callbacks, events, and extensions on your program.

Chapter 5: Running TypeScript in a Browser: a thorough walk-through including working with the Document Object Model, AJAX, session and local storage, IndexedDB, geolocation, hardware sensors, and web workers as well as information on packaging your program for the web.

Chapter 6: Running TypeScript on a Server: an explanation of running programs on a JavaScript server with examples for Node and a basic end-to-end application example written in Express and Mongoose.

Chapter 7: Exceptions, Memory, and Performance: describes exceptions and exception handling with information on memory management and garbage collection. Includes a simple performance testing utility to exercise and measure your program.

Chapter 8: Using JavaScript Libraries: explains how to consume any of the millions of JavaScript libraries from within your TypeScript program, including information on how to create your own type definitions and convert your JavaScript program to TypeScript.

Chapter 9: Automated Testing: a walk-through of automated testing in your TypeScript program with examples written using the Jasmine framework.

Appendix 1: JavaScript Quick Reference: an introduction to the essential JavaScript features for anyone who needs to brush up on their JavaScript before diving into TypeScript.

Appendix 2: TypeScript Compiler: explains how to use the compiler on the command line and describes many of the flags you can pass to customize your build.

Appendix 3: Bitwise Flags: dives into the details of bitwise flags including the low-level details of how they work as well as examples using TypeScript enumerations.

Appendix 4: Coding Katas: introduces the concept of coding katas and provides an example for you to try, along with techniques you can use to make katas more effective.

The TypeScript Components

TypeScript is made up of three distinct but complementary parts, which are shown in Figure 2.

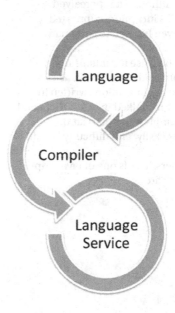

Figure 2. *The TypeScript components*

The language consists of the new syntax, keywords, and type annotations. As a programmer, the language will be the component you will become most familiar with. Understanding how to supply type information is an important foundation for the other components because the compiler and language service are most effective when they understand the complex structures you use within your program.

The compiler performs the type erasure and code transformations that convert your TypeScript code into JavaScript. It will emit warnings and errors if it detects problems and can perform additional tasks such as combining the output into a single file, generating source maps, and more.

The language service provides type information that can be used by development tools to supply autocompletion, type hinting, refactoring options, and other creative features based on the type information that has been gathered from your program.

Compile or Transpile?

The term *transpiling* has been around since the last century, but there is some confusion about its meaning. In particular, there has been some confusion between the terms *compilation* and *transpilation*. Compilation describes the process of taking source code written in one language and converting it into another language. Transpilation is a specific kind of compilation and describes the process of taking source code written in one language and transforming it into another language *with a similar level of abstraction*. So you might compile a high-level language into an assembly language, but you would transpile TypeScript to JavaScript as they are similarly abstracted.

Other common examples of transpilation include C++ to C, CoffeeScript to JavaScript, Dart to JavaScript, and PHP to C++.

Which Problems Does TypeScript Solve?

Since its first beta release in 1995, JavaScript (or LiveScript as it was known at the time it was released) has spread like wildfire. Nearly every computer in the world has a JavaScript interpreter installed. Although it is perceived as a browser-based scripting language, JavaScript has been running on web servers since its inception, supported on Netscape Enterprise Server, IIS (since 1996), and recently on Node. JavaScript can even be used to write native applications on operating systems such as Windows 8 and Firefox OS.

Despite its popularity, it hasn't received much respect from developers—possibly because it contains many snares and traps that can entangle a large program much like the tar pit pulling the mammoth to its death, as described by Fred Brooks (1975). If you are a professional programmer working with large applications written in JavaScript, you will almost certainly have rubbed up against problems once your program chalked up a few thousand lines. You may have experienced naming conflicts, substandard programming tools, complex modularization, unfamiliar prototypal inheritance that makes it hard to re-use common design patterns easily, and difficulty keeping a readable and maintainable code base. These are the problems that TypeScript solves.

Because JavaScript has a C-like syntax, it looks familiar to a great many programmers. This is one of JavaScript's key strengths, but it is also the cause of a number of surprises, especially in the following areas:

- Prototypal inheritance

- Equality and type juggling

- Management of modules

- Scope

- Lack of types

Typescript solves or eases these problems in a number of ways. Each of these topics is discussed in this introduction.

Prototypal Inheritance

Prototype-based programming is a style of object-oriented programming that is mainly found in interpreted dynamic languages. It was first used in a language called Self, created by David Ungar and Randall Smith in 1986, but it has been used in a selection of languages since then. Of these prototypal languages, JavaScript is by far the most widely known, although this has done little to bring prototypal inheritance into the mainstream. Despite its validity, prototype-based programming is somewhat esoteric; class-based object orientation is far more commonplace and will be familiar to most programmers.

TypeScript solves this problem by adding classes, modules, and interfaces. This allows programmers to transfer their existing knowledge of objects and code structure from other languages, including implementing interfaces, inheritance, and code organization. Classes and modules are an early preview of JavaScript proposals and because TypeScript can compile to earlier versions of JavaScript it allows you to use these features independent of support for the ECMAScript 6 specification. All of these features are described in detail in Chapter 1.

Equality and Type Juggling

JavaScript has always supported dynamically typed variables and as a result it expends effort at runtime working out types and coercing them into other types on the fly to make statements work that in a statically typed language would cause an error.

The most common type coercions involve strings, numbers, and Boolean target types. Whenever you attempt to concatenate a value with a string, the value will be converted to a string, if you perform a mathematical operation an attempt will be made to turn the value into a number and if you use any value in a logical operation there are special rules that determine whether the result will be true or false. When an automatic type conversion occurs it is commonly referred to as *type juggling*.

In some cases, type juggling can be a useful feature, in particular in creating shorthand logical expressions. In other cases, type juggling hides an accidental use of different types and causes unintended behavior as discussed in Chapter 1. A common JavaScript example is shown in Listing 1.

Listing 1. Type juggling

```
var num = 1;
var str = '0';

// result is '10' not 1
var strTen = num + str;

// result is 20
var result = strTen * 2;
```

TypeScript gracefully solves this problem by introducing type checking, which can provide warnings at design and compile time to pick up potential unintended juggling. Even in cases where it allows implicit type coercion, the result will be assigned the correct type. This prevents dangerous assumptions from going undetected. This feature is covered in detail in Chapter 2.

Management of Modules

If you have worked with JavaScript, it is likely that you will have come across a dependency problem. Some of the common problems include the following:

- Forgetting to add a script tag to a web page

- Adding scripts to a web page in the wrong order

- Finding out you have added scripts that aren't actually used

There is also a series of issues you may have come across if you are using tools to combine your scripts into a single file to reduce network requests or if you minify your scripts to lower bandwidth usage.

- Combining scripts into a single script in the wrong order

- Finding out that your chosen minification tool doesn't understand single-line comments

- Trying to debug combined and minified scripts

You may have already solved some of these issues using module loading as the pattern is gaining traction in the JavaScript community. However, TypeScript makes module loaders the normal way of working and allows your modules to be compiled to suit the two most prevalent module loading styles without requiring changes to your code. The details of module loading in web browsers are covered in Chapter 5 and on the server in Chapter 6.

Scope

In most modern C-like languages, the curly braces create a new context for scope. A variable declared inside a set of curly braces cannot be seen outside of that block. JavaScript bucks this trend by being functionally scoped, which means blocks defined by curly braces have no effect on scope. Instead, variables are scoped to the function they are declared in, or the global scope if they are not declared within a function. There can be further complications caused by the accidental omission of the var keyword within a function promoting the variable to the global scope. More complications are caused by *variable hoisting* resulting in all variables within a function behaving as if they were declared at the top of the function.

Despite some tricky surprises with scope, JavaScript does provide a powerful mechanism that wraps the current lexical scope around a function declaration to keep values to hand when the function is later executed. These closures are one of the most powerful features in JavaScript. There are also plans to add block level scope in the next version of JavaScript by using the let keyword, rather than the var keyword.

TypeScript eases scope problems by warning you about implicit global variables, provided you avoid adding variables to the global scope.

Lack of Types

The problem with JavaScript isn't that it has no types because each variable does have a type; it is just that the type can be changed by each assignment. A variable may start off as a string, but an assignment can change it to a number, an object, or even a function. The real problem here is that the development tools cannot be improved beyond a reasonable guess about the type of a variable. If the development tools don't know the types, the autocompletion and type hinting is often too general to be useful.

By formalizing type information, TypeScript allows development tools to supply specific contextual help that otherwise would not be possible.

Which Problems Are Not Solved

> *TypeScript is not a crutch any more than JSLint is a crutch. It doesn't hide JavaScript (as CoffeeScript tends to do).*

> — Ward Bell

TypeScript remains largely faithful to JavaScript. The TypeScript specification adds many language features, but doesn't attempt to change the ultimate style and behavior of the JavaScript language. It is just as important for TypeScript programmers to embrace the idiosyncrasies of the runtime as it is for JavaScript programmers. The aim of the TypeScript language is to make large-scale JavaScript programs manageable and maintainable. No attempt has been made to twist JavaScript development into the style of C#, Java, Python, or any other language (although it has taken inspiration from many languages).

Prerequisites

To benefit from the features of TypeScript, you'll need access to an integrated development environment that supports the syntax and compiler. The examples in this book were written using Visual Studio 2013, but you can use WebStorm/PHPStorm, Eclipse, Sublime Text, Vi, Emacs, or any other development tools that support the language; you can even try many of the simpler examples on the TypeScript Playground provided by Microsoft (2012).

From the Visual Studio 2013 Spring Update (Update 2), TypeScript is a first class language in Visual Studio. If you are using an older version you can download and install the TypeScript extension from Microsoft (2013). Although the examples in this book are shown in Visual Studio, you can use any of the development tools that were listed at the very start of this introduction.

It is also worth downloading and installing NodeJS (which is required to follow the example in Chapter 6) as it will allow you to access the Node Package Manager and the thousands of modules and utilities available through it. For example, you can use grunt-ts to watch your TypeScript files and compile them automatically each time you change them if your development tools don't do this for you.

Node is free and can be downloaded for multiple platforms from

```
http://nodejs.org/
```

TypeScript Alternatives

TypeScript is not the only alternative to writing to plain JavaScript. CoffeeScript is a popular alternative with a terse syntax that compiles to sensible JavaScript code. CoffeeScript doesn't offer many of the additional features that TypeScript offers, such as static type checking. It is also a very different language to JavaScript, which means you need to translate snippets of code you find online into CoffeeScript to use them. You can find out more about CoffeeScript on the official website

```
http://coffeescript.org/
```

Another alternative is Google's Dart language. Dart has much more in common with TypeScript. It is class-based, object oriented and offers optional types that can be checked by a static checker. Dart was originally conceived as a replacement for JavaScript, which could be compiled to JavaScript to provide wide support in the short term. It seems unlikely at this stage that Dart will get the kind of browser support that JavaScript has won, so the compile-to-JavaScript mechanism will remain core to Dart's future in the web browser. You can read about Dart on the official website for the language

```
https://www.dartlang.org/
```

There are also converters that will compile from most languages to JavaScript, including C#, Ruby, Java, and Haskell. These may appeal to programmers who are uncomfortable stepping outside of their primary programming language.

It is also worth bearing in mind that for small applications and web page widgets, you can defer the decision and write the code in plain JavaScript. With TypeScript in particular, there is no penalty for starting in JavaScript as you can simply paste your JavaScript code into a TypeScript file later on to make the switch.

Summary

TypeScript is an application-scale programming language that provides early access to proposed new JavaScript features and powerful additional features like static type checking. You can write TypeScript programs to run in web browsers or on servers and you can re-use code between browser and server applications.

TypeScript solves a number of problems in JavaScript, but respects the patterns and implementation of the underlying JavaScript language, for example, the ability to have dynamic types and the rules on scope.

You can use many integrated development environments with TypeScript, with several providing first class support including type checking and autocompletion that will improve your productivity and help eliminate mistakes at design time.

Key Points

- TypeScript is a language, a compiler, and a language service.

- You can paste existing JavaScript into your TypeScript program.

- Compiling from TypeScript to JavaScript is known specifically as transpiling.

- TypeScript is not the only alternative way of writing JavaScript, but it bears the closest resemblance to JavaScript.

CHAPTER 1

■ ■ ■

TypeScript Language Features

What if we could strengthen JavaScript with the things that are missing for large scale application development, like static typing, classes [and] modules...that's what TypeScript is about.

—Anders Hejlsberg

TypeScript is a superset of JavaScript. That means that the TypeScript language includes the entire JavaScript language plus a collection of useful additional features. This is in contrast to the various subsets of JavaScript and the various lint tools that seek to reduce the available features to create a smaller language with fewer surprises. This chapter will introduce you to the extra language features, starting with simple type annotations and progressing to more advanced features and structural elements of TypeScript. This chapter doesn't cover the features included in the ECMAScript 5 language specification so if you need a refresher on JavaScript take a look at Appendix 1.

The important thing to remember is that all of the standard control structures found in JavaScript are immediately available within a TypeScript program. This includes:

- Control flows
- Data types
- Operators
- Subroutines

The basic building blocks of your program will come from JavaScript, including if statements, switch statements, loops, arithmetic, logical tests, and functions. This is one of the key strengths of TypeScript—it is based on a language (and a family of languages) that is already familiar to a vast and varied collection of programmers. JavaScript is thoroughly documented not only in the ECMA-262 specification, but also in books, on developer network portals, forums, and question-and-answer websites.

Each of the language features discussed in this chapter has short, self-contained code examples that put the feature in context. For the purposes of introducing and explaining features, the examples are short and to the point; this allows the chapter to be read end-to-end. However, this also means you can refer back to the chapter as a reference later on. Once you have read this chapter, you should know everything you will need to understand the more complex examples described throughout the rest of the book.

JavaScript Is Valid TypeScript

Before we find out more about the TypeScript syntax, it is worth stressing this important fact: All JavaScript is valid TypeScript, with just a small number of exceptions, which are explained below. You can take existing JavaScript code, add it to a TypeScript file, and all of the statements will be valid. There is a subtle difference between valid code and error-free code in TypeScript; because, although your code may work, the TypeScript compiler will warn you about any potential problems it has detected.

1

If you transfer a JavaScript listing into a TypeScript file you may receive errors or warnings even though the code is considered valid. A common example comes from the dynamic type system in JavaScript wherein it is perfectly acceptable to assign values of different types to the same variable during its lifetime. TypeScript detects these assignments and generates errors to warn you that the type of the variable has been changed by the assignment. Because this is a common cause of errors in a program, you can correct the error by creating separate variables, by performing a type assertion, or by making the variable dynamic. There is further information on type annotations later in this chapter, and the type system is discussed in detail in Chapter 2.

Unlike some compilers that will only create output where no compilation errors are detected, the TypeScript compiler will still attempt to generate sensible JavaScript code. The code shown in Listing 1-1 generates an error, but the JavaScript output is still produced. This is an admirable feature, but as always with compiler warnings and errors, you should correct the problem in your source code and get a clean compilation. If you routinely ignore warnings, your program will eventually exhibit unexpected behavior. In some cases, your listing may contain errors that are so severe the TypeScript compiler won't be able to generate the JavaScript output.

Listing 1-1. Using JavaScript's "with" statement

```
// Not using with
var radius = 4;
var area = Math.PI * radius * radius;

// Using with
var radius = 4;
with (Math) {
    var area = PI * radius * radius;
}
```

■ **Caution**   The only exceptions to the "all JavaScript is valid TypeScript" rule are the with statement and vendor specific extensions, such as Mozilla's const keyword.

The JavaScript with statement in Listing 1-1 shows two examples of the same routine. Although the first calls Math.PI explicitly, the second uses a with statement, which adds the properties and functions of Math to the current scope. Statements nested inside the with statement can omit the Math prefix and call properties and functions directly, for example the PI property or the floor function.

At the end of the with statement, the original lexical scope is restored, so subsequent calls outside of the with block must use the Math prefix.

The with statement is not allowed in strict mode in ECMAScript 5 and in ECMAScript 6 classes and modules will be treated as being in strict mode by default. TypeScript treats with statements as an error and will treat all types within the with statement as dynamic types. This is due to the following:

- The fact it is disallowed in strict mode.

- The general opinion that the with statement is dangerous.

- The practical issues of determining the identifiers that are in scope at compile time.

So with these minor exceptions to the rule in mind, you can place any valid JavaScript into a TypeScript file and it will be valid TypeScript. As an example, here is the area calculation script transferred to a TypeScript file.

■ **Note**   The ECMAScript 6 specification, also known as "ES6 Harmony," represents a substantial change to the JavaScript language. The specification is still under development at the time of writing.

In Listing 1-2, the statements are just plain JavaScript, but in TypeScript the variables radius and area will both benefit from type inference. Because radius is initialized with the value 4, it can be inferred that the type of radius is number. With just a slight increase in effort, the result of multiplying Math.PI, which is known to be a number, with the radius variable that has been inferred to be a number, it is possible to infer the type of area is also a number.

Listing 1-2. Transferring JavaScript in to a TypeScript file

```
var radius = 4;
var area = Math.PI * radius * radius;
```

With type inference at work, assignments can be checked for type safety. Figure 1-1 shows how an unsafe assignment is detected when a string is assigned to the radius variable. There is a more detailed explanation of type inference in Chapter 2.

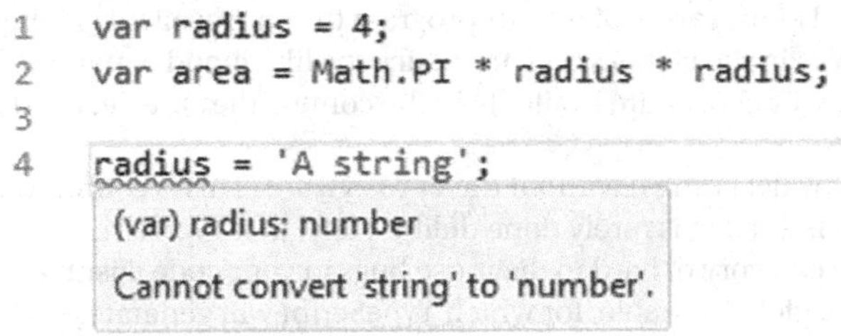

```
1    var radius = 4;
2    var area = Math.PI * radius * radius;
3
4    radius = 'A string';
```

(var) radius: number

Cannot convert 'string' to 'number'.

Figure 1-1. *Static type checking*

Variables

TypeScript variables must follow the JavaScript naming rules. The identifier used to name a variable must satisfy the following conditions.

The first character must be one of the following:

- an uppercase letter
- a lowercase letter
- an underscore
- a dollar sign
- a Unicode character from categories—*Uppercase letter* (Lu), *Lowercase letter* (Ll), *Title case letter* (Lt), *Modifier letter* (Lm), *Other letter* (Lo), or *Letter number* (Nl)

Subsequent characters follow the same rule and also allow the following:

- numeric digits

- a Unicode character from categories—*Non-spacing mark* (Mn), *Spacing combining mark* (Mc), *Decimal digit number* (Nd), or *Connector punctuation* (Pc)

- the Unicode characters U+200C (Zero Width Non-Joiner) and U+200D (Zero Width Joiner)

You can test a variable identifier for conformance to the naming rules using the JavaScript variable name validator by Mathias Bynens.

`http://mothereff.in/js-variables`

■ **Note** The availability of some of the more exotic characters can allow some interesting identifiers. You should consider whether this kind of variable name causes more problems than it solves. For example this is valid JavaScript: `var ಠ_ಠ = 'Dignified';`

Variables are functionally scoped. If they are declared at the top level of your program they are available in the global scope. You should minimize the number of variables in the global scope to reduce the likelihood of naming collisions. Variables declared inside of functions, modules, or classes are available in the context they are declared as well as in nested contexts.

In JavaScript it is possible to create a global variable by declaring it without the var keyword. This is commonly done inadvertently when the var keyword is accidentally missed; it is rarely done deliberately. In a TypeScript program, this will cause an error, which prevents a whole category of hard to diagnose bugs in your code. Listing 1-3 shows a valid JavaScript function that contains an implicit global variable, for which TypeScript will generate a `"Could not find symbol"` error. This error can be corrected either by adding the var keyword, which would make the variable locally scoped to the addNumbers function, or by explicitly declaring a variable in the global scope.

Listing 1-3. Implicit global variable

```
function addNumbers(a, b) {
    // missing var keyword
    total = a + b;
    return total;
}
```

Types

TypeScript is optionally statically typed; this means that types are checked automatically to prevent accidental assignments of invalid values. It is possible to opt out of this by declaring dynamic variables. Static type checking reduces errors caused by accidental misuse of types. You can also create types to replace primitive types to prevent parameter ordering errors, as described in Chapter 2. Most important, static typing allows development tools to provide intelligent autocompletion.

Figure 1-2 shows autocompletion that is aware of the variable type, and supplies a relevant list of options. It also shows the extended information known about the properties and methods in the autocompletion list. Contextual autocompletion is useful enough for primitive types—but most reasonable integrated development environments can replicate simple inference even in a JavaScript file. However, in a program with a large number of custom types, modules, and classes, the deep type knowledge of the TypeScript Language Service means you will have sensible autocompletion throughout your entire program.

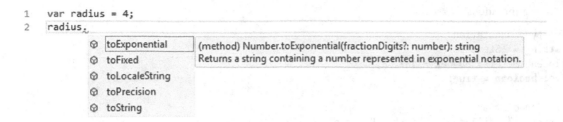

Figure 1-2. *TypeScript autocompletion*

Type Annotations

Although the TypeScript language service is expert at inferring types automatically, there are times when it isn't able to determine the type. There will also be times where you will wish to make a type explicit either for safety or readability. In all of these cases, you can use a type annotation to specify the type.

For a variable, the type annotation comes after the identifier and is preceded by a colon. Figure 1-3 shows the combinations that result in a typed variable. The most verbose style is to add a type annotation and assign the value. Although this is the style shown in many examples in this chapter, in practice this is the one you will use the least. The second variation shows a type annotation with no value assignment; the type annotation here is required because TypeScript cannot infer the type when there is no value present. The final example is just like plain JavaScript; a variable is declared and initialized on the same line. In TypeScript the type of the variable is inferred from the value assigned.

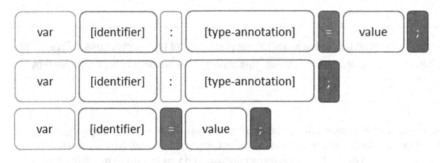

Figure 1-3. *Typed variable combinations*

To demonstrate type annotations in code, Listing 1-4 shows an example of a variable that has an explicit type annotation that marks the variable as a string. Primitive types are the simplest form of type annotation, but you are not restricted to such simple types.

Listing 1-4. Explicit type annotation

```
var name: string = 'Steve';
```

The type used to specify an annotation can be a primitive type, an array type, a function signature, or any complex structure you want to represent including the names of classes and interfaces you create. If you want to opt out of static type checking, you can use the special any type, which marks a variable's type as dynamic. No checks are made on dynamic types. Listing 1-5 shows a range of type annotations that cover some of these different scenarios.

Listing 1-5. Type annotations

```
// primitive type annotation
var name: string = 'Steve';
var heightInCentimeters: number = 182.88;
var isActive: boolean = true;

// array type annotation
var names: string[] = ['James', 'Nick', 'Rebecca', 'Lily'];

// function annotation with parameter type annotation and return type annotation
var sayHello: (name: string) => string;

// implementation of sayHello function
sayHello = function (name: string) {
    return 'Hello ' + name;
};

// object type annotation
var person: { name: string; heightInCentimeters: number; };

// Implementation of a person object
person = {
    name: 'Mark',
    heightInCentimeters: 183
};
```

■ **Note**   Although many languages specify the type before the identifier, the placement of type annotations in TypeScript after the identifier helps to reinforce that the type annotation is optional. This style of type annotation is also inspired by *type theory*.

If a type annotation becomes too complex, you can create an interface to represent the type to simplify annotations. Listing 1-6 demonstrates how to simplify the type annotation for the person object, which was shown at the end of the previous example in Listing 1-5. This technique is especially useful if you intend to reuse the type as it provides a re-usable definition. Interfaces are not limited to describing object types; they are flexible enough to describe any structure you are likely to encounter. Interfaces are discussed in more detail later in this chapter.

Listing 1-6. Using an interface to simplify type annotations

```
interface Person {
    name: string;
    heightInCentimeters: number;
}

var person: Person = {
    name: 'Mark',
    heightInCentimeters: 183
}
```

Primitive Types

Although the primitive types seem limited in TypeScript, they directly represent the underlying JavaScript types and follow the standards set for those types. String variables can contain a sequence of UTF-16 code units. A Boolean type can be assigned only the true or false literals. Number variables can contain a double-precision 64-bit floating point value. There are no special types to represent integers or other specific variations on a number as it wouldn't be practical to perform static analysis to ensure all possible values assigned are valid.

The any type is exclusive to TypeScript and denotes a dynamic type. This type is used whenever TypeScript is unable to infer a type, or when you explicitly want to make a type dynamic. Using the any type is equivalent to opting out of type checking for the life of the variable.

■ **Caution**   Before version 0.9 of TypeScript, the Boolean type was described using the `bool` keyword. There was a breaking change in the 0.9 TypeScript language specifications, which changed the keyword to `boolean`.

The type system also contains three types that are not intended to be used as type annotations but instead refer to the absence of values.

- The undefined type is the value of a variable that has not been assigned a value.

- The null type can be used to represent an intentional absence of an object value. For example, if you had a method that searched an array of objects to find a match, it could return null to indicate that no match was found.

- The void type is used only on function return types to represent functions that do not return a value or as a type argument for a generic class or function.

Arrays

TypeScript arrays have precise typing for their contents. To specify an array type, you simply add square brackets after the type name. This works for all types whether they are primitive or custom types. When you add an item to the array its type will be checked to ensure it is compatible. When you access elements in the array, you will get quality autocompletion because the type of each item is known. Listing 1-7 demonstrates each of these type checks.

Listing 1-7. Typed arrays

```
interface Monument {
    name: string;
    heightInMeters: number;
}

// The array is typed using the Monument interface
var monuments: Monument[] = [];

// Each item added to the array is checked for type compatibility
monuments.push({
    name: 'Statue of Liberty',
    heightInMeters: 46,
    location: 'USA'
});
```

```
monuments.push({
    name: 'Peter the Great',
    heightInMeters: 96
});

monuments.push({
    name: 'Angel of the North',
    heightInMeters: 20
});

function compareMonumentHeights(a: Monument, b: Monument) {
    if (a.heightInMeters > b.heightInMeters) {
        return -1;
    }
    if (a.heightInMeters < b.heightInMeters) {
        return 1;
    }
    return 0;
}

// The array.sort method expects a comparer that accepts two Monuments
var monumentsOrderedByHeight = monuments.sort(compareMonumentHeights);

// Get the first element from the array, which is the tallest
var tallestMonument = monumentsOrderedByHeight[0];

console.log(tallestMonument.name); // Peter the Great
```

There are some interesting observations to be made in Listing 1-7. When the monuments variable is declared, the type annotation for an array of Monument objects can either be the shorthand: Monument[] or the longhand: Array<Monument>—there is no difference in meaning between these two styles. Therefore, you should opt for whichever you feel is more readable. Note that the array is instantiated after the equals sign using the empty array literal ([]). You can also instantiate it with values, by adding them within the brackets, separated by commas.

The objects being added to the array using monuments.push(...) are not explicitly Monument objects. This is allowed because they are compatible with the Monument interface. This is even the case for the Statue of Liberty object, which has a location property that isn't part of the Monument interface. This is an example of structural typing, which is explained in more detail in Chapter 2.

The array is sorted using monuments.sort(...), which takes in a function to compare values. When the comparison is numeric, the comparer function can simply return a - b, in other cases you can write custom code to perform the comparison and return a positive or negative number to be used for sorting (or a zero if the values are the same).

The elements in an array are accessed using an index. The index is zero based, so the first element in the monumentsOrderedByHeight array is monumentsOrderedByHeight[0]. When an element is accessed from the array, autocompletion is supplied for the name and heightInMeters properties. The location property that appears on the Statue of Liberty object is not supplied in the autocompletion list as it isn't part of the Monument interface.

To find out more about using arrays and loops, refer to Appendix 1.

Enumerations

Enumerations represent a collection of named elements that you can use to avoid littering your program with hard-coded values. By default, enumerations are zero based although you can change this by specifying the first value, in which case numbers will increment from the specified value. You can opt to specify values for all identifiers if you wish to. In Listing 1-8 the VehicleType enumeration can be used to describe vehicle types using well-named identifiers throughout your program. The value passed when an identifier name is specified is the number that represents the identifier, for example in Listing 1-8 the use of the VehicleType.Lorry identifier results in the number 5 being stored in the type variable. It is also possible to get the identifier name from the enumeration by treating the enumeration like an array.

Listing 1-8. Enumerations

```
enum VehicleType {
    PedalCycle,
    MotorCycle,
    Car,
    Van,
    Bus,
    Lorry
}

var type = VehicleType.Lorry;

var typeName = VehicleType[type]; // 'Lorry'
```

In TypeScript enumerations are open ended. This means all declarations with the same name inside a common root will contribute toward a single type. When defining an enumeration across multiple blocks, subsequent blocks after the first declaration must specify the numeric value to be used to continue the sequence, as shown in Listing 1-9. This is a useful technique for extending code from third parties, in ambient declarations and from the standard library.

Listing 1-9. Enumeration split across multiple blocks

```
enum BoxSize {
    Small,
    Medium
}

//...

enum BoxSize {
    Large = 2,
    XLarge,
    XXLarge
}
```

■ **Note**   The term *common root* comes from graph theory. In TypeScript this term relates to a particular location in the tree of modules within your program. Whenever declarations are considered for merging, they must have the same fully qualified name, which means the same name at the same level in the tree.

Bit Flags

You can use an enumeration to define bit flags. Bit flags allow a series of items to be selected or deselected by switching individual bits in a sequence on and off. To ensure that each value in an enumeration relates to a single bit, the numbering must follow the binary sequence whereby each value is a power of two, e.g.,

---

1, 2, 4, 8, 16, 32, 64, 128, 256, 512, 1,024, 2,048, 4,096, and so on

---

Listing 1-10 shows an example of using an enumeration for bit flags. By default when you create a variable to store the state, all items are switched off. To switch on an option, it can simply be assigned to the variable. To switch on multiple items, items can be combined with the bitwise OR operator (|). Items remain switched on if you happen to include them multiple times using the bitwise OR operator. Bitwise Flags are explained in detail in Appendix 3.

Listing 1-10. Flags

```
enum DiscFlags {
        None = 0,
        Drive = 1,
        Influence = 2,
        Steadiness = 4,
        Conscientiousness = 8
}

// Using flags
var personality = DiscFlags.Drive | DiscFlags.Conscientiousness;

// Testing flags

// true
var hasD = (personality & DiscFlags.Drive) == DiscFlags.Drive;

// true
var hasI = (personality & DiscFlags.Influence) == DiscFlags.Influence;

// false
var hasS = (personality & DiscFlags.Steadiness) == DiscFlags.Steadiness;

// false
var hasC = (personality & DiscFlags.Conscientiousness) == DiscFlags.Conscientiousness;
```

Type Assertions

In cases in which TypeScript determines that an assignment is invalid, but you know that you are dealing with a special case, you can override the type using a type assertion. When you use a type assertion, you are guaranteeing that the assignment is valid in a scenario where the type system has found it not to be—so you need to be sure that you are right, otherwise your program may not work correctly. The type assertion precedes a statement, as shown in Listing 1-11. The avenueRoad variable is declared as a House, so a subsequent assignment to a variable declared as Mansion would fail. Because we know that the variable is compatible with the Mansion interface (it has all three properties required to satisfy the interface), the type assertion <Mansion> confirms this to the compiler.

Listing 1-11. Type assertions

```
interface House {
    bedrooms: number;
    bathrooms: number;
}

interface Mansion {
    bedrooms: number;
    bathrooms: number;
    butlers: number;
}

var avenueRoad: House = {
    bedrooms: 11,
    bathrooms: 10,
    butlers: 1
};

// Errors: Cannot convert House to Mansion
var mansion: Mansion = avenueRoad;

// Works
var mansion: Mansion = <Mansion>avenueRoad;
```

Although a type assertion overrides the type as far as the compiler is concerned, there are still checks performed when you assert a type. It is possible to force a type assertion, as shown in Listing 1-12, by adding an additional <any> type assertion between the actual type you want to use and the identifier of the variable.

Listing 1-12. Forced type assertions

```
var name: string = 'Avenue Road';

// Error: Cannot convert 'string' to 'number'
var bedrooms: number = <number> name;

// Works
var bedrooms: number = <number> <any> name;
```

Operators

All of the standard JavaScript operators are available within your TypeScript program. The JavaScript operators are described in Appendix 1. This section describes operators that have special significance within TypeScript because of type restrictions or because they affect types.

Increment and Decrement

The increment (++) and decrement (--) operators can only be applied to variables of type any, number, or enum. This is mainly used to increase index variables in a loop or to update counting variables in your program, as shown in Listing 1-13. In these cases you will typically be working with a number type. The operator works on variables with the any type, as no type checking is performed on these variables.

Listing 1-13. Increment and decrement

```
var counter = 0;

do {
    ++counter;
} while (counter < 10);

alert(counter); // 10
```

When incrementing or decrementing an enumeration, the number representation is updated. Listing 1-14 shows how incrementing the size variable results in the next element in the enumeration and decrementing the size variable results in the previous element in the enumeration. Beware when you use this method as you can increase and decrease the value beyond the bounds of the enumeration.

Listing 1-14. Increment and decrement of enumerations

```
enum Size {
    S,
    M,
    L,
    XL
}

var size = Size.S;
++size;
console.log(Size[size]); // M

var size = Size.XL;
--size;
console.log(Size[size]); // L

var size = Size.XL;
++size;
console.log(Size[size]); // undefined
```

Binary Operators

The operators in the following list are designed to work with two numbers. In TypeScript, it is valid to use the operators with variables of type number or any. Where you are using a variable with the any type, you should ensure it contains a number. The result of an operation in this list is always a number.

Binary operators: - * / % << >> >>> & ^ |

The plus (+) operator is absent from this list because it is a special case; a mathematical addition operator as well as a concatenation operator. Whether the addition or concatenation is chosen depends on the type of the variables on either side of the operator. As Listing 1-15 shows, this is a common problem in JavaScript programs in which an intended addition results in the concatenation of the two values, resulting in an unexpected value. This will be caught in a TypeScript program if you try to assign a string to a variable of the number type, or try to return a string for a function that is annotated to return a number.

Listing 1-15. Binary plus operator

```
// 6: number
var num = 5 + 1;

// '51': string
var str = 5 + '1';
```

The rules for determining the type resulting from a plus operation are

- If the type of either of the arguments is a `string`, the result is always a `string`.

- If the type of both arguments is either `number` or `enum`, the result is a `number`.

- If the type of either of the arguments is any, and the other argument is not a `string`, the result is any.

- In any other case, the operator is not allowed.

When the plus operator is used with only a single argument, it acts as a shorthand conversion to a number. This unary use of the plus operator is illustrated in Listing 1-16. The unary minus operator also converts the type to `number` and changes its sign.

Listing 1-16. Unary plus and minus operators

```
var str: string = '5';

// 5: number
var num = +str;

// -5: number
var negative = -str;
```

Bitwise Operators

Bitwise operators in TypeScript accept values of all types. The operator treats each value in the expression as a sequence of 32 bits and returns a number. Bitwise operators are useful for working with Flags, as discussed in the earlier section on Enumerations.

The full list of bitwise operators is shown in Table 1-1.

Table 1-1. *Bitwise Operators*

Operator	Name	Description
&	AND	Returns a result with a 1 in each position that both inputs have a 1.
|	OR	Returns a result with a 1 in each position where either input has a 1.
^	XOR	Returns a result with a 1 in each position where exactly one input has a 1.
<<	Left Shift	Bits in the left hand argument are moved to the left by the number of bits specified in the right hand argument. Bits moved off the left side are discarded and zeroes are added on the right side.

(continued)

13

Table 1-1. (*continued*)

Operator	Name	Description
>>	Right Shift	Bits in the left hand argument are moved to the right by the number of bits specified in the right hand argument. Bits moved off the right side are discarded and digits matching the left most bit are added on the left side.
>>>	Zero-fill Right Shift	Bits in the left hand argument are moved to the right by the number of bits specified in the right hand argument. Bits moved off the right side are discarded and zeroes are added on the left side.
~	NOT	Accepts a single argument and inverts each bit.

Logical Operators

Logical operators are usually used to test Boolean variables or to convert an expression into a Boolean value. This section explains how logical operators are used in TypeScript for this purpose, and also how logical AND and logical OR operators can be used outside of the context of Boolean types.

NOT Operator

The common use of the NOT (!) operator is to invert a Boolean value; for example, if (!isValid) conditionally runs code if the isValid variable is false. Using the operator in this way does not affect the type system.

The NOT operator can be used in TypeScript in ways that affect types. In the same way the unary plus operator can be used as a shorthand method for converting a variable of any type to a number, the NOT operator can convert any variable to a Boolean type. This can be done without inverting the truth of the variable by using a sequence of two unary NOT operators (!!). Both of these are illustrated in Listing 1-17. Traditionally, a single ! is used to invert a statement to reduce nesting in your code, whereas the double !! converts a type to a Boolean.

Listing 1-17. NOT operator

```
var truthyString = 'Truthy string';
var falseyString: string;

// False, it checks the string but inverts the truth
var invertedTest = ! truthyString;

// True, the string is not undefined or empty
var truthyTest = !! truthyString;

// False, the string is empty
var falseyTest = !! falseyString;
```

When converting to a Boolean using this technique, the JavaScript style type juggling rules apply. For this reason it is worth familiarizing yourself with the concepts of "truthy" and "falsey" that apply to this operation. The term *falsey* applies to certain values that are equivalent to false when used in a logical operation. Everything else is "truthy" and is equivalent to true. The following values are "falsey" and are evaluated as false

- undefined
- null

- `false: boolean`
- `'': string` (empty string)
- `0: number`
- NaN (the JavaScript Not a Number value)

All other values are evaluated as `true`. Surprising examples of this include:

- `'0': string`
- `'False': string`

This style of checking differs from other languages, but allows a rather powerful shorthand test of a variable as shown in Listing 1-18. Given that a variable can be `undefined` or `null`, and you probably don't want to check for both, this is a useful feature. If you want to perform a type-safe check with no juggling, you can use the three-character operators `===` or `!==`; for example, `if (myProperty === false)` tests that the type on both sides of the comparison are the same and their values are the same.

Listing 1-18. Shorthand Boolean test

```
var myProperty;

if (myProperty) {
    // Reaching this location means that...
    // myProperty is not null
    // myProperty is not undefined
    // myProperty is not boolean false
    // myProperty is not an empty string
    // myProperty is not the number 0
    // myProperty is not NaN
}
```

AND Operator

The common use of the logical AND operator (`&&`) is to assert that both sides of a logical expression are true, for example, `if (isValid && isRequired)`. If the left hand side of the expression is false (or is falsey, meaning it can be converted to false), the evaluation ends. Otherwise, the right hand side of the expression is evaluated.

The AND operator can also be used outside of a logical context because the right hand side of the expression is only evaluated if the left hand side is truthy. In Listing 1-19, the `console.log` function is only called if the console object is defined. In the second example the `player2` variable is only set if there is already a `player1` value. Where the result of the expression is assigned to a variable, the variable will always have the type of the right hand expression.

Listing 1-19. AND operator

```
// longhand
if (console) {
    console.log('Console Available');
}

// shorthand
console && console.log('Console Available');
```

15

```
var player1 = 'Martin';

// player2 is only defined if player1 is defined
var player2 = player1 && 'Dan';

// 'Dan'
alert(player2);
```

OR Operator

The common use of the logical OR (||) operator is to test that one of two sides to an expression are true. The left hand side is evaluated first and the evaluation ends if the left hand side is true. If the left hand side is not true, the right hand side of the expression is evaluated.

The less common use of the OR operator is to coalesce two values, substituting a value on the left with one on the right in cases where the left hand value is falsey. Listing 1-20 illustrates this usage. The result has the best common type between the two types in the expression. Best common types are explained in more detail in Chapter 2.

Listing 1-20. OR operator

```
// Empty strings are falsey
var errorMessages = '';

// result is 'Saved OK'
var result = errorMessages || 'Saved OK';

// Filled strings are truthy
errorMessages = 'Error Detected';

// result is 'Error Detected'
result = errorMessages || 'Saved OK';

var undefinedLogger;

// if the logger isn't initialized, substitute it for the result of the right-hand expression
var logger = undefinedLogger || { log: function (msg: string) { alert(msg); } };

// alerts 'Message'
logger.log('Message');
```

Short-Circuit Evaluation

Both the logical AND operator and the logical OR operator benefit from short-circuit evaluation. This means that as soon as the statement can be logically answered, evaluation stops. Whilst this saves the processing of the second statement, the real benefit is that it means you can ensure a value is defined before you use it.

In Listing 1-21, the if-statement would fail in a language that didn't support short-circuit evaluation because a property is being accessed on the caravan variable, which is undefined. Because an undefined variable is falsey, only the left hand of the expression needs to be evaluated to know that the whole expression is false, so the caravan.rooms property is never accessed.

Listing 1-21. Short-circuit evaluation

```
interface Caravan {
    rooms: number;
}

var caravan: Caravan;

if (caravan && caravan.rooms > 5) {
    //...
}
```

Conditional Operator

When you write an if-else statement that results in different values being assigned to the same variable (as shown in Listing 1-22), you can shorten your code using a conditional operator. The conditional operator is a shorthand way to assign one of two values based on a logical test, as illustrated in Listing 1-23. When a conditional operator is used in TypeScript, the result has the best common type between the two possible values. Best common types are described in Chapter 2.

Listing 1-22. The If-statement

```
var isValid = true;

// Long-hand equivalent
if (isValid) {
    message = 'Okay';
} else {
    message = 'Failed';
}
```

Listing 1-23. Conditional operator

```
var isValid = true;

// Conditional operator
var message = isValid ? 'Okay' : 'Failed';
```

Type Operators

There are a collection of operators available that can assist you when working with objects in JavaScript. Operators such as typeof, instanceof, in, and delete are particularly relevant to working with classes, you will find more information on these operators in the section on classes later in this chapter.

Functions

Now you have an understanding of the detailed minutia of types, you are ready to apply that knowledge to a subject that is right at the heart of a TypeScript program: functions. Although there are some interesting code organization options using classes and modules, functions are the building blocks of readable, maintainable, and re-usable code.

In TypeScript you are likely to find that most functions are actually written as methods that belong to a class. It makes sense to use modules and classes to organize your code into logical units. Whether you choose to use these structural elements, functions are improved by a number of TypeScript language features.

With variables, there is just a single location for a type annotation, which is directly after the identifier. With functions there are a number of places that can be annotated with type information. In Listing 1-24 you will see that each parameter can be given a type annotation. In the example in Listing 1-24, the getAverage function accepts three parameters and each one can have a different type. When the function is called, the type of each argument passed to the function is checked. The types are also known within the function, which allows sensible autocompletion suggestions and type checking inside the function body.

There is an additional type annotation outside of the parentheses that indicates the return type. In Listing 1-24 the function returns a string. Each return statement is checked against this annotation to ensure the return value is compatible with the return type. You can use the void type to indicate that the function does not return a value. This will prevent code inside the function from returning a value and stop calling code from assigning the result of the function to a variable.

Listing 1-24. Function type annotations

```
function getAverage(a: number, b: number, c: number): string {
    var total = a + b + c;
    var average = total / 3;
    return 'The average is ' + average;
}

var result = getAverage(4, 3, 8); // 'The average is 5'
```

Although it is possible to specify all of the types used in a function explicitly, you can rely on type inference rather than explicitly writing annotations for everything in your program. This is explained in detail in Chapter 2. For functions it is worth leaving out the return type unless the function returns no value. If you don't intend to return a value, an explicit void type will prevent a return value being added to a function at a later date that could break the design. In cases where a value is returned, TypeScript will check that all return statements are compatible with each other and issue the error "Could not find the best common type of types of all return statement expressions" if they are not.

Optional Parameters

In JavaScript, it is possible to call a function without supplying any arguments, even where the function specifies parameters. It is even possible in JavaScript to pass more arguments than the function requires. In TypeScript, the compiler checks each call and warns you if the arguments fail to match the required parameters in number or type.

Because arguments are thoroughly checked, you need to annotate optional parameters to inform the compiler that it is acceptable for an argument to be omitted by calling code. To make a parameter optional, suffix the identifier with a question mark, as shown in Listing 1-25, which is an updated version of the getAverage function, which accepts either two or three arguments.

Listing 1-25. Optional paramters

```
function getAverage(a: number, b: number, c?: number): string {
    var total = a;
    var count = 1;

    total += b;
    count++;
```

```
        if (typeof c !== 'undefined') {
            total += c;
            count++;
        }

        var average = total / count;
        return 'The average is ' + average;
}

var result = getAverage(4, 6); // 'The average is 5'
```

Optional parameters must be located after any required parameters in the parameter list. For example, the second parameter cannot be optional if the third parameter is required.

When you use an optional parameter you must check the value to see if it has been initialized. The typeof check is the common pattern for this check. If you used the shorthand check if (b), you would find that empty string and numeric zeroes would be treated as if the variable was undefined. The longer expression if (typeof b === 'undefined') avoids this by thoroughly checking the type and value.

Default Parameters

Default parameters are complementary to optional parameters. Wherever you consider using an optional parameter you should also consider the use of a default parameter as an alternative design. When you specify a default parameter, it allows the argument to be omitted by calling code and in cases where the argument is not passed the default value will be used instead.

To supply a default value for a parameter, assign a value in the function declaration as shown in Listing 1-26.

Listing 1-26. Default parameters

```
function concatenate(items: string[], separator = ',', beginAt = 0, endAt = items.length) {
        var result = '';

        for (var i = beginAt; i < endAt; i++) {
                result += items[i];
                if (i < (endAt - 1)) {
                        result += separator;
                }
        }

        return result;
}

var items = ['A', 'B', 'C'];

// 'A,B,C'
var result = concatenate(items);

// 'B-C'
var partialResult = concatenate(items, '-', 1);
```

The JavaScript code generated by default parameters includes a typeof check just as the one manually written for optional parameters in Listing 1-25. This means that the default parameters result in a check inside the function body that assigns the default value if no argument is passed. In the case of default parameters, though, these checks only appear in the output, which keeps the TypeScript code listing short and succinct. Because the checks are moved inside the function body, you can use a wide range of runtime values as default values—you aren't restricted to compile-time constants as you are in other languages. The default value could be calculated (as is the case for parameter endAt in Listing 1-26), or refer to any variable that could be accessed from within the function body.

Rest Parameters

Rest parameters allow calling code to specify zero or more arguments of the specified type. For the arguments to be correctly passed, rest parameters must follow these rules

- Only one rest parameter is allowed.

- The rest parameter must appear last in the parameter list.

- The type of a rest parameter must be an array type.

To declare a rest parameter, prefix the identifier with three periods and ensure that the type annotation is an array type, as shown in Listing 1-27.

Listing 1-27. Rest Parameters

```
function getAverage(...a: number[]): string {
    var total = 0;
    var count = 0;

    for (var i = 0; i < a.length; i++) {
        total += a[i];
        count++;
    }

    var average = total / count;
    return 'The average is ' + average;
}

var result = getAverage(2, 4, 6, 8, 10); // 'The average is 6'
```

Your function should expect to receive any number of arguments, including none. In your compiled JavaScript code, you will see that the compiler has added code to map the arguments list to your array variable within the method body.

■ **Note** If you require that at least one argument is passed, you would need to add a required parameter before the rest parameter to enforce this minimum requirement. This would be the correct signature for the getAverage function in Listing 1-27 to avoid a potential divide-by-zero error.

Overloads

I have deliberately covered optional, default, and rest parameters before introducing function overloads; in most cases you can write a method using parameter language features and avoid writing an overload. Where this isn't possible, you should consider writing separate, well-named functions that make their different intentions explicit. That isn't to say that there are no valid uses for function overloads and if you have considered the other options and chosen to use overloads that is a perfectly reasonable selection.

In many languages, each overload has its own implementation but in TypeScript the overloads all decorate a single implementation, as highlighted in Listing 1-28. The actual signature of the function appears last and is hidden by the overloads. This final signature is called an *implementation signature*. The implementation signature must define parameters and a return value that are compatible with all preceding signatures. As this implies, the return types for each overload can be different and the parameter lists can differ not only in types, but also in number of arguments. If an overload specifies fewer parameters than the implementation signature, the implementation signature would have to make the extra parameters optional, default, or rest parameters.

Listing 1-28. Overloads

```
function getAverage(a: string, b: string, c: string): string;
function getAverage(a: number, b: number, c: number): string;
// implementation signature
function getAverage(a: any, b: any, c: any): string {
    var total = parseInt(a, 10) + parseInt(b, 10) + parseInt(c, 10);
    var average = total / 3;
    return 'The average is ' + average;
}

var result = getAverage(4, 3, 8); // 5
```

When you call a function that has overloads defined, the compiler constructs a list of signatures and attempts to determine the signature that matches the function call. If there are no matching signatures the call results in an error. If one or more signature matches, the earliest of the matching signatures (in the order they appear in the file) determines the return type.

Overloads introduce a burden to the function as types may need to be tested or converted, and they may cause multiple logical branches within the function. In cases where the types are compatible and no additional code needs to be written within the function, overloads allow a single function to be used in multiple cases.

■ **Note** When you use overloads, the implementation signature cannot be called directly, so any calls must be compatible with one of the overloads.

Specialized Overload Signatures

Specialized overload signatures refer to the ability in TypeScript to create overloads based on string constants. Rather than the overloads being based on different parameters, they are based on the string value of an argument as shown in Listing 1-29. This allows a single implementation of a function to be re-used in many cases without requiring the calling code to convert the types.

Listing 1-29. Specialized overload signatures

```
class HandlerFactory {
    getHandler(type: 'Random'): RandomHandler;
    getHandler(type: 'Reversed'): ReversedHandler;
    getHandler(type: string): Handler; // non-specialized signature
    getHandler(type: string): Handler { // implementation signature
```

```
    switch (type) {
        case 'Random':
            return new RandomHandler();
        case 'Reversed':
            return new ReversedHandler();
        default:
            return new Handler();
    }
}
}
```

There are some rules to follow when using specialized overload signatures

- There must be at least one nonspecialized signature.

- Each specialized signature must return a subtype of a nonspecialized signature.

- The implementation signature must be compatible with all signatures.

The most common case for specialized signatures is that the nonspecialized signature returns a superclass, with each overload returning a more specialized subclass that inherits (or is structurally compatible with) the superclass. This is how the definition for the Document Object Model (DOM) method getElementsByTagName is declared in the TypeScript standard library, which means you get back an appropriately typed NodeList depending on the HTML tag name you pass to the function. An extract of this method signature is shown in Listing 1-30.

Listing 1-30. getElementsByTagName

```
// This example does not list all variations...
getElementsByTagName(name: "a"): NodeListOf<HTMLAnchorElement>;
getElementsByTagName(name: "blockquote"): NodeListOf<HTMLQuoteElement>;
getElementsByTagName(name: "body"): NodeListOf<HTMLBodyElement>;
getElementsByTagName(name: "button"): NodeListOf<HTMLButtonElement>;
getElementsByTagName(name: "form"): NodeListOf<HTMLFormElement>;
getElementsByTagName(name: "h1"): NodeListOf<HTMLHeadingElement>;
getElementsByTagName(name: string): NodeList; // Non-specialized signature
getElementsByTagName(name: string): NodeList { // implementation signature
    return document.getElementsByTagName(name);
}
```

When you write signatures that satisfy these rules, you may find that your implementation signature is identical to your nonspecialized signature. Remember that the implementation signature is hidden from calling code, so although it looks like duplication, it is necessary. This is illustrated in Listing 1-29, which shows how specialized subclasses are annotated as the return type where a specific value is passed in the type parameter.

This is an unusual technique, but is necessary for the purposes of defining the behavior you would expect from web browsers. The specialized overloads inspect the value being passed and select the overload based on that value, for example, if you pass a name argument with the value "blockquote", the second signature in Listing 1-31 will be matched and the return type is NodeListOf<HTMLQuoteElement>.

Listing 1-31. Arrow functions

```
var addNumbers = (a: number, b: number) => a + b;

var addNumbers = (a: number, b: number) => {
    return a + b;
}
var addNumbers = function (a: number, b: number) {
    return a + b;
}
```

Arrow Functions

TypeScript provides shorthand syntax for defining a function. The arrow function is inspired by proposed additions to the ECMAScript standard. Arrow functions allow you to leave out the function keyword and define your functions in an ultracompact way. All of the functions in Listing 1-31 result in identical JavaScript functions in the output when you target ECMAScript 3 or 5.

■ **Note**   The TypeScript compiler has options to target version 3 and version 5 of the ECMAScript specification and will support version 6 in the future. Version 4 of the ECMAScript specification was abandoned, so technically it doesn't exist.

Each of the addNumbers functions in Listing 1-31 defines a function that accepts two numbers and returns the sum of those numbers. In the shortest example, although there is no return keyword, the compiler will return the result of the single expression. If you want to write multiple expressions, you will need to wrap the function in braces and use the return keyword.

Sometimes the single expression to be returned by an arrow function will be an object, for example; { firstName: 'Mark', lastName: 'Rendle' }. The braces around the object declaration confuse the TypeScript compiler, so you need to mark it as an expression by surrounding it with parentheses, as shown in Listing 1-32.

Listing 1-32. Wrapping an object in parentheses

```
var makeName = (f: string, l: string) => ({first: f, last: l});
```

You can also use an arrow syntax to preserve the lexical scope of the this keyword. This is particularly useful when working with callbacks or events as these are two situations where you are likely to lose the current scope. This is discussed in more detail in the section on classes later in this chapter, but it is also useful outside of classes as shown in Listing 1-33.

Listing 1-33. Preserving scope with arrow syntax

```
var ScopeLosingExample = {
    text: "Property from lexical scope",
    run: function () {
        setTimeout(function() {
            alert(this.text);
        }, 1000);
    }
};

// alerts undefined
ScopeLosingExample.run();
```

```
var ScopePreservingExample = {
    text: "Property from lexical scope",
    run: function () {
        setTimeout(() => {
            alert(this.text);
        }, 1000);
    }
};

// alerts "Property from lexical scope"
ScopePreservingExample.run();
```

The ScopeLosingExample object uses the standard syntax to create the function that is called when the timer expires. The scope of this is lost when the function is invoked by the timer, so the value of this.text is undefined, as we are no longer in the object context. In the ScopePreservingExample the only change is the use of the arrow syntax, which fixes the scope problem and allows the correct value to be obtained.

Behind the scenes, the TypeScript compiler creates a variable named _this just before the arrow function is defined and sets its value to the current value of this. It also substitutes any usages of this within the function with the newly introduced _this variable, so the statement now reads _this.text in the JavaScript output. The use of the _this variable inside the function creates a closure around the variable, which preserves its context along with the function. You can follow this pattern yourself, which is useful if you ever need both the original meaning of this as well as the functionally scoped meaning of this, such as when you are handling events.

Interfaces

TypeScript interfaces can be used for several purposes. As you would expect, an interface can be used as an abstract type that can be implemented by concrete classes, but they can also be used to define any structure in your TypeScript program. Interfaces are also the building blocks for defining operations that are available in third-party libraries and frameworks that are not written in TypeScript. There is more detail on writing ambient declarations to define external code in Chapter 8.

Interfaces are declared with the interface keyword and contain a series of annotations to describe the contract that they represent. The annotations can not only describe properties and functions as you might expect, but also constructors and indexers. When writing interfaces to describe classes you intend to implement in your program, you won't need to define constructors or indexers. These features are included to help you describe external code with structures that may not be analogous to classes. This is discussed in Chapter 2.

Listing 1-34 demonstrates a set of interfaces to describe a vehicle, passengers, location, and destination. Properties and methods are declared using the familiar type annotations that have been used throughout this chapter. Constructors are declared using the new keyword.

Listing 1-34. Interfaces

```
interface Point {
        // Properties
        x: number;
        y: number;
}

interface Passenger {
        // Properties
        name: string;
}
```

```
interface Vehicle {
        // Constructor
        new() : Vehicle;

        // Properties
        currentLocation: Point;

        // Methods
        travelTo(point: Point);
        addPassenger(passenger: Passenger);
        removePassenger(passenger: Passenger);
}
```

Interfaces do not result in any compiled JavaScript code; this is due to type erasure, which is described in Chapter 2. Interfaces are used at design time to provide autocompletion and at compile time to provide type checking.

Just like enumerations, interfaces are open and all declarations with a common root are merged into a single interface. This means you must ensure that the combined interface is valid; you can't declare the same property in multiple blocks of the same interface (you'll receive a "duplicate identifier" error) and you can't define the same method (although you can add overloads to an existing one).

Declaring an interface in several blocks is not a particularly valuable feature when you are writing your own program, but when it comes to extending built-in definitions or external code, this feature is priceless. For example, Figure 1-4 shows the available items on a NodeList: the item method and the length property. The built-in interface definition for NodeList is shown in Listing 1-35; the length property, item method, and the indexer are all included.

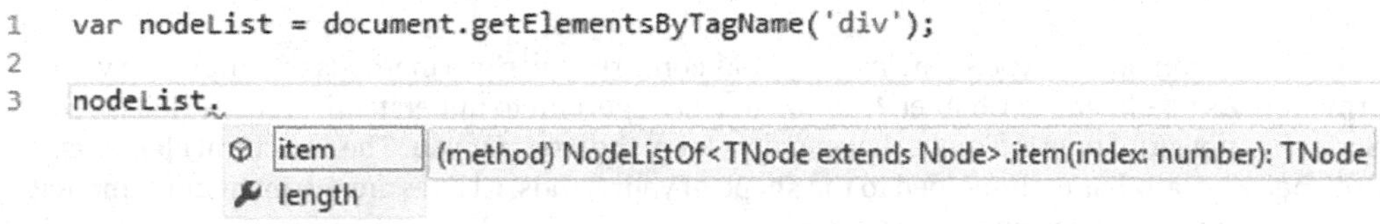

```
1    var nodeList = document.getElementsByTagName('div');
2
3    nodeList.
```

| | item | | (method) NodeListOf<TNode extends Node>.item(index: number): TNode |
| | length | | |

Figure 1-4. The native NodeList

Listing 1-35. Built-in NodeList interface

```
interface NodeList {
    length: number;
    item(index: number): Node;
    [index: number]: Node;
}
```

If interfaces were closed, you would be limited to the contract defined in the standard library that ships with TypeScript, but in Listing 1-36, an additional interface block extends the built-in NodeList interface to add an onclick property that is not available natively. The implementation isn't included in this example—it may be a new web standard that has yet to find its way into TypeScript's standard library or a JavaScript library that adds the additional functionality. As far as the compiler is concerned, the interface that is defined in the standard library and the interface that is defined in your TypeScript file are one interface. You can find out more about extending existing objects in Chapter 4, and about specifically extending native browser functionality in Chapter 5.

Listing 1-36 Extending the NodeList interface

```
interface NodeList {
    onclick: (event: MouseEvent) => any;
}

var nodeList = document.getElementsByTagName('div');

nodeList.onclick = function (event: MouseEvent) {
    alert('Clicked');
};
```

It is worth reiterating that interfaces can not only be used to describe a contract you intend to implement in a class, but also that interfaces can be used to describe any structure you can conceive in your program whether they are functions, variables, objects, or combinations thereof. When a method accepts an options object as a parameter, which is common in JavaScript frameworks such as jQuery, an interface can be used to provide autocompletion for the complex object argument.

There is one other slightly obscure feature related to interfaces in TypeScript that is worth keeping in mind. An interface can inherit from a class in the same way a subclass can inherit from a superclass. When you do this, the interface inherits all of the members of the class, but without any implementation. Anything added to the class will also be added to the interface. You'll find that this feature is particularly useful when used in conjunction with generics, which are explained later in this chapter.

Classes

Most of the preceding information on the TypeScript language has concerned various methods of annotating your code with type information. As you'll read in Chapter 2, although it is important to understand all the various type annotations, TypeScript has powerful type inference that can do a lot of the work for you. The structural elements, on the other hand, will become familiar tools molded to the shape of your hands. Classes are the most fundamental structural element when it comes to organizing you program.

There are quite a few aspects to learn when working with classes, but if you have any previous experience with class-based object orientation many of the features will be recognizable, even if the details or syntax are new.

Constructors

All classes in TypeScript have a constructor, whether you specify one or not. If you leave out the constructor, the compiler will automatically add one. For a class that doesn't inherit from another class, the automatic constructor will be parameterless and will initialize any class properties. Where the class extends another class, the automatic constructor will match the superclass signature and will pass arguments to the superclass before initializing any of its own properties.

Listing 1-37 shows two classes that have a manually written constructor. It is a slightly longer example than many of the other code listings in this chapter, but it is worth reading through it before each aspect is explained.

Listing 1-37. Constructors

```
class Song {
    constructor(private artist: string, private title: string) {

    }
```

```
    play() {
        console.log('Playing ' + this.title + ' by ' + this.artist);
    }
}

class Jukebox {
    constructor(private songs: Song[]) {
    }

    play() {
        var song = this.getRandomSong();
        song.play();
    }

    private getRandomSong() {
        var songCount = this.songs.length;
        var songIndex = Math.floor(Math.random() * songCount);

        return this.songs[songIndex];
    }
}

var songs = [
    new Song('Bushbaby', 'Megaphone'),
    new Song('Delays', 'One More Lie In'),
    new Song('Goober Gun', 'Stereo'),
    new Song('Sohnee', 'Shatter'),
    new Song('Get Amped', 'Celebrity')
];

var jukebox = new Jukebox(songs);

jukebox.play();
```

One of the first things that may strike you about the example is that the constructor parameters are not mapped to member variables. If you prefix a constructor parameter with an access modifier, such as private, it will automatically be mapped for you. You can refer to these constructor parameters as if they were declared as properties on the class, for example this.title, can be used anywhere within the Song class to obtain the song title on that instance. Listing 1-38 shows equivalent code where the parameters are manually mapped, but this is to illustrate the point that this creates a lot of redundant code, and you should avoid this approach.

Listing 1-38. Manually mapped constructor parameters

```
class Song {

    private artist: string;
    private title: string;

    constructor(artist: string, title: string) {
        this.artist = artist;
        this.title = title;
    }
```

```
    play() {
        console.log('Playing ' + this.title + ' by ' + this.artist);
    }
}
```

Access Modifiers

Access modifiers can be used to change the visibility of properties and methods within a class. By default, properties and methods are public—so you don't need to prefix properties and methods with the public keyword. You *do* need to prefix constructor parameters with the public keyword if you want them to be mapped to public properties automatically.

To hide a property or method, you prefix it with the private keyword. This restricts the visibility to within the class only, the member won't appear in autocompletion lists outside of the class and any external access will result in a compiler error. When you mark a class member as private, it can't even be seen by subclasses. If you need to access a property or method from a subclass, it must be made public. When you use the private access modifier, the TypeScript compiler will enforce the privacy of the member, but at runtime there will be no enforcement of the visibility because it would require an additional closure in every class with private members.

There are plans to introduce a protected keyword, which will make a class member available within the class and also the subclasses—but this feature is currently under consideration for release after TypeScript version 1.0. You can track this feature on the TypeScript Codeplex project: http://typescript.codeplex.com/workitem/125

Properties and Methods

Instance properties are typically declared before the constructor in a TypeScript class. A property definition consists of three parts; an optional access modifier, the identifier, and a type annotation. For example: public name: string; You can also initialize the property with a value: public name: string = 'Jane'; When your program is compiled, the property initializers are moved into the constructor. Instance properties can be accessed from within the class using the this keyword. If the property is public it can be accessed using the instance name.

You can also add static properties to your class, which are defined in the same way as instance properties, but with the static keyword between the access modifier (if one is specified) and the identifier. Static properties are accessed using the class name as shown in Listing 1-39, where the static maxSongCount property is accessed using Playlist.maxSongCount—even within a method on the class; this is because the property is not defined on each instance.

Listing 1-39. Properties and methods

```
class Playlist {

    private songs: Song[] = [];

    static maxSongCount: number = 30;

    constructor(public name: string) {
    }

    addSong(song: Song) {
        if (this.songs.length >=Playlist.maxSongCount) {
            throw new Error('Playlist is full');
        }

        this.songs.push(song);
    }
}
```

```typescript
// Creating a new instance
var playlist = new Playlist('My Playlist');

// Accessing a public instance property
var name = playlist.name;

// Calling a public instance method
playlist.addSong(new Song('Therapy?', 'Crooked Timber'));

// Accessing a public static property
var maxSongs = Playlist.maxSongCount;
```

Listing 1-39 also illustrates a typical method definition. Methods are defined a lot like functions, but they leave out the `function` keyword. You can annotate a method with all of the parameters and return value type annotations that were discussed earlier in the section on functions. You can prefix the method name with an access modifier to control its visibility, which is public by default. Just as with instance properties, methods can be accessed from within the class using the `this` keyword and if they are public they can be accessed outside of the class using the instance name.

You can create static methods by prefixing the method name with the `static` keyword. Static members can be called even when no instance of the class has been created and only a single instance of each static member exists in your program. All static members are accessed via the class name and not an instance name and static members have no access to nonstatic properties or methods.

TypeScript supports property getters and setters, as long as you are targeting ECMAScript 5 or above. The syntax for these is identical to method signatures as described in the following, except they are prefixed by either the get or set keyword. As shown in Listing 1-40, property getters and setters allow you to wrap property access with a method while preserving the appearance of a simple property to the calling code.

Listing 1-40. Property getters and setters

```typescript
interface StockItem {
        description: string;
        asin: string;
}

class WarehouseLocation {
        private _stockItem;

        constructor(public aisle: number, public slot: string) {

        }

        get stockItem() {
                return this._stockItem;
        }

        set stockItem(item: StockItem) {
                this._stockItem = item;
        }
}
```

```
var figure = { asin: 'B001TEQ2PI', description: 'Figure' };

var warehouseSlot = new WarehouseLocation(15, 'A6');

warehouseSlot.stockItem = figure;
```

Class Heritage

There are two types of class heritage in TypeScript. A class can implement an interface using the implements keyword and a class can inherit from another class using the extends keyword.

When you implement an interface, the implements declaration is entirely optional due to the structural types in TypeScript. If you do specify the interface using the implements keyword, your class will be checked to ensure that it complies with the contract promised by the interface. Listing 1-41 shows how the Song class implements the Audio interface. The play method must be implemented in the Song class, and its signature must be compatible with the Audio interface declaration. A class can implement multiple interfaces, with each interface being separated by a comma, for example: implements Audio, Video.

Listing 1-41. Class heritage

```
interface Audio {
    play(): any;
}

class Song implements Audio {
    constructor(private artist: string, private title: string) {
    }

    play() : void {
        console.log('Playing ' + this.title + ' by ' + this.artist);
    }

    static Comparer(a: Song, b: Song) {
        if (a.title === b.title) {
            return 0;
        }

        return a.title > b.title ? 1 : -1;
    }
}

class Playlist {
    constructor(public songs: Audio[]) {
    }

    play() {
        var song = this.songs.pop();
        song.play();
    }
```

```
    sort() {
        this.songs.sort(Song.Comparer);
    }
}

class RepeatingPlaylist extends Playlist {

    private songIndex = 0;

    constructor(songs: Song[]) {
        super(songs);
    }

    play() {
        this.songs[this.songIndex].play;

        this.songIndex++;

        if (this.songIndex >=this.songs.length) {
            this.songIndex = 0;
        }
    }
}
```

■ **Note**   A method on a class can have fewer parameters than the interface specifies. This allows a class to ignore arguments that it doesn't require to execute the method. Any parameters that are specified must match the parameters in the interface.

You inherit from a class using the extends keyword, as shown in Listing 1-41. An extends clause makes your class a derived class, and it will gain all of the properties and methods of the base class from which it inherits. You can override a public member of the base class by adding a member of the same name and kind as the base class member. The RepeatingPlaylist inherits from the Playlist class and uses the songs property from the base class using this.songs, but overrides the play method with a specialized implementation that plays the next song in a repeating loop.

The constructor on the RepeatingPlaylist class shown in Listing 1-41 could be omitted because the automatic constructor that would be generated would match it exactly.

If the subclass accepts additional arguments there are a couple of rules you need to follow. The super call to the base class must be the first statement in the subclass constructor and you cannot specify an access modifier for a parameter on the subclass if it has an access modifier on the base class.

There are some rules that must be followed for inheritance

- A class can only inherit from a single superclass.

- A class cannot inherit from itself, either directly or via a chain of inheritance.

It is possible to create a class that inherits from another class and also implements multiple interfaces. In this case, the class must be a subtype of the base class as well as each interface.

Scope

If you call a class method from an event, or use it as a callback, the original context of the method can be lost, which results in problems using instance methods and instance properties. When the context is changed, the value of the this keyword is lost.

Listing 1-42 shows a typical example of lost context. If the registerClick method is called directly against the clickCounter instance, it works as expected. When the registerClick method is assigned to the onclick event, the context is lost and this.count is undefined in the new context.

Listing 1-42. Lost context

```
class ClickCounter {
    private count = 0;

    registerClick() {
        this.count++;
        alert(this.count);
    }
}

var clickCounter = new ClickCounter();

document.getElementById('target').onclick = clickCounter.registerClick;
```

There are several techniques that can be used to preserve the context to enable this to work, and you may choose to use different approaches in different scenarios.

Property and Arrow Function

You can replace the method with a property and initialize the property using an arrow function as shown in Listing 1-43. This is a reasonable technique if you know that the class will be consumed with events or callbacks, but it is less of an option if your class has no knowledge of when and where it may be called.

Listing 1-43. Preserving context with a property and an arrow function

```
class ClickCounter {
    private count = 0;

    registerClick = () => {
        this.count++;
        alert(this.count);
    }
}
```

Function Wrapping at Point of Call

If you want to leave your class untouched, you can wrap the call to the instance method in a function to create a closure that keeps the context alongside the function. This is demonstrated in Listing 1-44, which allows the use of this within the registerClick method without converting the method to a property.

Listing 1-44. Preserving context with a closure

```
document.getElementById('target').onclick = function () {
        clickCounter.registerClick();
};
```

ECMAScript 5 Bind Function

Another technique that leaves the original class untouched is to use JavaScript's bind function, which is available in ECMAScript 5 and higher. The bind function permanently sets the context for the method. It can be used more generally to permanently replace the context, but in Listing 1-45 it is used to fix the context for the registerClick method to be the clickCounter instance.

Listing 1-45. Preserving context with bind

```
var clickHandler = clickCounter.registerClick.bind(clickCounter);

document.getElementById('target').onclick = clickHandler;
```

Choosing a Solution

There are several techniques you can use to ensure that your context is preserved when using a class instance method for callbacks and events. There are no fixed rules about which of these is the correct one to use; it depends on the specific use and your own design preferences.

If you are targeting slightly older browsers, the bind function may not be an option, but if older browsers aren't an issue you may find it more graceful than a closure and it certainly makes your intent much clearer. The property and arrow-function technique is a neat trick, but perhaps allows too much knowledge of where the method is called to leak into your class.

One thing to take into account when designing your program will be the number of instances of each class being created at runtime. If you are creating hundreds or thousands of instances it is more efficient for the methods to be normal instance methods, not arrow functions assigned to properties. This is because normal instance methods are defined once and used by all instances. If you use a property and arrow function, it will be duplicated on every instance. This duplication can become a big overhead when a large number of instances are created.

Type Information

Obtaining types at runtime is a topic to be treated with some care. If your program tests types to control the flow of the program, you should be hearing alarm bells in your head. Checking types and branching off in different directions based on the type is a strong indicator that you have broken encapsulation. With this in mind, the following section describes how you can check types and obtain type names at runtime.

To test the type of a class instance, you use the instanceof operator. The operator is placed between the instance and the type you want to test, as shown in listing 1-46. The test returns true if you have an instance of the specified class, or if the specified class appears anywhere in the inheritance chain. In all other cases, it returns false.

Listing 1-46. Using the instanceof operator

```
class Display {
    name: string = '';
}

class Television extends Display {

}

class HiFi {

}

var display = new Display();
var television = new Television();
var hiFi = new HiFi();

var isDisplay;

// true
isDisplay = display instanceof Display;

// true (inherits from Display)
isDisplay = television instanceof Display;

// false
isDisplay = hiFi instanceof Display;
```

You can also test the presence of specific properties using the in keyword. Expanding on the previous example from Listing 1-46, we can test for the presence of a name property as shown in Listing 1-47. The in operator will return true if the class has the property or if it inherits from a class that has the property.

Listing 1-47. The in property

```
var hasName;

// true
hasName = 'name' in display;

// false
hasName = 'name' in television;

// true
hasName = 'name' in hiFi;
```

It is important to note that due to the code generation in the TypeScript compiler, an uninitialized property will not be detected because unless the property has a value, it does not appear in the compiled JavaScript code. In Listing 1-48 the hasName property will be false because, although a name property is declared, the name property is never initialized. If the name property had been assigned a value, hasName would be true.

Listing 1-48. Uninitialized property

```
class Display {
    name: string;
}

var display = new Display();

// false
var hasName = 'name' in display;
```

■ **Note**   Don't forget the quotes around the property name when using the in keyword as you will need to pass a string. Without the quotes, you would be testing the value of a variable, which may not even be defined.

If you want to obtain the type name at runtime, you may be tempted to use the typeof operator. Unfortunately, this will return the type name 'object' for all classes. This means you need to inspect the constructor of the instance to find the type name. This can be done using a regular expression as shown in Listing 1-49. The static Describer.getName method can be used to obtain the class name of any instance in your program.

Listing 1-49. Obtaining runtime types

```
class Describer {
    static getName(inputClass) {
        // RegEx to get the class name
        var funcNameRegex = /function (.{1,})\(/;

        var results = (funcNameRegex).exec((<any> inputClass).constructor.toString());

        return (results && results.length > 1) ? results[1] : '';
    }
}

var tv = new Television();
var radio = new HiFi();

var tvType = Describer.getName(tv); // Television
var radioType = Describer.getName(radio); // HiFi
```

Modules

While classes are the most important structural element for code organization, because they lend themselves to common design patterns, modules are the most fundamental structural element when it comes to file organization and dynamically loading slices of your program. While modules give you some of the convenience of name spacing, their purpose is much more deliberate in TypeScript as they facilitate module loading.

There are two popular standards for loading modules at runtime. CommonJS is a framework class library for JavaScript and has a pattern for loading modules. There are many implementations of CommonJS designed both for servers and browsers. AMD (Asynchronous Module Definition) is simply an API for defining modules and is a popular style of loading modules in web browsers because of the asynchronous pattern.

Internal modules enclose their members within a function that limits their scope. The internal module name is added to the global scope and the exported members can be accessed via this globally scoped module identifier. External modules add nothing to the global scope. Instead, the members of an external module are made available via an alias when using CommonJS or limited to the scope of a callback function when using AMD.

There is further detail on module loading in web browsers using AMD in Chapter 5 and module loading on the server with CommonJS in Chapter 6.

Internal Modules

Internal modules can be used to group related features together. Each internal module is a singleton instance with all of the module's contents enclosed within the module's scope. By grouping variables, functions, objects, classes, and interfaces into modules, you can keep them out of the global scope and avoid naming collisions.

Modules are open ended and all declarations with the same name within a common root contribute toward a single module. This allows internal modules to be described in multiple files and will allow you to keep each file to a maintainable size.

Whereas class members are public by default, the content of a module body is hidden by default. To make an item available to code outside of the module body, you must prefix the item with the export keyword, as shown in Listing 1-50, where the Ship interface and Ferry class are the only items visible outside of the module.

Listing 1-50. Exporting from a module

```
module Shipping {

    // Available as Shipping.Ship
    export interface Ship {
        name: string;
        port: string;
        displacement: number;
    }

    // Available as Shipping.Ferry
    export class Ferry implements Ship {
        constructor(
            public name: string,
            public port: string,
            public displacement: number) {
        }
    }

    // Only available inside of the Shipping module
    var defaultDisplacement = 4000;

    class PrivateShip implements Ship {
        constructor(
            public name: string,
            public port: string,
            public displacement: number = defaultDisplacement) {
        }
    }

}

var ferry = new Shipping.Ferry('Assurance', 'London', 3220);
```

Although the export keyword makes module members available outside of the module, an import statement can be used within an internal module to provide an alias for another module or one of its members. In Listing 1-51 the Ship interface within the Shipping module is imported under the alias Ship. The alias can then be used throughout the Docking module as a short name, so wherever Ship appears within the module, it refers to Shipping.Ship. This is particularly useful if you have long module names or deep nesting in your program as it allows you to reduce the length of annotations.

Listing 1-51. Importing a module

```
module Docking {
    import Ship = Shipping.Ship;

    export class Dock {
        private dockedShips: Ship[] = [];

        arrival(ship: Ship) {
            this.dockedShips.push(ship);
        }
    }
}

var dock = new Docking.Dock();
```

Module names can contain periods. This allows you to create a naming hierarchy that acts like a namespace. For example, the following module names are all valid

- ```module Transport.Maritime.Shipping { //...```
- ```module Transport.Maritime.Docking { //...```
- ```module Transport.Railways.Ticketing { //...```

You do not need to have a Transport module for this to work (although you could if you wanted one); there will appear to be a Transport module that contains a Maritime module and a Railways module when autocompletion is shown. The naming allows features to be discovered logically using autocompletion. When you design your program structure, the discoverability of the features through autocompletion should be high on the list of factors that influence your naming.

Internal modules don't benefit from automatic module loading as external modules do. You are free to implement your own method of loading scripts. On a scale of elegance from least graceful to most, you could use any of the following options:

- Include each file in a script tag in your web page.

- Compile the program into a single file and include it using a script tag.

- Compile the program into a single file, minify it, and include it using a script tag.

- Switch to external modules and use a module loader.

The final two options are actually both valid depending on the size of your program. There is a threshold you may reach where internal modules just aren't a viable option any longer due to your program size. If your program becomes this large, loading smaller parts of the program as you need them may be the best bet and you are better off using external modules for this. For programs that can be combined and minified into a reasonably small file, internal modules can work well and result in fewer HTTP requests.

In some integrated development environments, the modules are recognized automatically and assumed to be present at runtime, which means in any given TypeScript file you will find autocompletion and type checking for all of the code in your program. In tools that don't automatically look for dependent files, you can supply a hint using a reference comment. Listing 1-52 shows the reference comment required to make the Shipping module visible within the Docking module.

Listing 1-52. Reference comments

```
///<reference path="Shipping.ts" />

module Docking {
    import Ship = Shipping.Ship;

    export class Dock {
        private dockedShips: Ship[] = [];

        arrival(ship: Ship) {
            this.dockedShips.push(ship);
        }
    }
}
```

■ **Tip**   Remember that with some development tools; reference comments are optional.

If you are compiling your project into a single file using the TypeScript compiler, the reference comments serve an additional purpose of helping the compiler to order your output correctly, based on the dependencies. You can read more about using the TypeScript compiler to generate a combined single output file in Appendix 2.

External Modules

External modules are the key to scaling really big programs. Although you can combine and minify all of your JavaScript files to squash the size of a program, ultimately this will not scale forever. If you are working on a seriously large application, external modules and module loading are both indispensable tools.

External modules have a name that matches the path of the source file, without the file extension. Listing 1-53 recreates the Shipping module, but using external modules rather than internal modules. The export keyword is used to make members available outside of the module.

Listing 1-53. External modules: Shipping.ts

```
export interface Ship {
    name: string;
    port: string;
    displacement: number;
}

export class Ferry implements Ship {
    constructor(
        public name: string,
        public port: string,
        public displacement: number) {
    }
}
```

```
var defaultDisplacement = 4000;

class PrivateShip implements Ship {
    constructor(
        public name: string,
        public port: string,
        public displacement: number = defaultDisplacement) {
    }
}
```

■ **Tip**   When using external modules, you don't need to wrap your code in a `module` block because the module is represented by the file.

To use an external module, you use an `import` statement along with a call to the `require` function as demonstrated in Listing 1-54. This is an important line of code in your program because it will be converted into code that loads your module at runtime. The `require` function accepts a string that represents the path to your source file, but without the file extension (i.e., no ".ts" on the end).

Listing 1-54. Importing external modules

```
import Shipping = require('./Shipping');

export class Dock {
    private dockedShips: Shipping.Ship[] = [];

    arrival(ship: Shipping.Ship) {
        this.dockedShips.push(ship);
    }
}
```

To organize your program, you can use a folder structure that represents your namespaces. You will only ever state this full path inside of an `import` statement, so the length shouldn't be a problem. All of the other code that references an external module will refer to it by the alias given in the `import` statement.

- ./Transport/Maritime/Shipping

- ./Transport/Maritime/Docking

- ./Transport/Railways/Ticketing

Module Loading

Module loading comes in two flavors. CommonJS is the pattern of choice for NodeJS and a program using CommonJS will simply load a module each time the `require` function is called. Execution of the program continues once the module is loaded. AMD also loads a module each time the `require` function is called. Rather than pausing execution while the file loads, AMD passes the code as a callback. The callback is executed once the module has been loaded, allowing other code to be executed in the interim.

You can tell the TypeScript compiler which pattern you will use for module loading and it will generate the appropriate JavaScript output. You can read more detail about all of the compiler flags, including the module type in Appendix 2. A comparison of the two different output styles is shown in Listing 1-55.

Listing 1-55. JavaScript output for module loading

```
// CommonJS style
var dependency = require("./CommonJSDependency");
// your code

// AMD style
define(["require", "exports", 'AmdDependency'], function (require, exports, __dependency__) {
    var dependency = __dependency__;
    // your code} );
```

In the CommonJS example, your code is placed after the dependency. Execution pauses until the module is loaded. In the AMD example, your code is wrapped in a callback function that is executed when the module has loaded.

Export Assignments

Although the term *module loading* is used to describe loading source file dependencies, the result of the import is not restricted to modules. You can specify any module member to be used in place of the module using an export assignment. Only one export assignment can be used within a source file.

You can substitute a module with a variable, object, function, interface, or class. Listing 1-56 replaces the module with the greet function. When this module is imported, the alias will be a direct reference to the function, which shortens the calling code as you no longer have navigate via the module alias name to get to the greet function, you can simply execute the alias as the function.

Listing 1-56. Export assignments

```
function greet(name: string): void {
    console.log('Hello ' + name);
}

export = greet;
```

Listing 1-57 shows the statement that imports the greet module and gives it an alias of hello. Because of the export statement in the greet module, the hello alias is a direct reference to the greet function, not to the whole module. This would still be the case even if the module contained other blocks of code such as interfaces and classes as the export declaration replaces the module.

Listing 1-57. Calling the greet function

```
import hello = require('./scripts/greet');

hello('Mark'); // instead of hello.greet('Mark');
```

Module Merging

This section describes a feature that can be used with care to create special relationships between functions and modules and between classes and modules. Listing 1-58 demonstrates merging between a class and a module, but it works identically with a function and a module. In all cases, the module must appear after the class or function for the merge to work.

Listing 1-58. Class and module merging

```
// Class/Module Merging
class Car {

}

module Car {
    export class Engine {

    }

    export class GloveBox {

    }

}

var car = new Car();
var engine = new Car.Engine();
var gloveBox = new Car.GloveBox();
```

The main use of this would be to logically group subcomponents below a master component and have the master component as well as all subcomponents creatable using the new keyword. You could simply wrap everything inside of a Car module, but instantiating a new `Car.Car` is a grating expression and the module would fail to describe the relationship between the master and subcomponents.

Module merging can be an expressive programming style as long as it accurately describes the relationships in the real objects being represented in the code.

Generics

Generic programming allows algorithms to be written in way that allows the types to be specified later. This allows the types to be processed identically without sacrificing type safety or requiring separate instances of the algorithm to handle each type. It is possible to constrain the possible types used by the algorithm by specifying a type constraint.

In TypeScript it is possible to create generic functions, including generic methods, generic interfaces, and generic classes.

Generic Functions

To make a function generic, you add a type parameter enclosed in angle brackets (< >) immediately after the function name. The type parameter can then be used to annotate function parameters, the return type, or types used within the function (or any combination thereof). This is illustrated in Listing 1-59.

Listing 1-59. Generic functions

```
function reverse<T>(list: T[]) : T[] {
    var reversedList: T[] = [];

    for (var i = (list.length - 1); i >=0; i--) {
        reversedList.push(list[i]);
    }

    return reversedList;
}

var letters = ['a', 'b', 'c', 'd'];
var reversedLetters = reverse<string>(letters); // d, c, b, a

var numbers = [1, 2, 3, 4];
var reversedNumbers = reverse<number>(numbers); // 4, 3, 2, 1
```

When you call a generic function, you can specify the type argument by placing it in angle brackets after the function name. If the type can be inferred (e.g., by inspecting the types of the arguments passed to the function), the type argument becomes optional.

■ **Tip** In both of the examples in Listing 1-59, the type arguments can be omitted because the compiler is able to infer the type based on the arguments passed to the function.

Generic Interfaces

To make a generic interface, the type parameters are placed directly after the interface name. Listing 1-60 shows a generic Repository interface that has two type parameters representing the type of a domain object and the type of an ID for that domain object. These type parameters can be used as annotations anywhere within the interface declaration.

Listing 1-60. Generic interfaces

```
class CustomerId {
    constructor(public customerIdValue: number) {
    }

    get value() {
        return this.customerIdValue;
    }
}

class Customer {
    constructor(public id: CustomerId, public name: string) {

    }
}

interface Repository<T, TId> {
    getById(id: TId): T;
    persist(model: T): TId;
}
```

```typescript
class CustomerRepository implements Repository<Customer, CustomerId> {
    constructor(private customers: Customer[]) {

    }

    getById(id: CustomerId) {
        return this.customers[id.value];
    }

    persist(customer: Customer) {
        this.customers[customer.id.value] = customer;
        return customer.id;
    }
}
```

When the CustomerRepository class implements the generic interface, it supplies the concrete Customer and CustomerId types as type arguments. The body of the CustomerRepository class is checked to ensure that it implements the interface based on these types.

Generic Classes

If generic interfaces can save some duplication in your code, generic classes can save even more by supplying a single implementation to service many different type scenarios. The type parameters follow the class name and are surrounded by angle brackets. The type parameter can be used to annotate method parameters, properties, return types, and local variables within the class.

Listing 1-61 uses a generic class to provide a single implementation for all named ID types in a domain model. This allows all ids to be named without requiring individual implementations for each named type. This is a common pattern described by P. J. Plauger (*Programming on Purpose*, Prentice Hall, 1993) that prevents accidental substitution of values. This technique can be used in TypeScript, although there are some details to bear in mind when you implement the technique; these are discussed in Chapter 2.

Listing 1-61. Generic classes

```typescript
class DomainId<T> {
    constructor(public id: T) {

    }

    get value(): T {
        return this.id;
    }
}

class OrderId extends DomainId<number> {
    constructor(public orderIdValue: number) {
        super(orderIdValue);
    }
}
```

```
class AccountId extends DomainId<string> {
    constructor(public accountIdValue: string) {
        super(accountIdValue);
    }
}
```

Type Constraints

A type constraint can be used to limit the types that a generic function, interface, or class can operate on. Listing 1-62 shows how an interface can be used to specify a contract that all types must satisfy to be used as a type argument. Type constraints are specified using the extends keyword, whether the constraint is an interface, a class, or a type annotation that describes the constraint.

Listing 1-62. Type constraints

```
interface HasName {
    name: string;
}

class Personalization {
    static greet<T extends HasName>(obj: T) {
        return 'Hello ' + obj.name;
    }
}
```

If a type argument is specified that does not satisfy the constraint, the compiler will issue an error. The constraint also allows the TypeScript language service to supply autocompletion suggestions for the generically typed members.

You can only specify a single class in a type constraint. Although you cannot specify multiple classes in a type constraint, you can create an interface that extends multiple classes and uses the interface as the constraint. Any types used with the constraint would then need to satisfy all of the class signatures that have been combined into the single interface.

TypeScript Futures

There are plans to add further features to the TypeScript language. In the short term, most language changes will be made to keep TypeScript in step with the ECMAScript 6 specification. The language will not be limited by ECMAScript developments though and the roadmap currently contains a range of features being considered for implementation, including

- Async/Await

- Mixins

- The protected access modifier

Summary

This chapter has introduced all of the language features you need to write large scale application using TypeScript. You can revisit this chapter if you need to refer back to any of these features.You should have an understanding of type annotations, be able to use operators to perform shorthand type conversions, create routines inside of classes and modules to structure your program, and take advantage of generics to avoid near-duplicate implementations.

The next chapter provides a deep dive into the type system, which is especially important if your background is in nominally typed languages.

Key Points

- All JavaScript is technically valid TypeScript.

- Primitive types are closely linked to JavaScript primitive types.

- Types are inferred in TypeScript, but you can supply annotations to make types explicit or deal with cases the compiler can't handle.

- Interfaces can be used to describe complicated structures, to make type annotations shorter.

- All TypeScript arrays are generic.

- You can use enumerations as bit flags.

- There are special cases where type coercion applies, but in most cases type checking will generate errors for invalid use of types.

- You can add optional, default, and rest parameters to functions and methods.

- Arrow functions provide a short syntax for declaring functions, but can also be used to preserve the lexical scope.

- Enumerations, interfaces, and modules are open, so multiple declarations that have the same name in the same common root will result in a single definition.

- Classes bring structure to your TypeScript program and make it possible to use common design patterns.

- Modules work as namespaces and external modules can help with module loading.

- You can obtain type information at runtime, but this should be used responsibly.

CHAPTER 2

■ ■ ■

The Type System

The fundamental problem addressed by a type theory is to insure that programs have meaning.
The fundamental problem caused by a type theory is that meaningful programs may not have
meanings ascribed to them. The quest for richer type systems results from this tension.

—Mark Manasse

In this chapter you will learn about the TypeScript type system, including some of the important ways in which it differs from other type systems that you may have encountered before. As TypeScript has drawn inspiration from a range of languages it is worth understanding the subtle details because leaning on your existing knowledge of other type systems may lead to some surprises. These details are explored by comparing structural and nominal type systems and by looking at the details of optional static types, type erasure, and the powerful type inference provided by the TypeScript language service.

At the end of the chapter is a section about ambient declarations, which can be used to fill in type information for code that hasn't been written in TypeScript. This allows you to consume external code with type checking and autocompletion, whether it is old JavaScript code you already have, additions to the runtime platform, or third party libraries and frameworks that you use within your program.

Type Systems

Type systems originate from type theory, which is credited to Bertrand Russell who developed the theory in the early 20th century and included it in his three volume *Principia Mathematica* (Whitehead and Russell, Cambridge University Press, 1910). Type theory is a system in which each term is given a type and operations are restricted based on the types. TypeScript in particular, with its type annotations, has a style reminiscent of the building blocks of type theory, as shown in Figure 2-1.

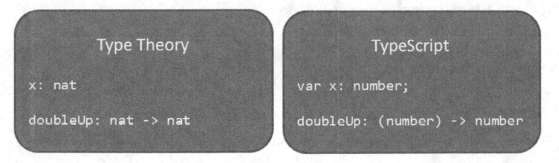

Figure 2-1. Type theory and TypeScript similarities

In type theory, a symbol is annotated with a type just like with TypeScript type annotation. The only difference in this respect is that type theory leaves out the var keyword and uses the nat type (a natural number) rather than the number type in TypeScript. Function annotations are also recognizable, with type theory leaving out the parentheses.

In general, a type system assigns a type to each variable, expression, object, function, class, or module in the system. These types are used alongside a set of rules designed to expose errors in the program. These checks can be performed at compile time (static checking) or at runtime (dynamic checking). Typical rules would include ensuring that the value used in an assignment is the same type as the variable it is being assigned to, or ensuring that a function call supplies arguments of the correct type based on the function signature.

All of the types used within a type system act as contracts that state the accepted interactions between all of the various components in the system. The kinds of errors that are detected based on these types are dependent on the rules in the type system and the level of complexity in the checking.

Optional Static Types

JavaScript is dynamically typed; variables do not have an associated type, so no type restrictions can be applied to operations. You can assign a value of one type to a variable and later assign a value of a completely different type to the same variable. You can perform an operation with two incompatible values and get unpredictable results. If you call a function, there is nothing to enforce that you pass arguments of the correct type and you can even supply too many or too few arguments. All of these are demonstrated in Listing 2-1.

Listing 2-1. JavaScript dynamic types

```
// Assignment of different types
var dynamic = 'A string';

dynamic = 52;

// Operations with different types
var days = '7';
var hours = 24;

// 168 (luckily, the hours string is coerced)
var week = days * hours;

// 77 (concatenate 7 and 7)
var fortnight = days + days;

// Calling functions
function getVolume(width, height, depth) {
        return width * height * depth;
}

// NaN (10 * undefined * undefined)
var volumeA = getVolume(10);

// 32 (the 8 is ignored)
var volumeB = getVolume(2, 4, 4, 8);
```

The JavaScript type system is incredibly flexible because of this, but sometimes this flexibility can cause problems.

TypeScript provides a system for inferring and specifying types, but allows types to be optional. The optionality is important because it means you can choose when to enforce types and when to allow dynamic types. Unless you opt out of type checking, using the any keyword, TypeScript will attempt to determine the types in your program and will check inferred types and explicit types you specify using type annotations. Type annotations are described in Chapter 1.

All of the checks are performed at compile time, which is what makes TypeScript statically typed. The compiler is responsible for constructing a schedule of all of the types, checking all expressions against the types and removing all of the type information when it converts the code into valid JavaScript.

If you were to paste the JavaScript code from Listing 2-1 into a TypeScript file, you would receive errors for all of the type errors found in the example. You can see the errors being flagged in the TypeScript listing in Figure 2-2 below.

```
1    // Assignment of different types
2    var dynamic = 'A string';
3
4    dynamic = 52;
5
6    // Operations with bad types
7    var days = 7;
8    var hours = '24';
9
10   var week = days * hours;
11
12   // Calling functions
13   function getVolume(width, height, depth) {
14       return width * height * depth;
15   }
16
17   var volumeA = getVolume(10);
18   var volumeB = getVolume(2, 4, 4, 8);
```

Figure 2-2. TypeScript compiler errors

■ **Note**   One of the key points in TypeScript's type system is the optionality of the types. This effectively means you are not restricted to static types and can opt to use dynamic behavior whenever needed.

Structural Typing

TypeScript is a structural type system; this contrasts with most C-like languages, which are typically nominative. A nominative, or *nominal*, type system relies on explicit named annotations to determine types. In a nominal system, a class would only be seen to implement an interface if it was decorated with the name of the interface (i.e., it must explicitly state that it implements the interface). In a structural type system, the explicit decoration is not required and a value is acceptable as long as its structure matches the specification of the required type.

A nominal type system is intended to prevent accidental type equivalence—just because something has the same properties does not mean it is valid—but as TypeScript is structurally typed accidental type equivalence is possible.

In a nominal type system you could use named types to ensure that correct arguments were being passed, for example, you could create a `CustomerId` type to wrap the identifier's value and use it to prevent assignment of a plain number, or `ProductId`, `CustomerTypeId`, or any other type. A type with identical properties, but a different name, would not be accepted. In a structural type system, if the `CustomerId` wrapped a public property named `value` that contained the ID number, any other type that had a `value` property with an equivalent type would be acceptable.

If you wanted to use custom types for this kind of type safety in TypeScript, you would have to ensure the types were not accidentally equivalent by making them structurally unique. You could do this by adding a public property with a unique name (such as `customerIdValue` on a `CustomerId` interface), or by adding a private member to a class. Whenever you add a private member to a class, it becomes impossible to match its structure. If you require the different ID objects to be polymorphic, you could achieve this by having an additional property or method that would have the same name on all of the objects.

In Listing 2-2 the `CustomerId` class uses the `getValue` method wherever it is needed to be substituted for `ObjectId` and the private `id` property avoids accidental equivalence.

Listing 2-2. Using and avoiding equivalence

```typescript
interface ObjectId {
    getValue(): number;
}

class CustomerId {
    constructor(private id: number) {

    }

    getValue() {
        return this.id;
    }
}

class ProductId {
    constructor(private id: number) {

    }

    getValue() {
        return this.id;
    }
}

class Example {
    static avoidAccidentalEquivalence(id: CustomerId) {
        // Implementation
    }

    static useEquivalence(id: ObjectId) {
        // Implementation
    }
}

var customerId = new CustomerId(1);
var productId = new ProductId(5);
```

```
// Allowed
Example.avoidAccidentalEquivalence(customerId);

// Errors 'Supplied parameters do not match signature of call target'
Example.avoidAccidentalEquivalence(productId);

// Allowed
Example.useEquivalence(customerId);

// Allowed
Example.useEquivalence(productId);
```

While structural typing may seem to cause difficulties in some situations, it has many advantages. For example, it is far easier to introduce compatible types without having to change existing code and it is possible to create types that can be passed to external code without inheriting from an external class. It is also impossible to create a new supertype in a nominally typed language without changing all of the subtypes, whereas in a structurally typed language you can easily create new supertypes without making changes elsewhere in your program.

One of the most significant benefits of structural typing is it saves myriad explicit type name decorations. In Listing 2-2 neither the CustomerId or ProductId classes have the interface declaration: implements ObjectId, but they can both be passed to the useEquivalence method because they are compatible with the ObjectId—*they have the same structure*. To satisfy a type requirement, the type must have matching properties and methods. The properties and methods should all be of the same type, or compatible types. A compatible type can be a subtype, a narrower type or a structurally similar type.

One thing to avoid in a structurally typed language, such as TypeScript, is empty structures. An empty interface or an empty class is essentially a valid supertype of practically everything in your program, which means any object could be substituted for the empty structure at compile time because there is no structure that the object would have to satisfy during type checking.

Structural typing complements the type inference in TypeScript. With these features, you can leave much of the work to the compiler and language service, rather than having to explicitly add type information and class heritage throughout your program.

■ **Note** You can't rely on named types to create restrictions in a TypeScript program, only unique structures. For interfaces, this means creating uniqueness using a uniquely named property or method. For classes, any private member will make the structure unique.

Type Erasure

When you compile your TypeScript program into plain JavaScript, the generated code is different in two ways: *code transformation* and *type erasure*. The code transformation converts language features that are not available in JavaScript into representations that are valid. For example, if you are targeting ECMAScript 5, where classes are not available, all of your classes will be converted into JavaScript functions that create appropriate representations using the prototypal inheritance available in ECMAScript 5. Type erasure is the process that removes all of the type annotations from your code, as they are not understood by JavaScript.

Type erasure removes both type annotations and interfaces. These are only required at design time and at compile time for the purpose of static checking. At runtime types are not checked, but you shouldn't encounter a problem because they have already been checked when you compiled your program (unless you used the any type).

Listing 2-3 shows an example TypeScript listing for an `OrderedArray` class. The class is generic, so the type of the elements in the array can be substituted. For complex types, an optional custom comparer can be supplied to evaluate the items in the array for the purposes of ordering, but for simple types it can be omitted. Following the class is a simple demonstration of the class in action. This code compiled into the JavaScript shown in Listing 2-4. In the compiled output all of the type information is gone and the class has been transformed into a common JavaScript pattern called a *self-executing anonymous function*.

Listing 2-3. TypeScript ordered array class

```
class OrderedArray<T> {
    private items: T[] = [];

    constructor(private comparer?: (a: T, b: T) => number) {
    }

    add(item: T): void {
        this.items.push(item);
        this.items.sort(this.comparer);
    }

    getItem(index: number) : T {
        if (this.items.length > index) {
            return this.items[index];
        }
        return null;
    }
}

var orderedArray: OrderedArray<number> = new OrderedArray<number>();

orderedArray.add(5);
orderedArray.add(1);
orderedArray.add(3);

var firstItem: number = orderedArray.getItem(0);

alert(firstItem); // 1
```

Listing 2-4. Compiled JavaScript code

```
var OrderedArray = (function () {
    function OrderedArray(comparer) {
        this.comparer = comparer;
        this.items = [];
    }

    OrderedArray.prototype.add = function (item) {
        this.items.push(item);
        this.items.sort(this.comparer);
    };
```

```
        OrderedArray.prototype.getItem = function (index) {
            if (this.items.length > index) {
                return this.items[index];
            }
            return null;
        };
        return OrderedArray;
})();

var orderedArray = new OrderedArray();

orderedArray.add(5);
orderedArray.add(1);
orderedArray.add(3);

var firstItem = orderedArray.getItem(0);

alert(firstItem); // 1
```

Despite the type erasure and transformations performed during compilation, the JavaScript output is remarkably similar to the original TypeScript program. Almost all transformations from TypeScript to JavaScript are similarly considerate of your original code. Depending on the version of ECMAScript you are targeting, there may be more or fewer transformations, for example, the ECMAScript 6 features that TypeScript transforms for compatibility with ECMAScript 3 and 5 wouldn't need to be transformed if you were to target ECMAScript 6.

Type Inference

Type inference is the polar opposite of type erasure. Type inference is the process by which types are determined at compile time in the absence of explicit type annotations.

Most basic examples of type inference, including the early examples in this book, show a simple assignment and explain how the type of the variable on the left of the assignment can be automatically set to the type of the value on the right hand side. This kind of type inference is really level one for TypeScript, and it is capable of some incredibly complex determinations of the types in use.

TypeScript performs deep inspections to create a schedule of types in your program and compares assignments, expressions, and operations using this schedule of types. During this process, there are some clever tricks that are employed when a direct type is not available, which allow the type to be found indirectly. One such trick is *contextual typing*, where TypeScript uses the context of an expression to determine the types.

Listing 2-5 shows how types can be inferred in progressively more indirect ways. The return value of the add function is determined by working backward from the return statement. The type of the return statement is found by evaluating the type of the expression a + b, which in turn is done by inspecting the types of the individual parameters.

In the very last expression in Listing 2-5, the result parameter type in the anonymous function can be inferred using the context that the function is declared in. Because it is declared to be used by the execution of callsFunction, the compiler can see that it is going to be passed a string, therefore the result parameter will always be a string type. A third example comes from the declaration of CallsFunction; because the variable has been typed using the CallsFunction interface, the compiler infers the type of the cb parameter based on the interface.

Listing 2-5. Bottom-up and top-down inference

```
function add(a: number, b: number) {
    /* The return value is used to determine
       the return type of the function */
    return a + b;
}

interface CallsFunction {
    (cb: (result: string) => any): void;
}

// The cb parameter is inferred to be a function accepting a string
var callsFunction: CallsFunction = function (cb) {
    cb('Done');

    // Supplied parameter does not match any signature of the call target
    // cb(1);
};

// The result parameter is inferred to be a string
callsFunction(function (result) {
    return result;
});
```

Best Common Type

The type of the example variable in Listing 2-6 looks a lot like the single object passed into the array literal. If you were writing the type annotation for this type it would be { a: string, b: number, c: boolean }[] and this is the type you will see if you hover over the example array in your development tools. This is the premise for understanding *best common types*.

Listing 2-6. Best common type premise

```
var bestCommonTypeExample = [
    { a: 'A', b: 1, c: true }
];

for (var i = 0; i < bestCommonTypeExample.length; i++) {
    var value = bestCommonTypeExample[i];

    console.log(value.a);

    console.log(value.b);

    console.log(value.c);
}
```

If you were to add a second item to the array literal with different properties, there are several possible outcomes.

- If the item is an object with an identical signature, the type of the example variable will be unaffected.

- If the item is an object with no matching properties, the type of the example variable will be updated to {}[]—simply an array of objects.

- If the item is an object with some matching properties, the type of the example variable will be updated to the *best common type*.

The best common type includes all properties with the same names and types that are present in all of the values in the expression. Any properties that fail to match throughout the expression are dropped from the best common type. In Listing 2-7, the type used for the example variable has been reduced to the only common property in all values, { b: number }[].

Listing 2-7. Best common type—example

```
var example = [
    { a: 'A', b: 1, c: true },
    { a: 'B', b: 2 },
    { b: 3 }
];

for (var i = 0; i < bestCommonTypeExample.length; i++) {
    var value = bestCommonTypeExample[i];

    // The property 'a' does not exist on value of type '{ b: number }'.
    // console.log(value.a);

    // OK
    console.log(value.b);

    // The property 'c' does not exist on value of type '{ b: number }'.
    // console.log(value.c);
}
```

The process of determining the best common type is not just used for array literal expressions; they also are used to determine the return type of a function or method that contains multiple return statements.

Contextual Types

Contextual types are a good example of how advanced type inference can be. Contextual typing occurs when the compiler bases its types on the location of an expression. In Listing 2-8, the type of the event parameter is determined by the known signature of the window.onclick definition. The inference is not just limited to the parameters, the entire signature, including the return value, can be inferred because of the existing knowledge of the window.onclick signature.

Listing 2-8. Contextual types

```
window.onclick = function(event) {
        var button = event.button;
};
```

Widened Types

The term *widened type* refers to situations in TypeScript where the type of a function call, expression, or assignment is null or undefined. In these cases, the type inferred by the compiler will be the widened any type. In Listing 2-9, the widened variable will have a type of any.

Listing 2-9. Widened types

```
function example() {
        return null;
}

var widened = example();
```

When to Annotate

Because type inference has been a key feature of TypeScript since day one, the discussion on when to make types explicit with type annotations can take place without controversy. This has been a tricky topic for statically typed languages that have later decided to add some level of support for type inference.

The final decision about the level of type annotations you add to your program should be made jointly between all team members, but you may wish to use the following suggestions as a starting point for your discussion.

Use as few type annotations as possible. If the type *can* be inferred, allow it to be inferred. You may want to make return types explicit (especially for void return types) and in most cases you should annotate parameters as part of a method signature, but outside of these cases you should put your faith in the compiler as far as you can. You can get the compiler to warn you about cases where it can't find a type using a special flag (--noImplicitAny) that prevents the any type from being inferred. You can read more about this flag in Appendix 2.

Duplicate Identifiers

On the whole, you should do your best to avoid name clashes in your program. TypeScript supplies the tools to make name clashes unnecessary by allowing you to move your program out of the global scope. However, there are some interesting features around identifiers in TypeScript including many situations where you are allowed to use the same name within the same scope.

In most cases, the use of an existing class or variable name within the same scope will result in a "Duplicate identifier" error. No particular structure gets preferential treatment; the later of the two identifiers will be the source of the error. If you create a module with a duplicate identifier, the error won't show until you implement the body of the module. This is because TypeScript is clever enough to delete empty modules from the compiled code (which in turn fixes the duplicate identifier error).

One valid use of a duplicate identifier is with interfaces. Once again, the compiler knows that there will be no duplicate identifier at runtime because interfaces are erased during compilation; its identifier will never appear in the JavaScript output. The use of a duplicate identifier for an interface and a variable is a common pattern in the TypeScript library, where the standard types are defined using an interface and then allocated to a variable declaration with a type annotation. Listing 2-10 shows the TypeScript library definition for DeviceMotionEvent. The interface for DeviceMotionEvent is immediately followed by a variable declaration with the same DeviceMotionEvent identifier.

Listing 2-10. TypeScript DeviceMotionEvent

```
interface DeviceMotionEvent extends Event {
    rotationRate: DeviceRotationRate;
    acceleration: DeviceAcceleration;
    interval: number;
```

```
        accelerationIncludingGravity: DeviceAcceleration;
        initDeviceMotionEvent(
                    type: string,
                    bubbles: boolean,
                    cancelable: boolean,
                    acceleration: DeviceAccelerationDict,
                    accelerationIncludingGravity: DeviceAccelerationDict,
                    rotationRate: DeviceRotationRateDict,
                    interval: number): void;
}

declare var DeviceMotionEvent: {
    prototype: DeviceMotionEvent;
    new (): DeviceMotionEvent;
}
```

Ambient Declarations are explained in more detail later in this chapter, but this technique works just as well without the declare keyword before the variable declaration. The use of interfaces in the standard library is a deliberate choice. Interfaces are open, so it is possible to extend the definitions in additional interface blocks. If a new web standard was published that added a motionDescription property to the DeviceMotionEvent object, you wouldn't have to wait for it to be added to the TypeScript standard library; you could simply add the code from Listing 2-11 to your program to extend the interface definition.

Listing 2-11. Extending the DeviceMotionEvent

```
interface DeviceMotionEvent {
    motionDescription: string;
}

// The existing DeviceMotionEvent has all of its existing properties
// plus our additional motionDescription property
function handleMotionEvent(e: DeviceMotionEvent) {
    var acceleration = e.acceleration;
    var description = e.motionDescription;
}
```

All of the interface definition blocks from the same common root are combined into a single type, so the DeviceMotionEvent still has all of the original properties from the standard library and also has the motionDescription property from the additional interface block.

Type Checking

Once a schedule of types has been gathered from your program, the TypeScript compiler is able to use this schedule to perform type checking. At its simplest, the compiler is checking that when a function is called that accepts a parameter of type number; all calling code passes an argument with a type that is compatible with the number type.

Listing 2-12 shows a series of valid calls to a function with a parameter named input, with a type of number. Arguments are accepted if they have a type of number, enum, null, undefined, or any. Remember, the any type allows dynamic behavior in TypeScript, so it represents a promise from you to the compiler saying that the values will be acceptable at runtime.

Listing 2-12. Checking a parameter

```
function acceptNumber(input: number) {
    return input;
}

// number
acceptNumber(1);

// enum
acceptNumber(Size.XL);

// null
acceptNumber(null);
```

As types become more complex, type checking requires deeper inspection of the objects. When an object is checked, each member of the object is tested. Public properties must have identical names and types; public methods must have identical signatures. When checking the members of an object, if a property refers to a nested object, the inspection continues to work down into that object to check compatibility.

Listing 2-13 shows three differently named classes and a literal object that show all are compatible as far as the compiler is concerned.

Listing 2-13. Compatible types

```
class C1 {
    name: string;

    show(hint?: string) {
        return 1;
    }
}

class C2 {
    constructor(public name: string) {

    }

    show(hint: string = 'default') {
        return Math.floor(Math.random() * 10);
    }
}

class C3 {
    name: string;

    show() {
        return <any> 'Dynamic';
    }
}
```

```
var T4 = {
    name: '',
    show() {
        return 1;
    }
};

var c1 = new C1();
var c2 = new C2('A name');
var c3 = new C3();

// c1, c2, c3 and T4 are equivalent
var arr: C1[] = [c1, c2, c3, T4];

for (var i = 0; i < arr.length; i++) {
        arr[i].show();
}
```

The notable parts of this example include the name property and the show method. The name *property* must exist on the object, it must be public, and it must be a string type. It doesn't matter whether the property is a constructor property. The show method must return a type compatible with number. The parameters must also be compatible—in this case the optional hint parameter can be matched using a default parameter or by omitting the parameter entirely. If a class had a mandatory hint parameter, it would not be compatible with the types in Listing 2-13. As shown in the fourth type, literal objects can be compatible with classes as far as the compiler is concerned, as long as they pass the type comparison.

Ambient Declarations

Ambient declarations can be used to add type information to existing JavaScript. Commonly, this would mean adding type information for your own existing code, or for a third-party library that you want to consume in your TypeScript program.

Ambient declarations can be gradually constructed by starting with a simple imprecise declaration and turning up the dial on the details over time. Listing 2-14 shows an example of the least precise ambient declaration you can write for the jQuery framework. The declaration simply notifies the compiler that an external variable will exist at runtime without supplying further details of the structure of the external variable. This will suppress errors for the $ variable, but will not supply deep type checking or useful autocompletion.

Listing 2-14. Imprecise ambient declaration

```
declare var $: any;

$('#id').html('Hello World');
```

All ambient declarations begin with the declare keyword. This tells the compiler that the following code block contains only type information and no implementation. Blocks of code created using the declare keyword will be erased during compilation and result in no JavaScript output. At runtime, you are responsible for ensuring the code exists and that it matches your declaration.

To get the full benefit of compile-time checking, you can create a more detailed ambient declaration that covers more of the features of the external JavaScript that you use. If you are building an ambient declaration, you can choose to cover the features you use the most, or the higher-risk features that you judge to be the most likely source of type errors. This allows you to invest in defining the type information that gives you the most return on your time investment.

In Listing 2-15 the jQuery definition has been extended to cover the two elements used in the first example; the selection of an element using a string query containing the element's id and the setting of the inner HTML using the html method. In this example, a class is declared called jQuery, this class has the html method that accepts a string. The $ function accepts a string query and returns an instance of the jQuery class.

Listing 2-15. Ambient class and function

```
declare class jQuery {
    html(html: string): void;
}

declare function $(query: string): jQuery;

$('#id').html('Hello World');
```

When this updated ambient declaration is used, autocompletion supplies type hints as shown in Figure 2-3. Any attempt to use a variable, function, method, or property that isn't declared will result in a compiler error and all arguments and assignments will also be checked.

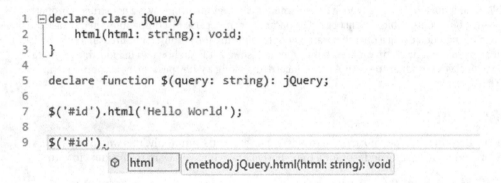

Figure 2-3. *Ambient declaration autocompletion*

It is possible to create ambient declarations for variables, functions, classes, enumerations, and both internal and external modules. Interfaces appear to be missing from this list, but interfaces are already analogous to ambient declarations as they describe a type without resulting in any compiled code. This means you can write ambient declarations using interfaces, but you would not use the declare keyword for interfaces.

■ **Note**   In reality, it actually makes more sense to declare jQuery as an interface rather than a class because you cannot instantiate instances of jQuery using var jq = new jQuery();. All you would need to do is change the class keyword to the interface keyword because neither needs implementation when used in a declaration.

Declaration Files

Although it is possible to place ambient declarations in any of your TypeScript files, there is a special naming convention for files that contain only ambient declarations. The convention is to use a `.d.ts` file extension. Each module, variable, function, class, and enum in the file must be preceded by the `declare` keyword, and this is enforced by the TypeScript compiler.

To use a declaration file from within your program, you can refer to the file just like any other TypeScript file. You can use reference comments, or make the file the target of an import statement. When using import statements to target a file, the declaration file should be placed in the same folder and have the same name as the JavaScript file as shown in Figure 2-4.

jquery.d.ts   jquery.js

Figure 2-4. *Declaration files*

Definitely Typed

If you plan to write an ambient declaration for any of the common JavaScript libraries or frameworks, you should first check to see if someone has already done the hard work by visiting the online library for ambient declarations, Definitely Typed:

```
https://github.com/DefinitelyTyped
```

The Definitely Typed project, started by Boris Yankov, contains over 180 definitions for popular JavaScript projects including Angular, Backbone, Bootstrap, Breeze, D3, Ember, jQuery, Knockout, NodeJS, Underscore, and many others. There are even declarations for unit testing frameworks such as Jasmine, Mocha, and qUnit. Some of these external sources are incredibly complex, so using an existing declaration can save a great deal of time.

Summary

Working within the TypeScript type system requires at least a passing knowledge of the difference between nominal and structural typing. Structural typing can make some designs a little tricky, but doesn't prevent you from using any patterns that you may wish to transfer from a nominally typed system. Structural typing allows you to leave out type annotations in favor of allowing the types to be inferred throughout your program.

When you compile your program, the types are checked against the explicit and implicit types, allowing a large class of errors to be detected early. You can opt out of type checking for specific parts of your program using the any type.

You can add type information for JavaScript code by creating or obtaining ambient declarations for the JavaScript code. Usually these ambient declarations would be stored in a declaration file that sits alongside the JavaScript file.

Key Points

- Static type checking is optional.

- TypeScript is structurally typed.

- All type information is removed during compilation.

- You can let the compiler work out the types for you using type inference.

- Ambient declarations add type information to existing JavaScript code.

■ ■ ■

CHAPTER 3

Object Orientation in TypeScript

There are two ways of constructing a software design: One way is to make it so simple that there are obviously no deficiencies and the other way is to make it so complicated that there are no obvious deficiencies. The first method is far more difficult. It demands the same skill, devotion, insight, and even inspiration as the discovery of the simple physical laws which underlie the complex phenomena of nature.

—Tony Hoare

Object-oriented programming allows concepts from the real world to be represented by code that contains both the data and related behavior. The concepts are normally modelled as classes, with properties for the data and methods for the behavior, and the specific instances of these classes are called objects.

There have been many discussions about object orientation over the years and I'm sure that the debate remains lively enough to continue for many years to come. Because programming is a heuristic process, you will rarely find one absolute answer. This is why you will hear the phrase "it depends" so often in software development. No programming paradigm fits every situation so anyone telling you that functional programming, object-oriented programming, or some other programming style is the answer to all problems hasn't been exposed to a large enough variety of complex problems. Because of this, programming languages are becoming increasingly multiparadigm.

Object-oriented programming is a formalization of many good practices that emerged early on in computer programming. It supplies the concepts to make these good practices easier to apply. By modelling real-world objects from the problem domain using objects in the code, the program can speak the same language as the domain it serves. Objects also allow encapsulation and information hiding, which prevent different parts of a program from modifying data that another part of the program relies on.

The simplest explanation in favor of programming concepts such as object orientation comes not from the world of software, but from psychology. G. A. Miller published his famous paper, "The Magical Number Seven, Plus or Minus Two" (*Psychological Review*, 1956) describing the limitations on the number of pieces of information we can hold in short-term memory at any one time. Our information processing ability is limited by this number of between five and nine items of information that we can hold on to concurrently. This is the key reason for any technique of code organization and in object orientation it should drive you toward layers of abstraction that allow you to skim high-level ideas first and dive further into the levels of detail when you need to. If you organize it well, a programmer maintaining the code will need to hold onto less concurrent information when attempting to understand your program.

Robert C. Martin (Uncle Bob) presented this idea in a slightly different way during a group-refactoring session when he said well-written, "polite" code was like reading a newspaper. You could scan the higher level code in the program as if they were headlines. A programmer maintaining the code would scan through the headlines to find relevant areas in the code and then drill down to find the implementation details. The value in this idea comes from small readable functions that contain code at a similar level of abstraction. The newspaper metaphor supplies a clear vision of what clean code looks like, but the principle of reducing the amount of cognitive overhead is still present.

Object Orientation in TypeScript

TypeScript supplies all of the key tools that you need to use object orientation in your program.

- Classes

- Instances of classes

- Methods

- Inheritance

- Open recursion

- Encapsulation

- Delegation

- Polymorphism

Classes, instances of classes, methods, and inheritance were discussed in detail in Chapter 1. These are the building blocks of an object-oriented program and are made possible in a simple way by the language itself. All you need for each of these concepts is one or two language keywords.

The other terms in this list are worthy of further explanation, particularly in respect of how they work within the TypeScript type system. The following sections expand on the concepts of open recursion, encapsulation, delegation, and polymorphism along with code examples that demonstrate each concept.

■ **Note**   Although this chapter discusses object orientation in detail, don't forget that JavaScript, and therefore TypeScript, is a multiparadigm language.

Open Recursion

Open recursion is a combination of recursion and late binding. When a method calls itself within a class, that call can be forwarded to a replacement defined in a subclass. Listing 3-1 is an example of a class that reads the contents of a directory. The FileReader class reads the contents based on the supplied path. Any files are added to the file tree, but where directories are found, there is a recursive call to this.getFiles. These calls would continue until the entire path including all subfolders are added to the file tree. The fs.reaaddirSync and fs.statSync methods belong to NodeJS, which is covered in more detail in Chapter 6.

Listing 3-1. Open recursion

```
interface FileItem {
    path: string;
    contents: string[];
}

class FileReader {
    getFiles(path: string, depth: number = 0) {
        var fileTree = [];

        var files = fs.readdirSync(path);

        for (var i = 0; i < files.length; i++) {
            var file = files[i];
```

```typescript
            var stats = fs.statSync(file);
            var fileItem;

            if (stats.isDirectory()) {
                // Add directory and contents
                fileItem = {
                    path: file,
                    contents: this.getFiles(file, (depth + 1))
                };
            } else {
                // Add file
                fileItem = {
                    path: file,
                    contents: []
                };
            }

            fileTree.push(fileItem);
        }

        return fileTree;
    }
}

class LimitedFileReader extends FileReader {
    constructor(public maxDepth: number) {
        super();
    }

    getFiles(path: string, depth = 0) {
        if (depth > this.maxDepth) {
            return [];
        }

        return super.getFiles(path, depth);
    }
}

// instatiating an instance of LimitedFileReader
var fileReader = new LimitedFileReader(1);

// results in only the top level, and one additional level being read
var files = fileReader.getFiles('path');
```

■ **Note** I used the Sync versions of the NodeJS file system calls, readdirSync and statSync, because they make the examples much simpler. In a real program you should consider using the standard equivalents, readdir and stat, which accept a callback function.

The `LimitedFileReader` is a subclass of the `FileReader` class. When you create an instance of the `LimitedFileReader` class, you must specify a number that limits the depth of the file tree represented by the class. This example shows how the call to `this.getFiles` uses open recursion. If you create a `FileReader` instance, the call to `this.getFiles` is a simple recursive call. If you create an instance of the `LimitedFileReader`, the same call to `this.getFiles` within the `FileReader.getFiles` method will actually be dispatched to the `LimitedFileReader.getFiles` method.

This example of open recursion can be summarized as:

- When you create a new `FileReader`

  - `fileReader.getFiles` is a call to `FileReader.getFiles`

  - **this**.`getFiles` within **FileReader** is a call to **FileReader**.`getFiles`

- When you create a new `LimitedFileReader`

  - `fileReader.getFiles` is a call to `LimitedFileReader.getFiles`

  - `super.getFiles` is a call to `FileReader.getFiles`

  - **this**.`getFiles` within **FileReader** is a call to **LimitedFileReader**.`getFiles`

The beauty of open recursion is that the original class remains unchanged and needs no knowledge of the specialization offered by the subclass. The subclass gets to re-use the code from the superclass, which avoids duplication.

Encapsulation

Encapsulation is fully supported in TypeScript. A class instance can contain both properties and methods that operate on those properties; this is the encapsulation of data and behavior. The properties can also be hidden using the `private` access modifier, which hides the data from code outside of the class instance.

A common use of encapsulation is data hiding; preventing access to data from outside of the class except via explicit operations. The example in Listing 3-2 shows a `Totalizer` class that has a `private total` property, which cannot be modified by code outside of the `Totalizer` class. The property can change when external code calls the methods defined on the class. This removes the risk of

- External code adding a donation without adding the tax rebate

- External code failing to validate the amount is a positive number

- The tax rebate calculation appearing in many places in calling code

- The tax rate appearing in many places in external code

Listing 3-2. Encapsulation

```
class Totalizer {
    private total = 0;
    private taxRateFactor = 0.2;

    addDonation(amount: number) {
        if (amount <= 0) {
            throw new Error('Donation exception');
        }

        var taxRebate = amount * this.taxRateFactor;
        var totalDonation = amount + taxRebate;
```

```
            this.total += totalDonation;
        }

        getAmountRaised() {
            return this.total;
        }
    }

    var totalizer = new Totalizer();

    totalizer.addDonation(100.00);

    var fundsRaised = totalizer.getAmountRaised();

    // 120
    console.log(fundsRaised);
```

Encapsulation is the tool that can help you to prevent the largest amount of duplicated code in a program, but it doesn't do it magically. You have to hide your properties using the private keyword to prevent external code changing the value or controlling the program's flow using the value. One of the most common kinds of duplication is logical branching, for example the if and switch statements, which control the program based on a property that should have been hidden using the private keyword. When you change the property, you then need to hunt down all of these logical branches, which creates a worrying ripple of change throughout your code.

Delegation

One of the most important concepts in terms of re-use in your program is *delegation*. Delegation describes the situation where one part of your program hands over a task to another part of the system. In true delegation, the wrapper passes a reference to itself into the delegate, which allows the delegate to call back into the original wrapper, for example WrapperClass would call DelegateClass, passing the keyword this as an argument. DelegateClass can then call methods on WrapperClass. This allows the wrapper and delegate to behave as a subclass and superclass.

Where the wrapper doesn't pass a reference to itself, the operation is known as *forwarding* rather than delegation. In both delegation and forwarding you may call a method on one class, but that class hands off the processing to another class, as shown in Listing 3-3. Delegation and forwarding are often good alternatives to inheritance if the relationship between two classes fails the "is a" test.

Listing 3-3. Delegation

```
interface ControlPanel {
    startAlarm(message: string): any;
}

interface Sensor {
    check(): any;
}

class MasterControlPanel {
    private sensors: Sensor[] = [];
```

```typescript
    constructor() {
        // Instantiating the delegate HeatSensor
        this.sensors.push(new HeatSensor(this));
    }

    start() {
        for (var i= 0; i < this.sensors.length; i++) {
            // Calling the delegate
            this.sensors[i].check();
        }

        window.setTimeout(() => this.start(), 1000);
    }

    startAlarm(message: string) {
        console.log('Alarm! ' + message);
    }
}

class HeatSensor {
    private upperLimit = 38;
    private sensor = {
        read: function() { return Math.floor(Math.random() * 100); }
    };

    constructor(private controlPanel: ControlPanel) {
    }

    check() {
        if (this.sensor.read() > this.upperLimit) {
            // Calling back to the wrapper
            this.controlPanel.startAlarm('Overheating!');
        }
    }
}

var cp = new MasterControlPanel();

cp.start();
```

■ **Note** The "is a" test in object orientation involves describing the relationship between objects to validate that the subclass is indeed a specialized version of the superclass. For example, "a Cat *is a* Mammal" and "a Savings Account *is a* Bank Account". It is usually clear when the relationship is not valid, for example, "a Motor Car *is a* Chassis" doesn't work, but "a Car *has a* Chassis" does. A "has a" relationship requires delegation (or forwarding), not inheritance.

Listing 3-3 is a simple example of delegation. The ControlPanel class passes itself into the HeatSensor constructor, which enables the HeatSensor class to call the startAlarm method on the ControlPanel when required. The ControlPanel can coordinate any number of sensors and each sensor can call back into the ControlPanel to set off the alarm if a problem is detected.

It is possible to expand on this to demonstrate various decision points where either inheritance or delegation may be selected. Figure 3-1 describes the relationships between various car components. The *chassis* is the plain skeleton that a motor car is built on, the bare framework for a car. When the engine, driveshaft, and transmission are attached to the chassis, the combination is called a *rolling chassis*.

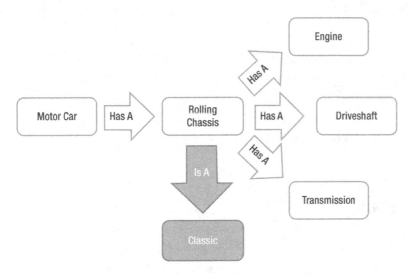

Figure 3-1. *Encapsulation and inheritance*

For each relationship in the diagram, try reading both the *is a* and the *has a* alternatives to see if you agree with the relationships shown.

Polymorphism

In programming, polymorphism refers to the ability to specify a contract and have many different types implement that contract. The code using a class that implements a contract should not need to know the details of the specific implementation. In TypeScript, polymorphism can be achieved using a number of different forms

- An interface implemented by many classes

- An interface implemented by many objects

- An interface implemented by many functions

- A superclass with a number of specialized subclasses

- Any structure with many similar structures

The final bullet point, "any structure with many similar structures," refers to TypeScript's structural type system, which will accept structures compatible with a required type. This means you can achieve polymorphism with two functions with the same signature and return type (or two classes with compatible structures, or two objects with similar structures) even if they do not explicitly implement a named type, as shown in Listing 3-4.

Listing 3-4. Polymorphism

```typescript
interface Vehicle {
    moveTo(x: number, y: number);
}

class Car implements Vehicle {
    moveTo(x: number, y: number) {
        console.log('Driving to ' + x + ' ' + y);
    }
}

class SportsCar extends Car {

}

class Airplane {
    moveTo(x: number, y: number) {
        console.log('Flying to ' + x + ' ' + y);
    }
}

function navigate(vehicle: Vehicle) {
    vehicle.moveTo(59.9436499, 10.7167959);
}

var airplane = new Airplane();

navigate(airplane);

var car = new SportsCar();

navigate(car);
```

Listing 3-4 illustrates polymorphism in TypeScript. The navigate function accepts any type compatible with the Vehicle interface. Specifically, this means any class or object that has a method named moveTo that accepts *up to* two arguments of type number.

■ **Note**   It is important to remember that a method is structurally compatible with another if it accepts fewer arguments. In many languages, you would be forced to specify the redundant parameter even though it isn't used in the method body, but in TypeScript you can omit it. The calling code may still pass the argument if the contract specifies it, which preserves polymorphism.

The navigate function in Listing 3-4 sends the specified Vehicle to the Norwegian Computing Centre is Oslo—where polymorphism was created by Ole-Johan Dahl and Kristen Nygaard.

All of the types defined in the example are compatible with the Vehicle definition; Car explicitly implements the interface, SportsCar inherits from Car so also implements the Vehicle interface. Airplane does not explicitly implement the Vehicle interface, but it has a compatible moveTo method and will be accepted by the navigate function. The acceptance of compatible types based on their structure is a feature of TypeScript's structural type system, which is described in Chapter 2.

SOLID Principles

Object orientation, as with any programming paradigm, doesn't prevent confusing or unmaintainable programs. This is the reason for the five heuristic design guidelines commonly referred to as the SOLID principles.

The SOLID principles were cataloged by R. C. Martin (http://www.objectmentor.com/resources/articles/Principles_and_Patterns.pdf, 2000; *Agile Principles, Patterns, and Practices in C#*. Prentice Hall, 2006), although the "SOLID" acronym was spotted by Michael Feathers. Luckily, the order of the principles isn't important, so they can be ordered to suit this more memorable form. The principles were intended to be the basic tenets that underpin object-oriented programming and design. In general, the principles provide guidance for creating readable and maintainable code.

It is important to remember that software design is a heuristic process. It is not possible to create rules that can be followed like a checklist. The SOLID principles are guidelines to help you think about your program's design in terms of object orientation and can help you to make an informed design decision that works in your specific context. The principles also supply a shared language that can be used to discuss designs with other programmers.

The five SOLID principles are

- *Single responsibility principle*—a class should have one, and only one, reason to change.

- *Open–closed principle*—it should be possible to extend the behavior of a class without modifying it.

- *Liskov substitution principle*—subclasses should be substitutable for their superclasses.

- *Interface segregation principle*—many small, client-specific interfaces are better than one general-purpose interface.

- *Dependency inversion principle*—depends on abstractions not concretions.

The five SOLID principles are discussed individually in the sections that follow.

The Single Responsibility Principle (SRP)

The SRP requires that a class should have only one reason to change. When designing your classes, you should aim to put related features together, ensuring that they are likely to change for the same reason, and keep features apart if they will change for different reasons. A program that follows this principle has classes that perform just a few related tasks. Such a program is likely to be highly cohesive.

The term *cohesion* refers to a measure of the relatedness of features within a class or module. If features are unrelated, the class has low cohesion and is likely to change for many different reasons. High cohesion results from the application of the SRP.

When you are adding code to your program, you need to make a conscious decision about where it belongs. Most violations of this principle do not come from obvious cases where a method is clearly mismatched to its enclosing class. It is far more common for a class to gradually overstep its original purpose over a period of time and under the care of many different programmers.

You don't need to limit your thinking to classes when considering the SRP. You can apply the principle to methods, ensuring that they do just one thing and therefore have just one reason to change. You can apply the principle to modules, ensuring that at a general level the module has one area of responsibility.

Listing 3-5 shows a typical violation of the SRP. At first glance all of the methods seem to belong to the Movie class, because they all perform operations using the properties of a movie. However, the appearance of persistence logic blurs the line between the use of the Movie class as an object, and its use as a data structure.

Listing 3-5. Single responsibility principle (SRP) violation

```typescript
class Movie {
    private db: DataBase;

    constructor(private title: string, private year: number) {
        this.db = DataBase.connect('user:pw@mydb', ['movies']);
    }

    getTitle() {
        return this.title + ' (' + this.year + ')';
    }

    save() {
        this.db.movies.save({ title: this.title, year: this.year });
    }
}
```

To fix this class before it grows into a bigger problem, the two concerns can be divided between the Movie class that takes care of movie related behavior and a MovieRepository that is responsible for storing the data as shown in Listing 3-6. If features are added to the Movie class, the MovieRepository requires no changes. If you were to change your data storage device, the Movie class wouldn't need to change.

Listing 3-6. Separate reasons for change

```typescript
class Movie {
    constructor(private title: string, private year: number) {
    }

    getTitle() {
        return this.title + ' (' + this.year + ')';
    }
}

class MovieRepository {
    private db: DataBase;

    constructor() {
        this.db = DataBase.connect('user:pw@mydb', ['movies']);
    }

    save(movie: Movie) {
        this.db.movies.save(JSON.stringify(movie));
    }
}

// Movie
var movie = new Movie('The Internship', 2013);

// MovieRepository
var movieRepository = new MovieRepository();

movieRepository.save(movie);
```

Keeping an eye on the class level responsibilities is usually straightforward if you keep in mind the SRP, but it can be even more important at the method level, ensuring that each method performs just one task and is named in a way that reveals the intended behavior of the method. Uncle Bob coined the phrase "extract 'til you drop," which refers to the practice of refactoring your methods until each one has so few lines it can only do a single thing. This method of refactoring methods extensively is easily worth the effort of reworking the design.

The Open–Closed Principle (OCP)

The OCP is often summed up by the sentence: *software entities should be open for extension but closed for modification.* In pragmatic terms, no matter how much you design your program up front, it is almost certain that it won't be entirely protected from modification. However, the risk of changing an existing class is that you will introduce an inadvertent change in behavior. This can be mitigated somewhat (but not entirely) by automated tests, which is described in Chapter 9.

To follow the OCP, you need to consider the parts of your program that are likely to change. For example, you would attempt to identify any class that contains a behavior that you may want to replace or extend in the future. The slight hitch with this is that it is usually not possible to predict the future and there is a danger that if you introduce code intended to pay off later on, it almost always will not. Trying to guess what may happen can be troublesome either because it turns out the code is never needed or because the real future turns out to be incompatible with the prediction. So you will need to be pragmatic about this principle, which sometimes means introducing the code to solve a problem only when you first encounter the problem in real life.

So with these warnings in mind, a common way to follow the OCP is to make it possible to substitute one class with another to get different behaviors. This is a reasonably simple thing to do in most object-oriented languages and TypeScript is no exception. Listing 3-7 shows a reward card point calculation class named RewardPointsCalculator. The standard number of reward points is four points per whole dollar spent in the store. When the decision is made to offer double points to some VIP customers, instead of adding a conditional comment within the original RewardPointsCalculator class, a subclass named DoublePointsCalculator is created to deal with the new behavior. The subclass in this case calls the original getPoints method on the superclass, but it could ignore the original class entirely and calculate the points any way it wishes.

Listing 3-7. Open-closed principle (OCP)

```typescript
class RewardPointsCalculator {
    getPoints(transactionValue: number) {
        // 4 points per whole dollar spent
        return Math.floor(transactionValue) * 4;
    }
}

class DoublePointsCalculator extends RewardPointsCalculator {
    getPoints(transactionValue: number) {
        var standardPoints = super.getPoints(transactionValue);
        return standardPoints * 2;
    }
}

var pointsCalculator = new DoublePointsCalculator();

alert(pointsCalculator.getPoints(100.99));
```

If the decision was taken to only give reward points on particular qualifying purchases, a class could handle the filtering of the transactions based on their type before calling the original RewardPointsCalculator—again, extending the behavior of the application rather than modifying the existing RewardPointsCalculator class.

By following the OCP, a program is more likely to contain maintainable and re-usable code. By avoiding changes, you also avoid the shock waves that can echo throughout the program following a change. Code that is known to work is left untouched and new code is added to handle the new requirements.

The Liskov Substitution Principle (LSP)

In *Data Abstraction and Hierarchy* Barbara Liskov (`http://www.sr.ifes.edu.br/~mcosta/disciplinas/20091/tpa/recursos/p17-liskov.pdf`, 1988) wrote,

> *What is wanted here is something like the following substitution property: If for each object o[1] of type S there is an object o[2] of type T such that for all programs P defined in terms of T, the behavior of P is unchanged when o[1] is substituted for o[2] then S is a subtype of T.*

—Barbara Liskov

The essence of this is that if you substitute a subclass for a superclass, the code that uses the class shouldn't need to know that the substitution has taken place. If you find yourself testing the type of an object in your program, there is a high probability that you are violating the LSP. The specific requirements of this principle are described later, using the example of a super `Animal` class, and a subclass of `Cat` that inherits from `Animal`.

- *Contravariance of method arguments in the subtype*: If the superclass has a method accepting a `Cat`, the subclass method should accept an argument of type `Cat` or `Animal`, which is the superclass for `Cat`.

- *Covariance of return types in the subtype*: If the superclass has a method that returns an `Animal`, the subclass method should return an `Animal`, or a subclass of `Animal`, such as `Cat`.

- *The subtype should throw either the same exceptions as the supertype, or exceptions that are subtypes of the supertype exceptions*: In TypeScript, you are not limited to using exception classes; you can simply specify a string to throw an exception. It is possible to create classes for errors in TypeScript, as shown in Listing 3-8. The key here is that if calling code has an exception handling block, it should not be surprised by the exception thrown by a subclass. There is more information on exception handling in Chapter 7.

   Listing 3-8. Error classes

   ```
   class ApplicationError implements Error {
       constructor(public name: string, public message: string) {

       }
   }

   throw new ApplicationError('Example Error', 'An error has occurred');
   ```

The LSP supports the OCP by ensuring that new code can be used in place of old code when a new behavior is added to a program. If a subclass couldn't be directly substituted for a superclass, adding a new subclass would result in changes being made throughout the code and may even result in the program flow being controlled by conditions that branch based on the object types.

The Interface Segregation Principle (ISP)

It is quite common to find that an interface is in essence just a description of an entire class. This is usually the case when the interface was written after the class. Listing 3-9 shows a simple example of an interface for a printer that can copy, print, and staple documents. Because the interface is just a way of describing all of the behaviors of a printer, it grows as new features are added, for example, folding, inserting into envelopes, faxing, scanning, and e-mailing may eventually end up on the `Printer` interface.

Listing 3-9. Printer interface

```
interface Printer {
    copyDocument();
    printDocument(document: Document);
    stapleDocument(document: Document, tray: number);
}
```

The ISP states that we should not create these big interfaces, but instead write a series of smaller, more specific, interfaces that are implemented by the class. Each interface would describe an independent grouping of behavior, allowing code to depend on a small interface that provides just the required behavior. Different classes could provide the implementation of these small interfaces, without having to implement additional unrelated functionality.

The `Printer` interface from Listing 3-9 makes it impossible to implement a printer that can print and copy, but not staple—or even worse, the staple method be implemented to throw an error that states the operation cannot be completed. The likelihood of a printer satisfying the `Printer` interface as the interface grows larger decreases over time and it becomes hard to add a new method to the interface because it affects multiple implementations. Listing 3-10 shows an alternative approach that groups methods into more specific interfaces that describe a number of contracts that could be implemented individually by a simple printer or simple copier, as well as by a super printer that could do everything.

Listing 3-10. Segregated interfaces

```
interface Printer {
    printDocument(document: Document);
}

interface Stapler {
    stapleDocument(document: Document, tray: number);
}

interface Copier {
    copyDocument();
}

class SimplePrinter implements Printer {
    printDocument(document: Document) {
        //...
    }
}

class SuperPrinter implements Printer, Stapler, Copier {
    printDocument(document: Document) {
        //...
    }
```

```
    copyDocument() {
        //...
    }

    stapleDocument(document: Document, tray: number) {
        //...
    }
}
```

When you follow the ISP, client code is not forced to depend on methods it doesn't intend to use. Large interfaces tend to encourage calling code that is organized in similar large chunks, whereas a series of small interfaces allows the client to implement small maintainable adapters to communicate with the interface.

The Dependency Inversion Principle (DIP)

In a conventional object-oriented program, the high-level components depend on low-level components in a hierarchical structure. The coupling between components results in a rigid system that is hard to change, and one that fails when changes are introduced. It also becomes hard to reuse a module because it cannot be moved into a new program without also bringing along a whole series of dependencies.

Listing 3-11 shows a simple example of conventional dependencies. The high-level LightSwitch class depends on the lower-level Light class.

Listing 3-11. High-level dependency on low-level class

```
class Light {
    switchOn() {
        //...
    }

    switchOff() {
        //...
    }
}

class LightSwitch {
    private isOn = false;

    constructor(private light: Light) {
    }

    onPress() {
        if (this.isOn) {
            this.light.switchOff();
            this.isOn = false;
        } else {
            this.light.switchOn();
            this.isOn = true;
        }
    }
}
```

The DIP simply states that high-level modules shouldn't depend on low-level components, but instead depend on an abstraction. In turn, the abstractions should not depend on details, but on yet more abstractions. In simple terms, you can satisfy the DIP by depending on an interface, rather than a class.

Listing 3-12 demonstrates the first step of DIP in practice, simply adding a LightSource interface to break the dependency between the LightSwitch and Light classes. We can continue this design by abstracting the LightSwitch into a Switch interface, the Switch interface would depend on the LightSource interface, not on the low-level Light class.

Listing 3-12. Implementing the dependency inversion principle (DIP)

```
interface LightSource {
    switchOn();
    switchOff();
}

class Light implements LightSource {
    switchOn() {
        //...
    }

    switchOff() {
        //...
    }
}

class LightSwitch {
    private isOn = false;

    constructor(private light: LightSource) {
    }

    onPress() {
        if (this.isOn) {
            this.light.switchOff();
            this.isOn = false;
        } else {
            this.light.switchOn();
            this.isOn = true;
        }
    }
}
```

The DIP extends the concepts of the OCP and the LSP. By depending on abstractions, code is less tightly bound to the specific implementation details of a class. This principle has a big impact, yet it is relatively simple to follow, as all you need to do is supply an interface to depend on rather than a class.

Design Patterns

In software, design patterns provide a catalog of known problems along with a design solution for each problem described. These patterns are not overly prescriptive, instead they provide a set of tools that you can arrange in a different way each time you use them. The definitive source for the most common design patterns is the original "Gang of Four" book, *Design Patterns: Elements of Reusable Object-Oriented Software* (Gamma, Helm, Johnson, & Vlissides, Addison Wesley, 1995).

It is possible to transfer these design patterns to JavaScript, as shown by Diaz and Harmes (*Pro JavaScript Design Patterns*, Apress, 2007), and if it can be done in plain JavaScript it can be done in TypeScript. The translation from traditional design pattern examples to TypeScript is more natural in many cases, due to the class-based object orientation offered in TypeScript.

TypeScript is a natural fit for design patterns because it supplies all of the language constructs required to use all of the creational, structural, and behavioral patterns in the original catalog as well as many more documented since then. A small sample of design patterns are described following along with TypeScript code examples.

The following example demonstrates the strategy pattern and the abstract factory pattern. These are just two of the 24 patterns described in the original Gang of Four book. The patterns are described in general below and then used to improve the design of a small program.

■ **Note** Although you may have an up-front idea about the design patterns that may improve the design of your program, it is far more common and often more desirable to let the patterns emerge as your program grows. If you predict the patterns that may be required, you could be guessing wrong. If you let the code reveal problems as you extend it, you are less likely to create a large number of unnecessary classes, and you are less likely to get lost down the rabbit hole following the wrong design.

The Strategy Pattern

The strategy pattern allows you to encapsulate different algorithms in a way that makes each one substitutable for another. In Figure 3-2 the Context class would depend on Strategy, which provides the interface for concrete implementations. Any class that implements the interface could be passed to the Context class at runtime.

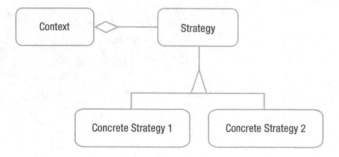

Figure 3-2. *The strategy pattern*

An example of the strategy pattern is shown in the practical example later in this section.

The Abstract Factory Pattern

The abstract factory pattern is a creational design pattern. It allows you to specify an interface for the creation of related objects without specifying their concrete classes. The aim of this pattern is for a class to depend on the behavior of the abstract factory, which will be implemented by different concrete classes that are either changed at compile time or runtime.

An example of the abstract factory pattern is shown in the practical example in Figure 3-3 and in the following text.

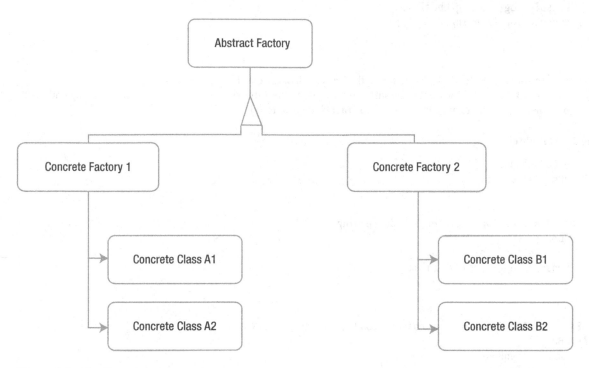

Figure 3-3. *The abstract factory pattern*

Practical Example

To illustrate the use of Strategy and Abstract Factory design patterns we use a car wash example. The car wash is able to run different grades of wash depending on how much the driver spends. Listing 3-13 illustrates the wheel cleaning strategy, which consists of an interface for wheel cleaning classes, and two strategies that provide either a basic or executive clean.

Listing 3-13. Wheel cleaning.

```
interface WheelCleaning {
    cleanWheels(): void;
}

class BasicWheelCleaning implements WheelCleaning {
    cleanWheels() {
        console.log('Soaping Wheel');
        console.log('Brushing wheel');
    }
}
```

```typescript
class ExecutiveWheelCleaning extends BasicWheelCleaning {
    cleanWheels() {
        super.cleanWheels();
        console.log('Waxing Wheel');
        console.log('Rinsing Wheel');
    }
}
```

Listing 3-14 shows the strategies for cleaning the bodywork of the car. This is similar to the WheelCleaning example in Listing 3-13, but it does not necessarily need to be. Neither the WheelCleaning nor BodyCleaning code will change when we convert the example to use the abstract factory pattern later.

Listing 3-14. Body cleaning

```typescript
interface BodyCleaning {
    cleanBody(): void;
}

class BasicBodyCleaning implements BodyCleaning {
    cleanBody() {
        console.log('Soaping car');
        console.log('Rinsing Car');
    }
}

class ExecutiveBodyCleaning extends BasicBodyCleaning {
    cleanBody() {
        super.cleanBody();
        console.log('Waxing car');
        console.log('Blow drying car');
    }
}
```

Listing 3-15 shows the CarWashProgram class before it is updated to use the abstract factory pattern. This is a typical example of a class that knows too much. It is tightly coupled to the concrete cleaning classes and is responsible for creating the relevant classes based on the selected program.

Listing 3-15. CarWashProgram class before the abstract factory pattern

```typescript
class CarWashProgram {
    constructor(private washLevel: number) {

    }

    runWash() {
        var wheelWash: WheelCleaning;
        var bodyWash: BodyCleaning;

        switch (this.washLevel) {
            case 1:
                wheelWash = new BasicWheelCleaning();
                wheelWash.cleanWheels();
```

```
                bodyWash = new BasicBodyCleaning();
                bodyWash.cleanBody();

                break;
            case 2:
                wheelWash = new BasicWheelCleaning();
                wheelWash.cleanWheels();

                bodyWash = new ExecutiveBodyCleaning();
                bodyWash.cleanBody();

                break;
            case 3:
                wheelWash = new ExecutiveWheelCleaning();
                wheelWash.cleanWheels();

                bodyWash = new ExecutiveBodyCleaning();
                bodyWash.cleanBody();

                break;
        }
    }
}
```

The abstract factory itself is an interface that describes the operations each concrete factory can perform. In Listing 3-16 the ValetFactory interface provides method signatures for obtaining the class providing the wheel cleaning feature and the class providing the body cleaning feature. A class that requires wheel cleaning and body cleaning can depend on this interface and remain de-coupled from the classes that specify the actual cleaning.

Listing 3-16. Abstract factory

```
interface ValetFactory {
    getWheelCleaning() : WheelCleaning;
    getBodyCleaning() : BodyCleaning;
}
```

In Listing 3-17, three concrete factories are declared that provide either a bronze, silver, or gold level wash. Each factory provides appropriate cleaning classes that match the level of wash required.

Listing 3-17. Concrete factories

```
class BronzeWashFactory implements ValetFactory {
    getWheelCleaning() {
        return new BasicWheelCleaning();
    }

    getBodyCleaning() {
        return new BasicBodyCleaning();
    }
}
```

```typescript
class SilverWashFactory implements ValetFactory {
    getWheelCleaning() {
        return new BasicWheelCleaning();
    }

    getBodyCleaning() {
        return new ExecutiveBodyCleaning();
    }
}

class GoldWashFactory implements ValetFactory {
    getWheelCleaning() {
        return new ExecutiveWheelCleaning();
    }

    getBodyCleaning() {
        return new ExecutiveBodyCleaning();
    }
}
```

Listing 3-18 shows the updated class with the abstract factory pattern in action. The CarWashProgram class no longer has any knowledge of the concrete classes that will perform the car cleaning actions. The CarWashProgram is now constructed with the appropriate factory that will provide the classes to perform the clean. This could either be done via a compile time mechanism or a dynamic runtime one.

Listing 3-18. Abstract factory pattern in use

```typescript
class CarWashProgram {
    constructor(private cleaningFactory: ValetFactory) {

    }

    runWash() {
        var wheelWash = this.cleaningFactory.getWheelCleaning();
        wheelWash.cleanWheels();

        var bodyWash = this.cleaningFactory.getBodyCleaning();
        bodyWash.cleanBody();
    }
}
```

Mixins

Mixins provide an alternate way of composing your application that isn't explicitly covered in books on design patterns.

Mixins take their name from a customizable ice-cream dessert that was first available at Steve's Ice Cream in Somerville, Massachusetts. The idea behind the mix-in dessert was that you choose an ice cream and add another product to flavor it, for example, a candy bar. The mix-in, or smoosh-in, ice-cream concept has gone global since its appearance on Steve Herrell's menu back in 1973.

In programming, mixins are based on a very similar concept. Augmented classes are created by adding together a combination of mixin classes that each provides a small reusable behavior. These mixin classes are partly an interface and partly an implementation.

TypeScript Mixins

Although mixins are not 100% natively supported in TypeScript yet, it is possible to implement them with the aid of just one additional function that performs the wiring. The function to apply the mixins is shown in Listing 3-19. This function walks the instance members of each of the mixin classes passed in the baseCtors array and adds each of them to the derivedCtor class. You will use this function each time you want to apply mixins to a class and you'll see this function used in the examples throughout this section.

Listing 3-19. Mixin enabler function

```
function applyMixins(derivedCtor: any, baseCtors: any[]) {
    baseCtors.forEach(baseCtor => {
        Object.getOwnPropertyNames(baseCtor.prototype).forEach(name => {
            if (name !== 'constructor') {
                derivedCtor.prototype[name] = baseCtor.prototype[name];
            }
        })
    });
}
```

Once you have added this function somewhere within your program, you are ready to start using mixins. In Listing 3-20 a series of small reusable mixin classes are defined. There is no specific syntax for these classes. In this example, we define a series of possible behaviors, Sings, Dances, and Acts. These classes act as the menu of behaviors that can be mixed together to create different flavors composed of different combinations.

Listing 3-20. Reusable classes

```
class Sings {
    sing() {
        console.log('Singing');
    }
}

class Dances {
    dance() {
        console.log('Dancing');
    }
}

class Acts {
    act() {
        console.log('Acting');
    }
}
```

On their own, these classes are too small to be useful, but they adhere very closely to the single responsibility principle. You are not restricted to a single method, but the idea is that each class represents one behavior that you can sum up in the class name. To make these mixins useful, you need to compose them into usable augmented classes.

In TypeScript, you compose your class using the implements keyword, followed by a comma-separated list of mixins. The implements keyword pays homage to the fact that mixins are like interfaces that come with an implementation. You will also need to supply temporary properties that match all of the mixins that you combine, as shown in listing 3-21. These properties will be replaced when the applyMixins function is called directly after the class declaration.

Listing 3-21. Composing classes

```
class Actor implements Acts {
    act: () => void;
}

applyMixins(Actor, [Acts]);

class AllRounder implements Acts, Dances, Sings {
    act: () => void;
    dance: () => void;
    sing: () => void;
}

applyMixins(AllRounder, [Acts, Dances, Sings]);
```

There is nothing to ensure that you call the applyMixins function with the same collection of classes that you listed in the implements statement. You are responsible for keeping the two lists synchronized.

The Actor and AllRounder classes have no real implementation, only placeholders for the implementation that is supplied by the mixins. This means that there is only one place in the program that needs to be changed for any given behavior. Using an augmented class is no different to using any other class in your program, as shown in Listing 3-22.

Listing 3-22. Using the classes

```
var actor = new Actor();
actor.act();

var allRounder = new AllRounder();
allRounder.act();
allRounder.dance();
allRounder.sing();
```

■ **Note**   You may have spotted that mixins look a little bit like multiple inheritance. Multiple inheritance is not permitted in TypeScript. The key to mixins is the use of the implements keyword, rather than the extends keyword, which makes them like interfaces rather than superclasses.

When to Use Mixins

Mixins already have some support in TypeScript—but what should you bear in mind when using them? First and foremost, the mechanism for adding the implementation to the augmented class is not checked, so you have to be very careful about calling the applyMixins function with the correct list of class names. This is one area that you will want to fully test to avoid any nasty surprises.

The decision about whether to use mixins or classical inheritance usually comes down to the relationship between the classes. When deciding between inheritance and delegation, it is common to use the "is a" verses "has a" test. As described earlier in this chapter.

- A car *has a* chassis.

- A rolling chassis *is a* chassis.

Inheritance would only be used where the "is a" relationship works in a sentence, and delegation would be used where "has a" makes more sense. With mixins, the relationship is best described by a "can do" relationship, for example

- *An actor can do acting.*

Or

- *An actor acts.*

You can reinforce this relationship by naming your mixins with names such as `Acting` or `Acts`. This makes your class read like a sentence, for example, "Actor implements Acting."

Mixins are supposed to allow small units to be composed into larger ones, so the following scenarios are good candidates for using mixins:

- Composing classes with optional features, mixins are options.

- Reusing the same behavior on many classes

- Creating many variations based on similar lists of features

Restrictions

You cannot use mixins with private members because the compiler will generate an error if the members are not implemented in the augmented class. The compiler will also generate an error if both the mixin and the augmented class define a private member with the same name.

The other restriction on mixins is that although method implementations are mapped to the augmented class, property values are not mapped; this is demonstrated in Listing 3-23. When you implement a property from a mixin you need to initialize it in the augmented class. To avoid confusion, it is best to define a required property in the mixin, but provide no default value.

Listing 3-23. Properties not mapped

```
class Acts {
    public message = 'Acting';

    act() {
        console.log(this.message);
    }
}

class Actor implements Acts {
    public message: string;
    act: () => void;
}

applyMixins(Actor, [Acts]);

var actor = new Actor();

// Logs 'undefined', not 'Acting'
actor.act();
```

If the property does not need to be tied to the instance, you can use static properties as these would remain available from within the methods that are mapped from the mixin to the augmented class. Listing 3-24 is an update to Listing 3-23 that solves the problem using a static property. If you do need different values on each instance, the instance property should be initialized within the augmented class.

Listing 3-24. Static properties are available

```
class Acts {
    public static message = 'Acting';

    act() {
        alert(Acts.message);
    }
}
```

Summary

The basic building blocks of object orientation are all present in TypeScript. The language tools make it possible to bring all of the principles and practices of object orientation from other languages into your program, using the SOLID principles to guide your composition and design patterns as a reference for well-established solutions to common problems.

Object orientation, in itself doesn't solve the problems of writing and maintaining a program that solves complex problems. It is just as possible to write poor code using object orientation as it is to write bad code in any other programming paradigm; this is why the patterns and principles are so important. The elements of object orientation in this chapter compliment the unit testing techniques in Chapter 9.

You can practice and improve your object-oriented design skills as well as your unit testing skills using coding katas. These are described in Appendix 4 and there are some example katas for you to try out.

Key Points

- TypeScript has all of the tools needed to write object-oriented programs.

- The SOLID principles aim to keep your code malleable and prevent it from rotting.

- Design patterns are existing well-known solutions to common problems.

- You don't have to implement a design pattern exactly as it is described.

- Mixins provide an alternative mechanism for composition.

■ ■ ■

CHAPTER 4

Understanding the Runtime

The difference between a bad programmer and a good programmer is understanding. That is, bad programmers don't understand what they are doing and good programmers do.

—Max Kanat-Alexander

Once your TypeScript program has been compiled to plain JavaScript, you can run it anywhere. JavaScript happily runs in a browser or on a server; you just have to bear in mind that the available features differ depending on where the code runs. This chapter explains some of the differences you will encounter between browser and server runtimes and also explains some important concepts that are common to all runtimes, such as the event loop, scope and events.

Runtime Features

Even an aged browser will give you access to the Document Object Model (DOM), mouse and keyboard events, forms, and navigation. A modern browser will add offline storage, an indexed database, HTTP requests, geolocation, and suite of application program interfaces (APIs) for device sensors such as light and proximity. JavaScript isn't just the most common language in web browsers; it has been running on servers since the early nineties. JavaScript's prominence as a server-side language has really gained traction with NodeJS, which is a server technology built on the V8 JavaScript engine. Running on the server gives you access to databases, the file system, cryptography, domain name resolution, streams, and countless other modules and utilities. Figure 4-1 illustrates how JavaScript as a language is made powerful by the APIs supplied by browsers or servers.

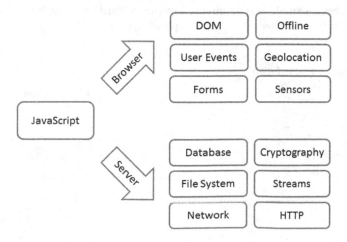

Figure 4-1. JavaScript features in browser vs. server environments

Unless you explicitly use an API that allows thread creation, such as web workers or a child process, the statements in your program will be queued to execute on a single thread. Running a program on a single thread removes many of the headaches that would be caused by multiple threads trying to manipulate the same data, but it does mean you need to bear in mind that your code could be queued. A long running event handler can block other events from firing in a timely manner and the order in which the queue gets executed can vary in subtle ways. The queue is usually processed in first-in first-out order, but different runtime environments may revisit the queue at different times. For example, one environment may return to the queue only when a function has been completed, but another may revisit the queue if the first function calls out to a second function. In the latter case, another statement may be executed before the second function is called. Despite the alarming nature of these potential differences, it is rare to find that they cause any problems in practice.

As well as processing the queue containing all of the events, the runtime may have other tasks to perform that need to be processed on the same thread; for example a browser may need to redraw the screen. If you have a function that takes too long to run, you could affect the redraw speed of the browser. To allow a browser to draw 60 frames per second, you would need to keep the execution of any function to less than 17 ms. Keeping functions fast is very easy in practice, except where you deal with an API with blocking calls, such as `localStorage`, or if you execute a long running loop.

One of the most common side effects of the single-threaded approach at runtime is that intervals and timers may appear to take longer than the specified time to execute. This is because they have to wait in the queue to be executed. Listing 4-1 provides an example to test this behavior. Calling the `test` function sets up the 50-ms timer and measures how long it takes to fire. Running this test a few times will show you that you get a result in the range of 50 to 52 ms, which is what you'd expect.

Listing 4-1. Queued timer

```
function test() {
    var testStart = performance.now();

    window.setTimeout(function () {
        console.log(performance.now() - testStart);
    }, 50);
}

test();
```

To simulate a long running process, a loop that runs for 100 ms has been added to the `test` function in Listing 4-2. The loop starts after the timer is set up, but because nothing is de-queued until the original `test` function is completed, the timer executes much later than before. The times logged in this example are typically in the range of 118 to 130 ms.

Listing 4-2. Queued timer, delayed, waiting for the test method to finish

```
function test() {
    var testStart = performance.now();

    window.setTimeout(function () {
        console.log(performance.now() - testStart);
    }, 50);
```

```
    // Simulated long running process
    var start = +new Date();
    while (true) {
        if (+new Date() - start > 100) {
            break;
        }
    }
}

test();
```

■ **Note**   The `performance.now` high resolution timer is not yet supported everywhere, but this method of measuring execution times is more accurate than using the `Date` object. Dates are based on the system clock, which is synchronized as often as every 15 minutes. If synchronization occurs while you are timing an operation, it will affect your result. The `performance.now` value comes from a high resolution timer that can measure submillisecond intervals, starts at 0 when the page begins to load, and isn't adjusted during synchronization.

Scope

The term *scope* refers to the set of available identifiers that can be resolved in a given context. In most C-like languages, identifiers are block scoped, meaning they are available within the same set of curly-braces that they are defined in. Variables declared within a set of curly braces are not available outside of those braces, but statements within the curly braces can access variables declared outside of the braces. Listing 4-3 shows this general C-like scoping in action.

This is not currently the case in JavaScript (and therefore TypeScript). If the code in Listing 4-3 was executed in a JavaScript runtime, the value logged in both statements would be *Outer: 2*, rather than *Outer: 1*. This is because scope is defined by functions, rather than curly braces.

Listing 4-3. C-like scope

```
var scope = 1;

{
    var scope = 2;

    // Inner: 2
    console.log('Inner: ' + scope);
}

// Outer: 1
console.log('Outer: ' + scope);
```

To provide the same restricted scope to the inner variable and logging statement in JavaScript, the curly braces would need to be replaced by a function definition, as shown in Listing 4-4.

Listing 4-4. Functional scope

```
var scope = 1;

(function () {
    var scope = 2;

    // Inner: 2
    console.log('Inner: ' + scope);
}());

// Outer: 1
console.log('Outer: ' + scope);
```

As ECMAScript 6 gains traction, block-level scope will be made available using the let keyword. The let keyword can be used anywhere you previously used the var keyword, but variables declared with let are block scoped rather than function scoped.

Listing 4-5 shows an example where a variable is wrapped in curly braces, but because variables have function scope it can be accessed from outside of the block.

Listing 4-5. Using the var keyword

```
{
    var name = 'Scope Example';
    console.log('A: ' + name);
}

// 'B: Scope Example'
console.log('B: ' + name);
```

Using the let keyword as shown in Listing 4-6 restricts the scope of the name variable to the block, and the attempt to access the value of the variable outside of the braces fails.

Listing 4-6. Using the let keyword

```
{
    let name = 'Scope Example';
    console.log('A: ' + name);
}

// 'B: undefined'
console.log('B: ' + name);
```

Block-level scoping applies wherever a set of curly braces is used, for example, when writing loops, if-statements, switch-statements, or even just a pair of curly braces without an expression as shown in these examples.

As with all new features in the ECMAScript 6 proposal, browser support is currently limited. TypeScript currently does not allow the use of the let keyword unless the compiler is targeting ES6 mode (which is currently planned, but not available). The compiler flags are described in detail in Appendix 2.

Variable Hoisting

When you declare a variable with the var keyword, the declaration is hoisted to the top of the function it is declared in. This variable hoisting is usually irrelevant to your program, but there are subtle scenarios that will result in strange behavior.

It is important to declare local variables with the var keyword; otherwise the variable contributes to the global scope, rather than the local scope. The TypeScript compiler will warn you if you accidentally omit the var keyword, as long as there isn't already a global variable with the same name. If there is already a global variable with the same name, the compiler will assume you intended to re-use the global variable.

Listing 4-7 shows one such example. The global type variable is declared first. The use of the type variable at the top of the function looks like a reference to the global variable because the local variable has not yet been declared. Because of variable hoisting, the local variable declaration is moved to the top of the function at runtime, hiding the global variable of the same name. The assignment remains in the original location. This results in an undefined value being logged, rather than the global 'Ring Tailed Lemur' value or the local 'Ruffed Lemur' value. The local type variable is declared, but not assigned when console.log is called.

Listing 4-7. Variable hoisting

```
var type = 'Ring Tailed Lemur';

function Lemur() {
    console.log(type);
    var type = 'Ruffed Lemur';
}

Lemur();
```

Variable hoisting also applies to the let keyword, although the declaration in this case is hoisted to the top of the block scope rather than to the top of the function scope. This keeps the behavior consistent between block-scoped variables and function-scoped variables.

■ **Note**   In your program, the best way to avoid confusion is to avoid adding to the global scope wherever possible. The absence of global variables means the TypeScript compiler can warn you about usage of variables before they are declared and accidental omission of the var or let keywords.

Callbacks

Almost all modern JavaScript APIs, including the new browser APIs that supply access to readings from device sensors, avoid blocking the main thread by accepting a callback. A callback is simply a function that you pass as an argument, which is called when an operation has completed.

To illustrate the benefits of callbacks, Figure 4-2 shows the program flow while waiting for a blocking sensor to respond to a request. Because the request is blocking the thread for the duration of the request, no other statements can be executed. Blocking the event queue for more than a few milliseconds is undesirable and must be avoided for long operations. Operations involving calls to the file system, hardware devices, or calls across a network connection all have the potential to block your program for unacceptable lengths of time.

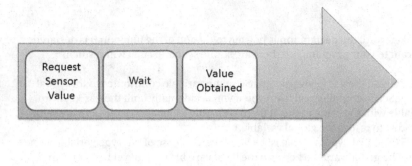

Figure 4-2. *Blocking call*

Callbacks are very useful for avoiding these blocking requests. Figure 4-3 shows how this pattern is used to avoid blocking the main thread during a long-running process. When the request is made, a function is passed along with the request. The main thread is then able to process the event queue as normal. When the long-running process ends, the callback function is then called, being passed any relevant arguments. The callback is placed on the event queue and is executed in turn.

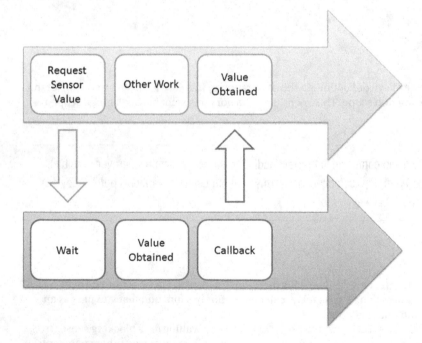

Figure 4-3. *Using a callback*

Although callbacks are commonly used to avoid blocking the program during a long-running process, you can freely pass a function as an argument anywhere in your program. Listing 4-8 demonstrates this. The go function accepts a function argument. The `callback` parameter has a type annotation that restricts the functions that can be passed to only those that accept a `string` argument. The `callbackFunction` satisfies this type annotation.

Listing 4-8. Passing a function as an argument

```
function go(callback: (arg: string) => void) {
    callback.call(this, 'Example Argument');
}

function callbackFunction(arg: string) {
    alert(arg);
}

go(callbackFunction);
```

In the body of the go function, the callback is executed using the `call` method, which is available on all functions in JavaScript.

There are three ways to execute the callback from within the go function. In Listing 4-8, the `call` method was used. When you use `call`, you must supply a variable that will be used to set the context of the `this` keyword within the callback. You can follow the context argument with any number of additional arguments; these will be passed into the callback. You can also use the `apply` method, which is almost identical to `call`, except you pass the arguments as an array, as shown in Listing 4-9.

Listing 4-9. Using apply

```
function go(callback: (arg: string) => void) {
    callback.apply(this, ['Example Argument']);
}
```

The third method of executing a callback is to simply append the parameter name with parentheses as demonstrated in Listing 4-10. This technique doesn't allow the context to be set, but you can pass arguments in the usual way by placing them within the parentheses.

Listing 4-10. Simple function call

```
function go(callback: (arg: string) => void) {
    callback('Example Argument');
}
```

There is an additional use for the `apply` method outside of the context of callbacks. Because it accepts an array containing arguments, you can use `apply` to extract arguments from an array. This is demonstrated in Listing 4-11. To find the maximum number in the `numbers` array you would either write a loop to test each one or pass each value individually into the `Math.max` function using each index. Using the `apply` method means you can simply pass the `numbers` array and have the `apply` method convert the array into the argument list. Because you aren't using `apply` to modify the scope, you can pass `null` as the first argument.

Listing 4-11. Using apply to convert array to arguments

```
var numbers = [3, 11, 5, 7, 2];

// A fragile way of finding the maximum number
// var max = Math.max(numbers[0], numbers[1], numbers[2], numbers[3], numbers[4]);

// A solid way to find the maximum
var max = Math.max.apply(null, numbers);

// 11
console.log(max);
```

The pattern of using callbacks is one example of functions passed as arguments. The next section describes how powerful this language feature is and how it can be used in other ways.

Passing Functions as Arguments

Functions are first-class citizens in JavaScript, which means they can be passed as arguments, returned from another function as a return value, assigned to variables, and stored as properties on an object. Passing a function as an argument is the mechanism used to provide callbacks.

You can use the ability to pass functions as arguments to create a simple implementation of the observer pattern, storing a collection of subscribers and publishing an event to them all from a single class. This simple observer design is shown in Listing 4-12. Any number of subscribers can be added, and when the publisher receives a message, it distributes it to all of the subscribers.

Listing 4-12. Simple observer

```
interface Subscriber {
    () : any;
}

class Publisher {
    private subscribers: Subscriber[] = [];

    addSubscriber(subscriber: Subscriber) {
        this.subscribers.push(subscriber);
    }

    notify(message: string) {
        for (var i = 0; i < this.subscribers.length; i++) {
            this.subscribers[i].apply(message);
        }
    }
}

var publisher = new Publisher();

publisher.addSubscriber(function () {
    console.log('A: ' + this);
});
```

```
publisher.addSubscriber(function () {
    console.log('B: ' + this);
});

// A: Test message
// B: Test message
publisher.notify('Test message');
```

___

■ **Note** When you pass a function as an argument, you must omit the parentheses; for example, go(callbackFunction) rather than go(callbackFunction()), otherwise the function is executed and the return value is passed as the argument.

___

First-class functions are one of the most powerful features in any language. You can create higher-order functions that accept functions as arguments and return functions as results; this allows greater flexibility as well as granular code reusability in your program.

Events

Events are a fundamental concept in the JavaScript runtime, so they are of great interest to any TypeScript programmer. Event listeners are commonly attached to user-initiated events such as touch, click, keypress, and other interactions on a web page, but events can also be used as a mechanism for decoupling code that needs to trigger processing and the code that undertakes the work.

Events are handled across two distinct phases—capturing and bubbling. During capturing, the event is sent to the topmost elements in the document hierarchy first and then to more deeply nested elements. During bubbling it is sent to the target element first and then to its ancestors. The phase is supplied as a property of the event argument and can be accessed using e.eventPhase where your event argument is named e.

At the risk of overstating the point about running in an event loop on a single thread, it is worth remembering that multiple event listeners attached to the same event will execute sequentially, not in parallel, and a long-running listener may delay the execution of the subsequent listeners attached to the same event. When an event is triggered, each event listener is queued in the same order it is attached, if the first listener takes 2 s to run, the second listener is blocked for at least 2 s and will only execute once it reaches the top of the event queue.

Listing 4-13. Event listeners

```
class ClickLogger {
    constructor () {
        document.addEventListener('click', this.eventListener);
    }

    eventListener(e: Event) {
        // 3 (Bubbling Phase)
        var phase = e.eventPhase;

        var tag = (<HTMLElement>e.target).tagName;

        console.log('Click event in phase ' + phase +
            ' detected on element ' + tag + ' by ClickLogger.');
    }
}

var clickLogger = new ClickLogger();
```

Listing 4-13 shows a class that attaches one of its methods, eventListener, to the click event on the document. When used in conjunction with the HTML page in Listing 4-14, this ClickLogger class will output messages based on the element clicked, for example

- Click event detected on element DIV by ClickLogger.

- Click event detected on element P by ClickLogger.

- Click event detected on element BLOCKQUOTE by ClickLogger.

- Click event detected on element FOOTER by ClickLogger.

Listing 4-14. Example document

```
<!DOCTYPE html>
<html lang="en">
<head>
    <meta http-equiv="content-type" content="text/html; charset=UTF-8">
    <title>Event Demo</title>
</head>
<body>
    <div>
        Clicking on different parts of this document logs appropriate messages.
        <blockquote>
            <p>Any fool can write code that a computer can understand.
                Good programmers write code that humans can understand.</p>
            <footer>
                -Martin Fowler
            </footer>
        </blockquote>
    </div>
</body>
</html>
```

■ **Note** The correct way to add an event listener is the addEventListener call. Versions of Internet Explorer prior to version 9 use an alternative attachEvent method. You can target both of these methods of attaching an event using the custom addEventCrossBrowser function shown in Listing 4-15. An improved version of this function appears in Chapter 5.

Listing 4-15. Cross-browser events

```
function addEventCrossBrowser(element, eventName, listener) {
    if (element.addEventListener) {
        element.addEventListener(eventName, listener, false);
    } else if (element.attachEvent) {
        element.attachEvent('on' + eventName, listener);
    }
}
```

```
class ClickLogger {
    constructor () {
        addEventCrossBrowser(document, 'click', this.eventListener);
    }

    eventListener(e: Event) {
        // 3 (Bubbling Phase)
        var phase = e.eventPhase;

        var tag = (<HTMLElement>e.target).tagName;

        console.log('Click event detected on element ' + tag + ' by ClickLogger.');
    }
}

var clickLogger = new ClickLogger();
```

You are not limited to the finite list of supported events in a given runtime; you can listen for, and dispatch, your own custom events.

TypeScript's Custom-Event Mechanism

Listing 4-16 shows the custom-event mechanism. In some environments, it is as simple as using addEventListener and dispatchEvent. You can pass custom data as part of the event to use in the listener.

Listing 4-16. Custom events

```
// Polyfill for CustomEvent:
// https://developer.mozilla.org/en/docs/Web/API/CustomEvent
(function () {
    function CustomEvent(event, params) {
        params = params || { bubbles: false, cancelable: false, detail: undefined };
        var evt = <any>document.createEvent('CustomEvent');
        evt.initCustomEvent(event, params.bubbles, params.cancelable, params.detail);
        return evt;
    };

    CustomEvent.prototype = (<any>window).Event.prototype;

    (<any>window).CustomEvent = CustomEvent;
})();

// Fix for lib.d.ts
interface StandardEvent {
    new (name: string, obj: {}): CustomEvent;
}
var StandardEvent = <StandardEvent><any> CustomEvent;
```

```
// Code for custom events is below:

enum EventType {
    MyCustomEvent
}

class Trigger {
    static customEvent(name: string, detail: {}) {
        var event = new StandardEvent(name, detail);

        document.dispatchEvent(event);
    }
}

class ListeningClass {
    constructor() {
        document.addEventListener(
            EventType[EventType.MyCustomEvent],
            this.eventListener,
            false);
    }

    eventListener(e: Event) {
        console.log(EventType[EventType.MyCustomEvent] + ' detected by ClickLogger.');
        console.log('Information passed: ' + (<any>e).detail.example);
    }
}

var customLogger = new ListeningClass();

Trigger.customEvent(
    EventType[EventType.MyCustomEvent],
    {
        "detail": {
            "example": "Example Value"
        }
    }
);
```

You can choose to use events, or code events, such as the simple observer from the earlier example in Listing 4-12, to distribute work throughout your program.

Event Phases

An event is dispatched to an event target along a propagation path that flows from the root of the document to the target element. Each progression along the path from the root to the target element is part of the capture phase of the event and the phase will be 1. Then the event reaches the event target, and the phase changes to the target phase, which is phase 2. Finally, the event flows in the reverse direction from the event target back to the root in the bubbling phase, which is phase 3.

These event phases are shown in Figure 4-4. The footer element in the figure is not part of the hierarchy between the root and the event target, so it is not included in the propagation path.

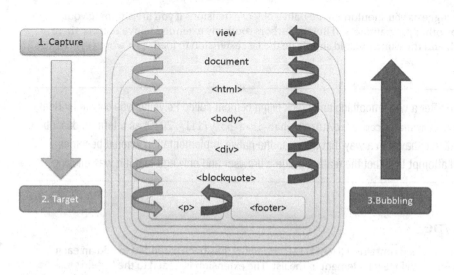

Figure 4-4. *Event phases*

Events provide a powerful mechanism for decoupling the code in your program. If you trigger events rather than directly call code to perform an action, it is a simple task to divide the action into small event listeners with a single responsibility. It is also a trivial matter to add additional listeners later.

Extending Objects

Almost everything in JavaScript is an object that consists of a set of properties. Each property is a key-value pair with a string key and value of any type, including primitive types, objects, and functions. If the value is a function, it is commonly called a method. Whenever you create a class in TypeScript, it is represented using JavaScript objects, but there are also many built-in objects that you can use.

The native objects all remain open, which means you can extend them as easily as you can your own objects. You need to take care when extending a native object for the following reasons:

- If everyone extended native objects, the chances are the extensions would overwrite each other or combine in incompatible ways.

- It is possible that the native object definition may later clash with yours and your implementation will hide the native implementation.

So although it is possible to extend native objects, in general it is only recommended as a technique to be used as a *polyfill*, which is a way of adding current features to older runtimes. Although you may decide to live by a less restrictive rule, it is worth writing extensions to native objects in the style of a polyfill so you can at least detect when one of the following happens:

- Native functionality is added with a name that clashes with your extension.

- Another programmer adds another extension with the same name.

- A third-party library or framework adds an extension with the same name.

The third item in particular suggests you shouldn't write native object extensions if you are shipping your program to be used as a library by other programmers. If library authors routinely extended native objects, there would be a high chance of a clash and the winner would simply be the last extension to load, as it would overwrite all previous ones.

■ **Note**   The term *polyfill* (named after a wall smoothing and crack filling cement called Polyfilla) was coined by Remy Sharp (*Remy Sharp's Blog,* `http://remysharp.com/2010/10/08/what-is-a-polyfill/`, 2010) as a term to describe a technique used to add missing native behavior in a way that defers to the native implementation when it becomes available. For example, you would attempt to detect the feature inside a browser and only add to it if it was missing.

Extending the Prototype

In Listing 4-17, the native NodeList, which contains a list of HTML elements, has been extended to add an each method that executes a callback function for each element in the list. The extension is added to the NodeList. prototype, which means it will be available on all NodeList instances. Calling document.querySelectorAll returns a NodeList of matching elements and now the each method can be used to display the contents of each element using the getParagraphText function. The use of the each method means the for loop can be defined in just a single place.

Listing 4-17. Extending objects in JavaScript

```javascript
NodeList.prototype.each = function (callback) {
    for (var i = 0; i < this.length; i++) {
        callback.call(this[i]);
    }
};

var getParagraphText = function () {
    console.log(this.innerHTML);
};

var paragraphs = document.querySelectorAll('p');
paragraphs.each(getParagraphText);
```

Rather than passing each element into the callback function as an argument, the call method is used to bind the element to the function's context, which means the getParagraphText function can use the this keyword to refer to the element.

When you add this code to a TypeScript program, errors will be generated to warn you that the each method doesn't exist on the NodeList interface. You can remove these errors and get intelligent autocompletion by adding to the interface in your program, as shown in Listing 4-18. The added benefit is that if the native object is updated in a way that clashes with your extension, the TypeScript compiler will warn you about the duplicate declaration.

Listing 4-18. Extending objects in TypeScript

```
interface NodeList {
        each(callback: () => any): void;
}

NodeList.prototype.each = function (callback) {
    for (var i = 0; i < this.length; i++) {
        callback.call(this[i]);
    }
};

var getParagraphText = function () {
    console.log(this.innerHTML);
};

var paragraphs = document.querySelectorAll('p');
paragraphs.each(getParagraphText);
```

In this example, the this keyword within the each method has no type because it can't be inferred. This can be improved as shown in Listing 4-19. By moving the elements from the contextual this keyword into a parameter, the autocompletion and type checking in your program is improved. This also means the function can be re-used more easily.

Listing 4-19. Improved TypeScript object extensions

```
interface NodeList {
        each(callback: (element: HTMLElement) => any): void;
}

NodeList.prototype.each = function (callback) {
    for (var i = 0; i < this.length; i++) {
        callback.call(null, this[i]);
    }
};

var getParagraphText = function (element: HTMLElement) {
    console.log(element.innerHTML);
};

var paragraphs = document.querySelectorAll('p');
paragraphs.each(getParagraphText);
```

To make this solution more like a polyfill, the code should check for the existence of the each method before adding it. This is how you would add an interim feature that is planned but not yet available on your target runtime. You can see this in action in Listing 4-20.

Listing 4-20. Turning an extension into a polyfill

```
if (!NodeList.prototype.each) {
    NodeList.prototype.each = function (callback) {
        for (var i = 0; i < this.length; i++) {
            callback.call(null, this[i]);
        }
    };
}
```

Extending objects via the prototype is a technique that can be used on any object in TypeScript, even your own—although it is a convoluted way to add behavior to objects that are under your control. You may be tempted to use the technique to extend a library that you consume, as it would allow you to upgrade the library without losing your additions.

Sealing Objects

If you are concerned about your code being extended, you can prevent extensions being made to your instances by using Object.seal. Listing 4-21 shows a typical extension that someone else may make to your code, and Listing 4-22 shows how to prevent it. Object.seal prevents new properties from being added and marks all existing properties as nonconfigurable. It is still possible to modify the values of the existing properties.

Listing 4-21. Extended instance

```
class Lemur {
    constructor(public name: string) {

    }
}

var lemur = new Lemur('Sloth Lemur');

// new property
lemur.isExtinct = true;

// true
console.log(lemur.isExtinct);
```

Listing 4-22. Sealing an instance

```
class Lemur {
    constructor(public name: string) {

    }
}
```

```
var lemur = new Lemur('Sloth Lemur');
```

Object.seal(lemur);

```
// new property
lemur.isExtinct = true;

// undefined
console.log(lemur.isExtinct);
```

You can check whether an object is sealed using the `Object.isSealed` method, passing in the object you want to check. There are a series of similar operations that may be useful—each could be used in Listing 4-21 in place of the `Object.seal` call to get the results described in the following example.

- `Object.preventExtensions/Object.isExtensible` is a more permissive version of `Object.seal`, allowing the properties to be deleted and to be added to the prototype.

- `Object.freeze/Object.isFrozen` is a more restrictive alternative to `Object.seal` that prevents properties from being added or removed and also prevents values being changed.

There is an excellent overview of creating, extending, and sealing JavaScript objects in *Expert JavaScript* by Mark Daggett (Apress, 2013).

Alternatives to Extending

It would be somewhat irresponsible to advise against extending native objects without presenting an alternative solution to the problem. This section shows an example of the `classList` property that is available on HTML elements in modern web browsers. The polyfill is shown, and then an alternative solution is supplied that uses a façade to marshal the call between either the native `classList` or the substitute version.

Listing 4-23 shows a call to retrieve the list of classes from an element that will fail in old browsers. The `classList` API actually supplies options to add, remove, and toggle classes—but for this example just the retrieval of the array of class names is shown.

Listing 4-23. Using the native classList

```
var elem = document.getElementById('example');

console.log(elem.classList);
```

One common solution to the potential absence of this feature is to use a polyfill. Listing 4-24 shows a simple polyfill that tests for the presence of the `classList` API and then adds it to the `HTMLElement` or `Element` prototype. The replacement function splits the string of class names to create an array, or returns an empty array if there are no class names.

Listing 4-24. Polyfill

```
if (typeof document !== "undefined" && !("classList" in document.documentElement)) {
    var elementPrototype = (HTMLElement || Element).prototype;
    if (elementPrototype) {
        Object.defineProperty(elementPrototype, 'classList',{
            get : function () {
                var list = this.className ? this.className.split(/\s+/) : [];
                console.log('Polyfill: ' + list);
            }
        });
    }
}

var elem = document.getElementById('example');

console.log(elem.classList);
```

Although using a polyfill is the right solution in this particular case (due to its close match to the native behavior and safety check that ensures it doesn't overwrite the native implementation if it is present), it is worth looking at the alternative design too. In many cases, the solution in Listing 4-25 is a more stable option as it won't ever clash with native or library code. The downside to this approach is that the calling code must be changed to reference the façade.

Listing 4-25. Façade

```
class Elements {
    static getClassList(elem) {
        if ('classList' in elem) {
            return elem.classList;
        }
        return elem.className ? elem.className.split(/\s+/) : [];
    }
}

var elem = document.getElementById('example');

console.log(Elements.getClassList(elem));
```

The façade option has one major benefit in addition to being better isolated than the polyfill. The intent of this code is clear. When it comes to maintaining your code, the less cluttered and more straightforward method in the Elements class trumps the polyfill every time. Clean and maintainable code is always preferable to a clever but complex solution.

Summary

The JavaScript runtime is well known for its quirks and surprises, but on the whole the TypeScript compiler will shield you from most of the common faux pas. Keeping the global scope clear can help the compiler to help you, so it is worth using the structural features of TypeScript such as modules and classes to enclose functions and variables.

Most of your code will execute on a single thread, and the callback pattern helps to avoid blocking this thread during long-running operations. Keeping functions short not only makes your program easier to maintain, it can also make your program more responsive as each time a function is called it is added to the back of the event queue and the runtime has an opportunity to process the oldest entry on the queue.

You can listen to native events and create custom events, or you can use the observer pattern to dispatch and listen to custom events in your program.

You can extend objects, including native objects, but it is often more appropriate to use mediating code to marshal the call to avoid clashing with other libraries or future extensions to native code. You can prevent extensions on your own objects by sealing, freezing, or preventing extensions.

Key Points

- JavaScript is functionally scoped, with block-level variables added in ECMAScript 6.

- Callbacks can help to avoid blocking the main thread.

- Events can prevent tight coupling, whether using native events or your own publisher.

- You can extend all JavaScript objects and almost everything in JavaScript is an object.

- You can seal or freeze objects to prevent further changes.

- You can polyfill missing behavior to make new features available on old platforms.

CHAPTER 5

■ ■ ■

Running TypeScript in a Browser

All modern web browsers—on desktops, game consoles, tablets and smart phones—include JavaScript interpreters, making JavaScript the most ubiquitous programming language in history.

—David Flanagan

Although there are many different environments you might target with your TypeScript program, one of the widest categories of runtime will surely be the web browser. This chapter introduces the general design of the web browser before introducing practical examples for interacting with web pages, making asynchronous requests to the web server, storing data on the user's local machine, and accessing hardware sensors. At the end of the chapter there is information about modularizing your program and loading modules on demand.

■ **Note**   Some of the features described in this chapter are experimental and have limited browser support. To find out which browsers support any specific feature, visit the "Can I use" project by Deveria (`http://caniuse.com/`, 2014).

The Anatomy of a Web Browser

Web browsers have quickly evolved from the simple document displays of the 1990s to fully fledged application environments and 3D gaming displays today. The reliance on plugins, applets, and downloads is diminishing fast as video, audio, and gaming all join documents, images, and applications inside of the web browser.

It is worth knowing a little about web browsers if your program is going to rely on them to work, but if the details of browsers and the history of some of the important features aren't causing a general feeling of excitement or if you already know everything there is to know about browsers, feel free to skip to the next section, which is more hands-on. If you'd like to know a bit more about how web browsers work read on.

Web browsers are typically made up of several components as shown in Figure 5-1.

- User interface
- Browser engine
- Rendering engine
- Widget engine
- JavaScript interpreter
- Networking
- Storage

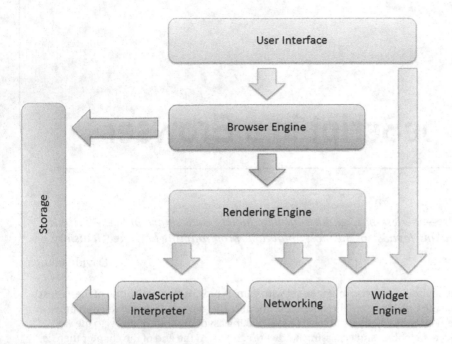

Figure 5-1. *Web browser components*

The user interface includes all the buttons and text boxes that appear on all web browser windows, for example, the address bar, back and forward buttons, and the refresh button. The browser engine and rendering engine handle the content display, which takes up the main area of the web browser's display. The widget engine supplies common user controls to the user interface and to the rendering engine, such as text inputs, drop-down lists, and buttons.

To display a web page, the browser engine relies on the rendering engine to display the HTML along with the appropriate styles defined in the cascading style sheets (CSS) or by the user if they are overriding page styles. The rendering engine relies on networking to fetch resources such as the web page, stylesheets, JavaScript files, and images. The widget engine is used whenever a user interaction component is needed, such as a text box. The JavaScript interpreter runs the downloaded JavaScript, which in turn may access storage, networking, and any other available application programming interfaces (APIs).

On the whole, the user interface, browser engine, rendering engine, and widget engine do a grand job and you don't need to know all of the minute details; the one exception to this is a process known as *reflows*, which can affect the perceived performance of your program.

Reflows

Each time the layout of the web page is changed by JavaScript or CSS, the layout is flagged as being invalid, but isn't immediately updated. The reflow, which recalculates the size and position of all elements in the document, would typically occur just before drawing the page. Additional reflows can be triggered if the JavaScript code requests the size or position of an element when the layout has the invalid flag. This additional reflow is needed to ensure the information supplied for the size or position is up to date.

Listing 5-1 shows a function that has a typical reflow problem, invalidating the layout on two occasions and causing two reflows. Each time a value is set on the document that can affect the layout; the layout is flagged as being invalid. Each time a value is retrieved from the document when the layout is invalid, the reflow is triggered. Although the example in the listing results in two reflows, if the mistake is repeated, it can result in many more. Reflows slow down your program and the page, which needs to wait for its turn to rerender.

Listing 5-1. Triggering multiple reflows

```typescript
var image = document.getElementById('mainImage');
var container = document.getElementById('content');

function updateSizes() {
    // Flags the layout as invalid
    image.style.width = '50%';

    // Causes a reflow to get the value
    var imageHeight = image.offsetHeight;

    // Flags the layout as invalid
    container.classList.add('highlight');

    // Causes a reflow to get the value
    var containerHeight = container.offsetHeight;

    return {
        'imageHeight': imageHeight,
        'containerHeight': containerHeight
    };
}

var result = updateSizes();
```

Multiple reflows can be avoided by performing the layout-invalidating operations before attempting to retrieve any values from the document, as shown in Listing 5-2. By grouping all of the operations that invalidate the layout at the start of the function and before any operations that require a reflow, we reduce the total number of reflows required during the function.

Listing 5-2. Triggering a single reflow

```typescript
var image = document.getElementById('mainImage');
var container = document.getElementById('content');

function updateSizes() {
    // Operations that invalidate the layout
    image.style.width = '50%';
    container.classList.add('highlight');

    // Operations that require a reflow
    var imageHeight = image.offsetHeight;
    var containerHeight = container.offsetHeight;

    return {
        'imageHeight': imageHeight,
        'containerHeight': containerHeight
    };
}

var result = updateSizes();
```

The only situation that can prevent you from avoiding multiple reflows is one in which you need to obtain a measurement after making a change. For example, finding the width of an element after you have changed its contents and then using the width to reposition the element, which cannot be done without a reflow. You can still carefully plan your operations to reduce the overall number of reflows to the minimum number possible.

The Interesting Components

The JavaScript interpreter along with the network and storage APIs are the most interesting components of a web browser when it comes to TypeScript. Each is described in more detail in the following sections.

The JavaScript Interpreter

The JavaScript interpreter, or JavaScript engine as it is also known, has a lot of work to do. Not only does it parse and execute the JavaScript program; it must manage objects and memory, work the event loop, and handle interactions with APIs such as storage, network, and sensors.

One of the things that make JavaScript programming in the browser so interesting (and at times frustrating) is that you will encounter many different JavaScript interpreters. In some rare cases, you may even encounter no interpreter and your program won't run. Having to support a number of interpreters can increase the amount of testing you need to perform as you will need to check that your program works in each web browser. However, there are upsides to the plethora of interpreters. One of the upsides is that browser vendors all want to be able to claim that their particular implementation of a JavaScript engine is the fastest and as a result interpreters have become many times faster as they each fight for the top spot.

The main things to watch for when relying on all of these different interpreters to run your program are

- They may only support an older version of the ECMAScript standard.

- They are allowed to implement additional features that are not part of the ECMAScript specification.

- They all run different code at different speeds especially on different operating systems.

- At some point in time you will encounter an end user who has JavaScript switched off entirely.

■ **Note**   The vast majority of browsers currently support ECMAScript version 5 as well as various parts of the ECMAScript 6 standard. Some older browsers are still stuck on the much older ECMAScript 3 standard, so you'll need to know whether you need to support these browsers as it will restrict the language features you can use in JavaScript (and to a lesser extent TypeScript, see Chapter 1).

A Brief History of Networking

The evolution of networking in the web browser can be tracked through several stages. The earliest mechanism for updating a part of the web page, without replacing the entire document, was to use a frameset. Framesets were a proposal for the HTML 3.0 specification. Websites would typically have a three-part frameset with individual frames for the header, navigation, and content. When a link was selected in the navigation frame, the content frame would be replaced with a new web page without reloading the header or the navigation. Framesets had the dual purpose of allowing parts of the display to update independently and also allowed re-usable widgets such as headers and navigation to be included without server-side processing.

A major problem with framesets was that the web address for the page was not updated as the user navigated because the user was still viewing the frameset, no matter which pages were being displayed in the frames within the frameset. When users bookmarked a page or shared a link to a page, it would not lead them back to the display they navigated to, but instead simply displayed the landing page for the website. In addition, framesets caused various problems for screen readers and text browsers.

The replacement for framesets was inline frames (the iframe element). Inline frames were placed inside the body of another document and could be updated independently.

But what do frames have to do with networking? In the days before networking in JavaScript, enterprising and creative programmers would use frames to give the appearance of live updates. For example, a hidden iframe pointing to a server-generated web page would be refreshed using a timer every ten seconds. Once the page has loaded, JavaScript would be used to grab new data from the iframe and update parts of the visible page based on the hidden page in the iframe. The architecture of this mechanism is shown in Figure 5-2.

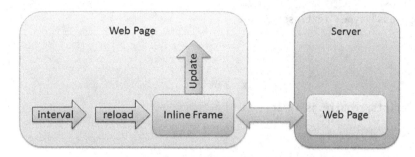

Figure 5-2. *Updating a web page by refreshing a second page in an iframe*

It was this creative use of frames and inline frames to transfer data from the server to a web page that inspired the invention of XMLHTTP communication and later the standardized XmlHttpRequest. These asynchronous requests were revolutionary because of the part they played in enabling web-based applications. There are various complications with using asynchronous requests, which are detailed later in this chapter, but their importance cannot be overstated.

The latest networking technology to hit the web browser is web sockets, which provides a persistent full-duplex communication between the browser and the server. This allows simultaneous communication in both directions. Web sockets are also discussed in more detail later in this chapter.

Storing Data on the Client

For a long time, the only storage available to a JavaScript program was a few miserly kilobytes in a cookie that could disappear without warning at any time. Many browsers offer a setting that clears all cookies each time the browser is closed. At best, cookies could be used to store a token to keep a user logged in for a time, and this was really its only major usefulness to a web application.

In modern browsers, there are many options for storage on the user's machine from simple key/value local storage to NoSQL indexed databases. Even the initial limit of a few megabytes can be increased with the user's permission. Concrete examples of storage options are explained later in this chapter.

The ability to store a reasonable amount of data on the user's machine allows caching of data locally. This can speed up your program and reduce the number of round trips to the server. It also allows your web application to run offline and synchronize with the server the next time a connection is available.

The Document Object Model

The Document Object Model, or DOM, is a web browser interface for interacting with HTML and XML documents. The interface allows you to find elements, obtain and update information about their contents, and attributes and listen to user events. If you are interacting with a web page from your program, you are using the DOM.

All of the examples in this section use the HTML document in Listing 5-3.

Listing 5-3. HTML document for DOM examples

```
<!DOCTYPE html>
<html lang="en">
<head>
    <meta charset="utf-8" />
    <title>Running in a Browser</title>
    <link rel="stylesheet" href="app.css" type="text/css" />
</head>
<body>
    <h1>Running in a Browser</h1>

    <div id="content"></div>
    <script data-main="app" src="/Scripts/require.js"></script>
</body>
</html>
```

The document is an HTML5 web page with a heading and a division with an id of "content". The aim of the following examples is to obtain a reference to this element, make changes to it, and listen to events generated within it.

Finding Elements

One of the most common interactions with the DOM is finding an element within the document. There are several ways to get an element as shown in Listing 5-4. Using document.getElementById has long been the standard method of obtaining an element on the web page and in TypeScript this returns an object of the HTMLElement type. Although this is a common way to find elements, it specifically only obtains elements based on their id attribute.

Listing 5-4. Finding DOM elements

```
// HTMLElement
var a = document.getElementById('content');

// Element
var b = document.querySelector('#content');

// HTMLDivElement (due to type assertion)
var c = <HTMLDivElement> document.querySelector('#content');
```

The traditional alternative to document.getElementById has been document.getElementsByTagName. Whereas obtaining elements based on the id is too specific; finding them by tag name is typically too general. For this reason, the document.querySelector and document.querySelectorAll methods were introduced in the Selectors API specification, allowing CSS query selectors to be used to find elements. When there are multiple possible matches, document.querySelector returns the first matching element, whereas document.querySelectorAll returns all matching elements.

112

When you obtain elements using getElementById it will return the general HTMLElement type. Using querySelector will get you the even more general Element type. The TypeScript compiler is not able to determine the exact kind of element that is returned. If you want to use members from a specific type of element, you can use a type assertion to tell the compiler which element type to expect. This doesn't guarantee that the type will be correct at runtime; it just gives you the right autocompletion information and type checking.

Type assertions are not required when you use document.getElementsByTagName because TypeScript uses specialized overload signatures to return the correct type based on the tag name you supply. This is shown in Listing 5-5, where the NodeList is returned with elements of the HTMLDivElement type automatically.

Listing 5-5. Getting elements by HTML tag

```
// NodeListOf<HTMLDivElement>
var elements = document.getElementsByTagName('div');

// HTMLDivElement
var a = elements[0];
```

The final type you will come across is the NodeList returned from the document.querySelectorAll method, in which each element is of type Node, rather than Element or HTMLElement as shown in Listing 5-6. Despite this, you can still use a type assertion to work with the specialized HTML element of your choice.

Listing 5-6. Getting elements using CSS selectors

```
// NodeList
var elements = document.querySelectorAll('#content');

// Node
var a = elements[0];

// HTMLDivElement
var b = <HTMLDivElement> elements[0];
```

■ **Note**   You may have noticed that the various methods of finding elements in the DOM all return different types of objects and different collections. Be prepared for another variation when the DOM4 specification, van Kesteren and Gregor (2014), gains adoption—as the query and queryAll methods return the single Element type and Elements collection type, respectively.

Changing Elements

Once you have located an element, or elements, that you want to change, there are several options available to you to update the contents of each element.

Listing 5-7 shows a simple replacement of the entire contents of the element by supplying a new string of HTML. The existing contents of the element will be discarded in favor of the string you supply. There are downsides to this approach; not only does this involve hard-coding HTML strings in your program, but also there can be security risks if you use this method to insert user-generated or third-party content. On the positive side, this is simplest way to completely replace the entire contents of an element.

Listing 5-7. Updating the element's HTML

```
var element = <HTMLDivElement> document.querySelector('#content');

element.innerHTML = '<span>Hello World</span>';
```

In many cases, rather than replacing the entire contents of an element, you will want to add to the element without losing all of the existing contents. Listing 5-8 shows multiple additions to the content division, which results in all of the new elements being appended. The listing also shows the use of the document.createElement method to generate elements, rather than using strings.

Listing 5-8. Using appendChild

```
var element = <HTMLDivElement> document.querySelector('#content');

var newElement1 = document.createElement('div');
newElement1.textContent = 'Hello World';

element.appendChild(newElement1);

var newElement2 = document.createElement('div');
newElement2.textContent = 'Greetings Earth';

element.appendChild(newElement2);
```

When you use element.appendChild, the newest element appears last. To add the newest element to the top of the element, you can use the element.insertBefore method as shown in Listing 5-9. The first argument passed to insertBefore is the new element and the second argument is the element used to position the new element. In the example the current first child element is used to ensure the new element appears first, but you can use the same method to place a new element anywhere in the DOM.

Listing 5-9. Using insertBefore

```
var newElement2 = document.createElement('div');
newElement2.textContent = 'Greetings Earth';

element.insertBefore(newElement2, element.firstChild);
```

If you plan to create a nested set of elements to add to the page, it is more efficient to construct the whole hierarchy before adding it to the DOM. This will ensure you only invalidate the layout once, which in turn ensures the page is only redrawn once to reflect your changes.

Events

There are many different ways of attaching event listeners, with some browsers lagging behind the standards-compliant method of adding listeners. The addEventListener method is the standards-compliant way to add an event listener for a DOM event, but some browsers still rely on the attachEvent method (which also requires that the event name is prefixed with 'on').

To solve the problems of cross-browser compatibility, Remy Sharp created an addEvent method that not only eases the browser differences, but also allows collections of elements to be passed as an argument, not just single elements. Listing 5-10 is an adapted version of Remy's original script with the addition of type information for the method.

Listing 5-10. Cross-browser enhanced events

```typescript
var addEvent: (elem: any, eventName: string, callback: Function) => void = (function () {
    if (document.addEventListener) {
        return function (elem, eventName, callback) {
            if (elem && elem.addEventListener) {
                // Handles a single element
                elem.addEventListener(eventName, callback, false);
            } else if (elem && elem.length) {
                // Handles a collection of elements (recursively)
                for (var i = 0; i < elem.length; i++) {
                    addEvent(elem[i], eventName, callback);
                }
            }
        };
    } else {
        return function (elem, eventName, callback) {
            if (elem && elem.attachEvent) {
                // Handles a single element
                elem.attachEvent('on' + eventName, function () {
                    return callback.call(elem, window.event);
                });
            } else if (elem && elem.length) {
                // Handles a collection of elements (recursively)
                for (var i = 0; i < elem.length; i++) {
                    addEvent(elem[i], eventName, callback);
                }
            }
        };
    }
})();

export = addEvent;
```

The two major branches of the addEvent method handle the browser differences, with a check inside each branch that handles either a single element of a collection of elements. When all browsers support the addEventListener method, the second half of the method will become redundant.

This addEvent method will be used wherever events are needed in this chapter.

Frameworks and Libraries

There are many frameworks and libraries that can help with all of these DOM interactions. A select few are described below, although there are many more to choose from. The incredible selection of libraries is summed up neatly by Martin Beeby.

> *If you pick a noun and add .js or .io, you'll probably get a library.*

—Martin Beeby

Despite a sometimes overwhelming range of libraries, the high quality ones tend to float to the top thanks to a discerning and vocal community. Most of the available libraries can be added to your program using your preferred package manager, such as NuGet in Visual Studio, or NPM if you are using NodeJS, or you can just download the scripts and add them manually. For a third-party library that is written in plain JavaScript, you can usually find a matching type definition within the Definitely Typed project repository on GitHub:

```
https://github.com/borisyankov/DefinitelyTyped
```

Figure 5-3 shows the installation of RequireJS using the NuGet package manager screen within Visual Studio. The type definition file is also listed in the search results. The package manager will install the library as well as any dependencies and perform any project configuration required.

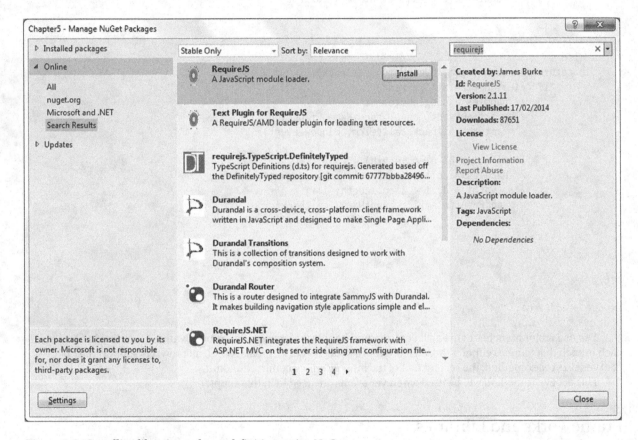

Figure 5-3. *Installing libraries and type definitions using NuGet*

Figure 5-4 shows the local installation of KnockoutJS using Node Package Manager and the command `npm install [library-name]`. This will install the library and any dependencies in the local project within a folder named `node_modules`.

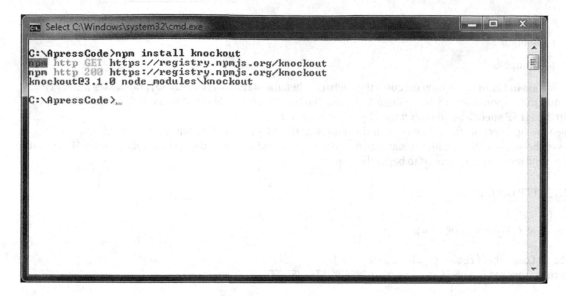

Figure 5-4. *Installing libraries with Node Package Manager*

The ability to find and change elements on a web page becomes more powerful when you combine this feature with real-time data from your server. The next section covers making background requests to a web server to save and retrieve information without reloading the entire web page.

Network

Since its invention towards the end of the 1990s, AJAX has dominated the networking requirements for JavaScript in the web browser. Despite its dominance, there have been some newer entrants into the networking space that are useful for browser-based applications. This section introduces the three major techniques for communicating from the browser; allowing you to pick and choose the methods that best serve your program.

AJAX

AJAX stands for asynchronous JavaScript and XML. This is a poor name because XML is not the only format used for data, and it may not even be the most common format. An AJAX request is initiated using JavaScript in the browser. The request is sent to the server, which sends an HTTP response that can include a body in plain text, JSON, HTML, XML or even a custom format.

The HTTP request and response occur asynchronously, which means it doesn't block the JavaScript event loop described in Chapter 4.

HTTP Get

Listing 5-11 shows a simple Ajax class with a single public method for performing HTTP GET requests. The method creates a new XMLHttpRequest object, which is the standard way to make AJAX requests. A callback is then attached to the onreadystatechange event on the request. This is called for each of the states that a request transitions to, but normally you will be primarily interested in the *completed* state. The potential states are

- 0—Uninitialized
- 1—Set up, but not sent

- 2—Sent

- 3—In flight

- 4—Complete

The Ajax class in Listing 5-11 only executes the callback when the status is 4 (Complete) and passes the HTTP status code and the response text to the callback function. The HTTP status code could potentially be any of the codes described in the HTTP specification maintained by the W3C (1999).

The open method accepts the HTTP verb for the request and the URL. The third parameter sets whether the request is asynchronous. Finally, with the state change listener attached and with the request set up with a HTTP verb and URL, the send method can be used to begin the request.

Listing 5-11. HTTP Get method

```
class Ajax {
    private READY_STATUS_CODE = 4;

    private isCompleted(request: XMLHttpRequest) {
        return request.readyState === this.READY_STATUS_CODE;
    }

    httpGet(url: string, callback: (status: number, response: string) => any) {
        // Create a request
        var request = new XMLHttpRequest();

        // Attach an event listener
        request.onreadystatechange = () => {
            var completed = this.isCompleted(request);
            if (completed) {
                callback(request.status, request.responseText);
            }
        };

        // Specify the HTTP verb and URL
        request.open('GET', url, true);

        // Send the request
        request.send();
    }
}

export = Ajax;
```

■ **Note**   You should always make your AJAX requests asynchronous and use a callback to execute dependent code. Although making a request synchronous appears convenient, you will tie up the event loop for a long period of time and your application will appear unresponsive.

HTTP Post

The example code in Listing 5-12 is an httpPost method that can be added to the Ajax class from Listing 5-9. As well as changing the HTTP verb to 'POST', the content type request header is added and the data are sent in the request body. The data in this example must formatted as key/value pairs, for example 'type=5&size=4'. To send a JSON string containing the data, you would have to set the content type to 'application/json'.

Listing 5-12. HTTP Post method

```typescript
httpPost(url: string, data: string, callback: (status: number, response: string) => any) {
    var request = new XMLHttpRequest();

    request.onreadystatechange = () => {
        var completed = this.isCompleted(request);
        if (completed) {
            callback(request.status, request.responseText);
        }
    };

    request.open('POST', url, true);
    request.setRequestHeader('Content-type', 'application/x-www-form-urlencoded');
    request.send(data);
}
```

You can send different data formats by specifying the appropriate Content-type, for example, application/json or application/xml, and by passing the data in the appropriate serialized format. You are only limited by what your server-side program accepts.

You can call the Ajax class whenever you need to make an HTTP request and an example call is shown in Listing 5-13. You could also extend the Ajax class to handle other HTTP requests, such as PUT and DELETE.

Listing 5-13. Using the Ajax class

```typescript
import Ajax = require('./Scripts/Ajax');

var ajax = new Ajax();

// The function to execute when the response is received
function onGetResponse(status: number, data: string) {
    document.getElementById('content').innerHTML = data;
}

// Making a GET request
ajax.httpGet('Data.html', onGetResponse);
```

If you attempt to make an AJAX request to a different domain, you will find that the request is blocked by a cross-origin security feature in modern browsers. You will encounter this even across subdomains on the same website or between HTTP and HTTPS pages. In cases where you want to enable cross-origin request sharing (CORS), and if the server supports it, you can add an additional header to your AJAX request, as shown in Listing 5-14. This header causes a preflight OPTIONS request to be sent to ask if the server will accept the actual request, which follows if the server confirms that it will accept the cross-origin communication.

Listing 5-14. Allowing CORS, client side

```
request.setRequestHeader('X-Requested-With', 'XMLHttpRequest');
```

Although server configuration is beyond the scope of this chapter, for a server to support CORS, it must accept and respond to the preflight `OPTIONS` request that is issued before the actual cross-origin request with an `Access-Control-Allow-Origin` response header. This header indicates the domains that the server is willing to communicate with. This acts as a handshake between the client and server to verify that the cross-domain communication can proceed.

WebSockets

One of the most common uses of AJAX has been to poll a server to check for updates. One particular implementation of this is long polling; the AJAX request is made, but the server delays responding to the request until it has an update to send. Long-polling implementations must deal with timeout issues and concurrent request limits. Long polling can also cause problems on some servers where the number of clients waiting for a response can tie up a large number of request threads.

The WebSocket specification solves this problem by establishing a persistent two-way communication channel between the server and client that can be used to send messages in either direction. This means you can send messages at any time without having to re-establish a connection and you can receive messages in the same way. Listing 5-15 is a simple example of establishing communication with a server using the `ws://` protocol, listening for messages, and sending a message to the server.

Listing 5-15. Establishing a WebSocket connection

```
var webSocket = new WebSocket('ws://localhost:8080/WS');

webSocket.onmessage = (message: MessageEvent) => {
    // Log message from server
    console.log(message.data);
}

webSocket.send('Message To Server');
```

When you are finished with a WebSocket connection, you can end the communication by calling `webSocket.close()`. If you want to learn more about web sockets, you can read *The Definitive Guide to HTML5 WebSockets* by Wang, Salim, and Moskovits (Apress, 2013).

Real-Time Communications

The next evolution in network communications is real-time peer-to-peer audio and video streaming. The WebRTC specification being drafted by the W3C (2013) allows streaming between browsers without the need for browser plugins or additional installed software. Although the specification currently has limited support, the potential for the technology is incredible. Video and audio calls would be possible between browsers without the need for a communication provider in the middle.

WebRTC is supported in several browsers in an experimental state, with most browsers offering the feature using a prefixed version that is subject to change. To use WebRTC in TypeScript you will need to extend the library definitions to include these transitional browser implementations.

A full implementation of WebRTC is outside of the scope of this book, but Listing 5-16 shows the additional definitions required to support the `getUserMedia` API, which gives access to the user's video and audio stream after obtaining the user's permission.

Listing 5-16. Interface extensions for transitional getUserMedia

```
interface GetUserMedia {
    (options: {}, success: Function, error: Function): any;
}

interface HTMLVideoElement {
    mozSrcObject: any;
}

interface Window {
    URL: any;
    webkitURL: any;
}

interface Navigator {
    getMedia: GetUserMedia;
    getUserMedia: GetUserMedia;
    webkitGetUserMedia: GetUserMedia;
    mozGetUserMedia: GetUserMedia;
    msGetUserMedia: GetUserMedia;
}

navigator.getMedia = (navigator.getUserMedia || navigator.webkitGetUserMedia ||
navigator.mozGetUserMedia || navigator.msGetUserMedia);
```

These definitions are not comprehensive, but they allow your program to use the key features of this API to obtain a stream and display it within an HTML video element. The final line of code in this example condenses all of the potential prefixed versions of the feature into a single navigator property. Listing 5-17 is a working example of displaying video within a web page.

Listing 5-17. Displaying a video stream

```
var video = document.createElement('video');
document.body.appendChild(video);

function videoObtained(stream) {
    if (navigator.mozGetUserMedia) {
        video.mozSrcObject = stream;
    } else {
        var vendorURL = window.URL || window.webkitURL;
        video.src = vendorURL.createObjectURL(stream);
    }
    video.play();
}

navigator.getMedia({ video: true, audio: false },
    videoObtained,
    (err) => console.log(err)
);
```

The getMedia method contains whichever version of getUserMedia is supported in the browser and accepts arguments for options, a success callback and an error callback. The success callback in the example is the videoObtained function, which adds the obtained stream to the video element and plays the video. The result of this script is usually the pleased face of a programmer being shown back to them on the web page.

Obtaining video and audio is the first step towards establishing a peer-to-peer stream and if you are interested in this technology there are entire books dedicated to this fascinating subject. Despite being a part of the WebRTC specification, the getUserMedia API has other potential uses outside of peer-to-peer communication. You may want to grab an image from the video stream to use in your program, or even use the stream in a more traditional manner to send to a server.

Networking provides the tools you need to communicate from the local browser to a server or remote peer. The next section covers storing data locally, which can allow your program to continue to work even when the network is unavailable.

Storage

Storage on the user's machine has come a long way since cookies, with their size limitations and terrible API. Depending on what you need, there are several available storage options with different lifespans, soft limits, and APIs that you can use to keep hold of data locally.

Both session storage and local storage have an identical API, but they offer different life-spans. However, IndexedDB offers a more advanced data storage mechanism. All three of these storage APIs are described in the following.

Session Storage

Session storage is attached to a page session. A page session starts when a page is opened and continues even if the page is reloaded or restored within a browser tab. Opening the same page in a separate tab or browser window results in a new page session.

Listing 5-18 shows how simple the session storage API is, allowing a simple key/value pair to be stored with the setItem method. Both the key and the value must be strings, so objects would need to be serialized to a string to be stored.

Listing 5-18. Session storage

```
var storageKey = 'Example';

// null the first time, 'Stored value' each subsequent time
console.log(sessionStorage.getItem(storageKey));

sessionStorage.setItem(storageKey, 'Stored value');
```

To demonstrate the life-span of this storage mechanism, the getItem method is called before the item is set; when the page first loads, the null value is logged, but on subsequent refreshes the stored value is logged. If you open the page in a new tab, once again the null value will be logged. If you view the page, visit an entirely separate page in the same tab, then load the original page once again, you'll see that the value has been retained. The session remains as long as the tab is open, even if other pages are loaded in the tab—the browser may even support the resumption of the session after a restart.

Listing 5-19 shows the methods for removing an item based on its key and for clearing all items from the session storage for the page. These methods follow the same scope and life cycle as the other session storage methods described earlier.

Listing 5-19. Removing and clearing session storage

```
// Remove an item using a key
sessionStorage.removeItem(storageKey);

// Clear all items
sessionStorage.clear();
```

Local Storage

The local storage API is identical to the session storage API, but the storage persists until it is deleted by the user or cleared for security reasons. Local storage can also be accessed from multiple pages on the same domain as well as in multiple browsers and tabs.

Because local storage items are shared across pages, tabs, and browsers it can be used to store a cache of data to reduce network traffic. It also can be used to store user-entered data while there is no connection or to store data that never needs to be transmitted, such as temporary application state.

Listing 5-20 describes a script that stores a value including the current date and time in local storage. An event listener is attached to the storage event, which should fire whenever a change is made in another tab or window.

Listing 5-20. Local storage and events

```
var storageKey = 'Example';

localStorage.setItem(storageKey, 'Stored value ' + Date.now());

addEvent(window, 'storage', (event: StorageEvent) => {
    console.log(event.key +
        ' "' + event.oldValue + '" changed to "' + event.newValue + '"');
});
```

If you run this script in multiple browser tabs, each tab will log the change in local storage except for the tab that initiated the change. This allows you to keep all of the tabs updated with changes in data made in any other tab.

Storage Restrictions

For both session storage and local storage, browsers are likely to follow a series of restrictions and configurations described in the Web Storage specification, once again maintained by the W3C (2014).

Browsers are likely to limit the amount of storage available to a page initially to prevent malicious attempts to exhaust the user's disk space. The limit applies across subdomains and, when reached, will cause a prompt to be shown to the user asking for permission to increase the allocated storage space. The recommended limit for storage is five megabytes before the user is prompted for permission.

To protect user privacy, browsers are likely to prevent third-party access to storage. This means that you will only be able to access storage on the same domain as it was stored. Browsers can clear out storage based on user preferences (e.g., every time the browser is closed or when it reaches a certain age) and there will also be options available to the user to view and clear storage as well as white list or blacklist sites. It may even be possible for blacklisted sites to be shared across a community, allowing automatic blocking of storage for a domain based on a number of users blacklisting it.

For security reasons, you should avoid using storage from a shared domain as storage would be available to other users of the shared domain. You cannot restrict access to storage by path. For example, the same storage could be accessed by both of the following paths:

- www.shared.com/your-site/

- www.shared.com/third-party-site/

IndexedDB

Although session storage and local storage are simple and convenient ways to store small amounts of data in a key/value store, IndexedDB allows much larger volumes of data to be stored in a structured way that allows fast searches using indexes.

IndexedDB is designed to work asynchronously, which means you supply a callback to each method on the API that executes when the operation has completed. A synchronous version of IndexedDB has a specification, but currently no browsers implement this style of the API. It is generally preferable to use asynchronous APIs to avoid blocking the event loop from running on the main thread, so learning to use the asynchronous version of IndexedDB is worth the additional effort.

The IndexedDB API is demonstrated using the Product class shown in Listing 5-21. The Product class has two public properties for productId and name. The productId will be used as the key for items stored in the database.

Listing 5-21. Product.ts

```
class Product {
    constructor(public productId: number, public name: string) {


    }
}

export = Product;
```

Listing 5-22 shows an empty ProductDatabase class. This will be expanded to perform database operations such as storing, retrieving, and deleting products. This class will also reduce the dependency on the IndexedDB API in the program code.

Listing 5-22. Empty ProductDatabase.ts

```
import Product = require('./Product');

class ProductDatabase {
    constructor(private name: string, private version: number) {
    }
}

export = ProductDatabase;
```

The ProductDatabase constructor takes the database name and the version number. The version number is used to detect if the database stored locally needs to be upgraded to a new version. Each time you change the schema, you should increment the version number. The version number must be an integer, even though there is no native integer type in JavaScript or TypeScript.

Upgrade Required

A database upgrade is determined by comparing the local version number with the version number in your program. If the program version number is larger than the local version number, an onupgradeneeded event is triggered. The event is also fired if there is no local database. You can specify a method to be executed in the event of an upgrade that handles the schema changes and adds any required data.

Listing 5-23 contains an updated constructor for the ProductDatabase class that issues a request to open the database and adds a listener to the onupgradeneeded event. If an upgrade is needed, the update method is called.

Listing 5-23. ProductDatabase supporting upgrades

```typescript
import Product = require('./Product');

class ProductDatabase {

    constructor(private name: string, private version: number) {
        var openDatabaseRequest = indexedDB.open(this.name, this.version);
        openDatabaseRequest.onupgradeneeded = this.upgrade;
    }

    upgrade(event: any) {
        var db = event.target.result;

        // The keyPath specifies the property that contains the id
        var objectStore = db.createObjectStore("products", { keyPath: 'productId' });

        objectStore.createIndex('name', 'name', { unique: false });

        // Example static data
        var products = [
            new Product(1, 'My first product'),
            new Product(2, 'My second product'),
            new Product(3, 'My third product')
        ];

        // Add records
        var productStore = db.transaction('products', 'readwrite').objectStore('products');
        for (var i = 0; i < products.length; i++) {
            productStore.add(products[i]);
        }
    }
}

export = ProductDatabase;
```

The update method in this example uses createObjectStore to create a products table. The options argument specifies a keyPath, which tells the database that the objects stored will have a productId property that should be used as the unique key. You can opt to have a key automatically created for you by passing the autoIncrement option with a value of true instead of passing the keyPath property.

The createIndex method adds an index to the name property to make searches by name faster. It is possible to make an index unique, although in the example duplicates have been allowed by setting unique to false. Attempting to create a unique index will fail if the database already contains duplicates.

Finally, a transaction is created on the products object store and used to add products to the database. This step is useful if you need to seed the database with static data.

Listing 5-24 shows the code that instantiates an instance of the ProductDatabase class. Although the constructor assigns the event handler for the onupgradeneeded event, the constructor will complete before the event fires.

Listing 5-24. Instantiating a ProductDatabase

```
import ProductDatabase = require('./Scripts/ProductDatabase');

var versionNumber = 1;

var db = new ProductDatabase('ExampleDatabase', versionNumber);
```

Querying the Database

Because IndexedDB is designed to work asynchronously, some operations seem to require more effort than you might expect. Despite this, it is worth taking advantage of asynchrony—even if the synchronous versions of these operations eventually get implemented by a browser.

Listing 5-25 shows a getProduct method for the ProductDatabase class, which handles the database opening request, transactions, and queries. This allows calling code to simply pass the productId and a callback to process the result.

Listing 5-25. getProduct method

```
getProduct(productId: number, callback: (result: Product) => void) {
    // Open the database
    var openDatabaseRequest = indexedDB.open(this.name, this.version);

    openDatabaseRequest.onsuccess = () => {
        // The database is open
        var db = openDatabaseRequest.result;

        // Start a transaction on the products store
        var productStore = db.transaction(['products']).objectStore('products');

        // Request the query
        var query = productStore.get(productId);
        query.onsuccess = () => {
            callback(query.result);
        };
    };
}
```

The getProduct method creates a request to open the database, supplies a callback to create a transaction, and runs the query when the connection has opened successfully. You can also supply a callback to be executed onerror, which will be called if the database could not be opened. The query request is also supplied with a callback that is passed the result of the query.

To use the product database, Listing 5-26 contains a simple HTML page for the user to enter a product ID and view the result obtained from the database.

Listing 5-26. HTML page

```html
<!DOCTYPE html>
<html lang="en">
<head>
    <meta charset="utf-8" />
    <title>IndexedDB</title>
    <link rel="stylesheet" href="app.css" type="text/css" />
</head>
<body>
    <h1>IndexedDB</h1>
    <div>
        <label>Product Id: <input type="number" id="productId" /></label>
    </div>
    <div id="content"></div>
    <script data-main="app" src="/Scripts/require.js"></script>
</body>
</html>
```

The code to collect the data entered by the user and call the `ProductDatabase` class is shown in Listing 5-27. The product ID entered into the input is collected using the keyup event and is passed to the `getProduct` method, along with a callback that displays the result on the web page if there is a matching record.

Listing 5-27. Calling getProduct

```typescript
import addEvent = require('./Scripts/AddEvent');
import Product = require('./Scripts/Product');
import ProductDatabase = require('./Scripts/ProductDatabase');

var db = new ProductDatabase('ExampleDatabase', 1);

// Wait for entry in the productId input
addEvent(document.getElementById('productId'), 'keyup', function () {
    // Get the id entered by the user, convert to number
    var productId = +this.value;

    // Search the database with the id
    db.getProduct(productId, (product) => {
        document.getElementById('content').innerHTML = product ?
        'The result for product id: ' + product.productId + ' is: ' + product.name :
        'No result';
    });
});
```

Running this example will confirm that despite some of the code appearing a little complex, the retrieval of records is blisteringly fast because no network round trip is required. The data is also available offline, which means your program can continue to work without a connection.

Adding a New Record

Adding a new record to the database is slightly simpler than obtaining a record with a query, as shown in the previous section, because adding a record requires one less callback. The general pattern is the same, as shown in Listing 5-28, requesting a connection and starting a transaction inside the success callback.

Listing 5-28. addProduct method

```
addProduct(product: Product) {
    // Open the database
    var openDatabaseRequest = indexedDB.open(this.name, this.version);

    openDatabaseRequest.onsuccess = () => {
        // The database is open
        var db = openDatabaseRequest.result;

        // Start a transaction on the products store
        var productStore = db.transaction('products', 'readwrite').objectStore('products');

        // Add the product
        productStore.add(product);
    };
}
```

The product is then stored using the add method, which takes in the product object and automatically finds the productId property to use as the unique key as per the database configuration in Listing 5-23.

The code to call the addProduct method is shown in Listing 5-29. Because the ProductDatabase class has handled the connection request, all the calling code needs to do is supply the new product that is to be stored.

Listing 5-29. Calling addProduct

```
import Product = require('./Scripts/Product');
import ProductDatabase = require('./Scripts/ProductDatabase');

var db = new ProductDatabase('ExampleDatabase', 1);

var newProduct = new Product(4, 'Newly added product');

db.addProduct(newProduct);
```

Because the database is available offline, it is possible to store records without a network connection and then later synchronize them to the server when a connection is available. You could use a holding table for the records to synchronize, or flag records to show whether they are synchronized.

Deleting a Record

The method for deleting a record from the database is shown in Listing 5-30. The unique key is used to identify the record to be removed. Once again there is the need to open the database and open a transaction on the product store.

Listing 5-30. deleteProduct method

```
deleteProduct(productId: number) {
    // Open the database
    var openDatabaseRequest = indexedDB.open(this.name, this.version);

    openDatabaseRequest.onsuccess = (event: any) => {
        // The database is open
        var db = openDatabaseRequest.result;

        // Start a transaction on the products store
        var productStore = db.transaction('products', 'readwrite').objectStore('products');

        // Add the product
        var deleteRequest = productStore.delete(productId);
    };
}
```

The calling code to delete a product is shown in Listing 5-31, which is as simple as calling deleteProduct with the unique key for the product.

Listing 5-31. Calling deleteProduct

```
import Product = require('./Scripts/Product');
import ProductDatabase = require('./Scripts/ProductDatabase');

var db = new ProductDatabase('ExampleDatabase', 1);

db.deleteProduct(4);
```

IDBRequest Interface

The IDBRequest is prevalent in the IndexedDB model. Any request you create against the database supports this interface whether it is indexedDB.open, objectStore.get, objectStore.add, or objectStore.delete.

The beauty of this convention is that you can add a listener to any of these operations to handle both success and error events. Within the event handler you can access the original request object, which contains the following information:

- result—the result of the request, if available

- error—the error message, if available

- source—the index or object store, if applicable to the request

- transaction—the transaction for the request, if the request is within a transaction; you can undo the changes in the transaction by calling transaction.abort()

- readyState—either pending or done

In all of these examples, event handlers could have been supplied as shown in Listing 5-32. If you are writing a robust program that uses IndexedDB you should use these events to ensure that database operations are successful and to detect any errors.

Listing 5-32. IDBRequest convention

```
var deleteRequest = productStore.delete(productId);

deleteRequest.onsuccess = () => {
    console.log('Deleted OK');
}

deleteRequest.onerror = () => {
    console.log('Failed to delete: ' + deleteRequest.error.name);
}
```

The examples in this section have all used the TypeScript arrow function syntax. This is not to preserve the meaning of the this keyword, but to reduce the noise of the many nested function declarations that would otherwise be present in the code.

Storage Roundup

This section introduced several options for storage within the browser. Although this has involved a great many examples, it really only described the most common aspects of the storage mechanisms that you may use.

Whatever storage mechanism you use, you cannot guarantee that the data you store will persist long term. All of the storage specifications describe instances where the data may be deleted, including when the user opts to clear it manually. For this reason, any storage supplied by the browser should be treated as potentially volatile.

Another consideration when using browser storage is that many users have different devices that they may use to access your browser-based application. Therefore, synchronization with your server will be required if you want their experience to persist across these devices.

Geolocation

The geolocation API provides a single mechanism for obtaining the user's location no matter whether the user's device supports location using the global position system or network-based inference to determine the actual location.

You can only obtain the user's location if they grant your application permission to access the information, so you will need to supply a fallback mechanism to handle denied requests as well as older browsers and failed lookups. The usual mechanism for obtaining a location when geolocation fails is to allow the user to enter a search term to find their location.

Listing 5-33 shows a one-off location lookup using the getCurrentPosition method. If the request is approved and succeeds the success callback will be called, with an argument containing the position information. The position object contains latitude and longitude and can also contain additional data about altitude, direction, and speed, if available. The output of Listing 5-33 assumes the user is located at the foot of the London Eye.

Listing 5-33. Geolocation getCurrentPosition

```
function success(pos: Position) {
    console.log('You are here: Lat=' + pos.coords.latitude +
        ' Long=' + pos.coords.longitude +
        ' Altitude=' + pos.coords.altitude +
        ' (Accuracy=' + pos.coords.altitudeAccuracy + ')' +
        ' Heading=' + pos.coords.heading +
        ' Speed=' + pos.coords.speed);
}
```

```
navigator.geolocation.getCurrentPosition(success);

// You are here: Lat = 51.5033 Long = 0.1197
// Altitude = 15 (Accuracy = 0)
// Heading = 0 Speed = 0
```

As well as obtaining a single reading of the user's position, you can watch the position for changes using the watchPosition method. Listing 5-34 reuses the success callback function from the previous example to listen to changes in the user's location. The output from this example assumes the user has travelled quickly between the top of the London Eye and the top of The Gherkin in one second, causing a speed of 3,379 meters per second to be registered. The heading is represented by degrees with north being 0, east being 90, south 180, and west 270 degrees.

Listing 5-34. Geolocation watchPosition

```
function success(pos: Position) {
    console.log('You are here: Lat=' + pos.coords.latitude +
        ' Long=' + pos.coords.longitude +
        ' Altitude=' + pos.coords.altitude +
        ' (Accuracy=' + pos.coords.altitudeAccuracy + ')' +
        ' Heading=' + pos.coords.heading +
        ' Speed=' + pos.coords.speed);
}

var watch = navigator.geolocation.watchPosition(success);

// You are here: Lat = 51.5033 Long = 0.1197
// Altitude = 135 (Accuracy = 15)
// Heading = 0 Speed = 0

// You are here: Lat = 51.5144 Long = 0.0803
// Altitude = 180 (Accuracy = 15)
// Heading = 60 Speed = 3379
```

If you want to stop tracking the user's location, you can call the clearWatch method, passing in a reference to the original watchPostion request to end listening to changes in location. The code in Listing 5-35 ends the watch from the previous example.

Listing 5-35. Clearing a watch

```
navigator.geolocation.clearWatch(watch);
```

In cases where you need to know that the request for the user's location has been denied or failed, you can pass an additional callback to be called if the request fails. Listing 5-36 shows an updated call to watchPosition that passes the additional error function. You can call getCurrentPosition with an error callback too.

Listing 5-36. Failing to obtain the location

```
function success() {
    console.log('Okay');
}

function error() {
    console.log('Position information not available.');
}

var watch = navigator.geolocation.watchPosition(success, error);
```

Geolocation is commonly used to customize a page based on the user's current location or to store the location as metadata when the user performs an action such as posting a message. Once the user has granted permission for your website, the browser may store this to avoid prompting the user every time they use the web application. The default behavior in most browsers is to remember the permission for pages served over a secure connection but not for unsecure pages.

Sensors

There are several APIs already published for working with sensors from within a browser. This is thanks in part to organizations such as Mozilla and Nokia (among others) pushing for features for smart phones, and the traction HTML, CSS, and JavaScript have on mobile platforms. (The entire user interface of Firefox OS is written in web technologies, as are all of the apps.)

Despite being influenced by mobile devices, the standards for these APIs are being published via the World Wide Web Consortium (W3C), which means they live alongside the existing web standards and can be implemented in browsers regardless of whether the device is mobile. There are likely to be more APIs published than the selection covered in this section, but you will notice from the examples given in the following that there is a distinct pattern to the implementation of sensor APIs.

Many of the APIs featured in this section were originally part of a general System Information API that was proposed by the W3C (2014), but the editors decided to work on individual specifications for each API to speed up the process of writing the standards. For example, a disagreement on the Vibration API could have delayed the Battery Status API if both were part of the same specification.

Battery Status

To get autocompletion and type checking for the battery status API, you will need to supply a type definition containing two interfaces. These interfaces are shown in Listing 5-37. The `BatteryManager` interface contains the properties and events that make up the battery status API. The `Navigator` interface extends the existing interface in the TypeScript library to add the battery property.

Listing 5-37. Type definitions for battery status

```
interface BatteryManager {
    charging: boolean;
    chargingTime: number;
    dischargingTime: number;
    level: number;
    onchargingchange: () => any;
```

```
        onchargingtimechange: () => any;
        ondischargingtimechange: () => any;
        onlevelchange: () => any;
}

interface Navigator {
        battery: BatteryManager;
        mozBattery: BatteryManager;
        webkitBattery: BatteryManager;
}
```

To obtain information from the battery API, you first need to detect the presence of the feature before calling the properties on the battery manager. Listing 5-38 is a complete example using the battery manager to display information on a web page.

Listing 5-38. Battery status

```
var battery = (<any>navigator).battery || (<any>navigator).mozBattery ||
(<any>navigator).webkitBattery;
if (battery) {
        var output = document.getElementById('content');

        function updateBatteryStatus() {
            // Gets the battery charge level
            var charge = Math.floor(battery.level * 100) + '%';

            // Detects whether the battery is charging
            var charging = battery.charging ? ' charging' : ' discharging';

            // Gets the time remaining based on charging or discharging
            var timeLeft = battery.charging ?
                ' (' + Math.floor(battery.chargingTime / 60) + ' mins)' :
                ' (' + Math.floor(battery.dischargingTime / 60) + ' mins)';

            output.innerHTML = charge + timeLeft + charging;
        }

        // Update the display when plugged in or unplugged
        battery.onchargingchange = updateBatteryStatus;

        // Update the display when the charging time changes
        battery.onchargingtimechange = updateBatteryStatus;

        // Update the display when the discharging time changes
        battery.ondischargingtimechange = updateBatteryStatus;

        // Update the display when the battery level changes
        battery.onlevelchange = updateBatteryStatus;
}
```

The battery level is supplied as a value between 0 and 1.0, so you can obtain the percentage charge by multiplying this value by 100. All of the times given in the battery information are supplied in seconds, which you can convert into minutes or hours as required. The charging flag indicates whether the battery is currently connected to a power source.

There are four events that you can subscribe to that allow you to detect a change in battery status. You may be interested in just one or a combination. For example, although the most likely case for using this API is to display the information obtained as shown in the example, you could use the onchargingchange event to sound an alarm if a device is taken off charge, either to warn the user or as a rudimentary security mechanism that detects the device is being stolen. You could also use the battery information to be sensitive to low battery situations—perhaps by throttling your application when the battery is below 20%.

Proximity Sensor

The proximity sensor is a very simple API that determines whether the user is very close to the device. Typically, the sensor is located at the top of a mobile phone, near the phone speaker. When the user holds the phone to their ear, the API detects that something is close to the speaker. When the phone is moved away, the device detects that the user is no longer near.

The primary purpose of this sensor is to hide the screen and disable touch when the user is speaking on the phone and then redisplay the screen when the user moves the phone away from their ear. Despite the humble purpose of the proximity sensor, you may determine a more innovative purpose for it in your program.

The proximity API allows for two different kinds of event: a user proximity event that supplies a property to state whether the user is near, and a device proximity event that supplies a measurement within a range. The device proximity event information will differ based on the specific implementation.

Listing 5-39. Proximity events

```
import addEvent = require('./AddEvent');

interface ProximityEvent {
    min: number;
    max: number;
    value: number;
    near: boolean;
}

var output = document.getElementById('content');

function sensorChange(proximity: ProximityEvent) {
    var distance =
        (proximity.value ? proximity.value + ' ' : '') +
        (proximity.near ? 'near' : 'far');

    output.innerHTML = distance;
}

// Near or far
addEvent(window, 'userproximity', sensorChange);

// Measurement within a range
addEvent(window, 'deviceproximity', sensorChange);
```

Unlike the battery sensor, which supplies a manager with properties that can be tested at any time, the proximity API is based on the userproximity and deviceproximity events, which pass an event argument containing the data. If the sensor is not available or the API is not supported on the device, these events will never fire; otherwise the event handler will be called whenever there is a change in the proximity status.

Light Sensor

The ambient light sensor supplies a single reading that represents the current ambient light as measured in lux units. Lux units represent one lumen per square meter, which is a reasonable representation of light intensity as seen by the human eye. A full moon on a clear night can supply up to one lux of light. Office lighting typically ranges from 300 to 500 lux, while a television studio might use 1,000 lux. Direct sunlight can achieve a range from 32,000 to 100,000 lux.

The light sensor API has a `devicelight` event, which supplies a single value as shown in Listing 5-40.

Listing 5-40. Ambient light sensor

```
import addEvent = require('./AddEvent');

interface DeviceLightEvent {
    value: number;
}

var output = document.getElementById('content');

function sensorChange(data: DeviceLightEvent) {
    output.innerHTML = 'Ambient light reading: ' + data.value;
}

addEvent(window, 'devicelight', sensorChange);
```

Although the `devicelight` event in the example supplies the greatest level of granularity, there is also a `lightlevel` event that returns the more abstract enum values `dim`, `normal`, or `bright` depending on the ambient light.

Motion and Orientation

The motion and orientation API is already contained within the TypeScript standard library, so no additional types need to be declared on top of the existing `DeviceMotionEvent` type.

The example in Listing 5-41 obtains the `motion`, measured as the acceleration in meters per second squared and the `rotation` measured in degrees.

Listing 5-41. Motion and orientation

```
import addEvent = require('./AddEvent');

var output = document.getElementById('content');

function sensorChange(event: DeviceMotionEvent) {
    var motion = event.acceleration;
    var rotation = event.rotationRate;

    output.innerHTML = '<p>Motion :<br />' +
            motion.x + '<br />' +
            motion.y + '<br />' +
            motion.z + '</p>' +
        '<p>Rotation:<br />' +
            rotation.alpha + '<br />' +
            rotation.beta + '<br />' +
            rotation.gamma + '</p>';
}

addEvent(window, 'devicemotion', sensorChange);
```

The `acceleration` property is normalized to remove the effects of gravity. This normalization can only take place on devices that have a gyroscope. In the absence of a gyroscope, an additional property named `accelerationIncludingGravity` is available, which includes an additional measurement of 9.81 on the axis currently facing up/down (or spread between multiple axes if the device is at an angle where no single axis is pointing directly up/down). For example, if the device was flat on its back with the screen facing up, you would get the following values:

- `acceleration: { x: 0, y: 0, z: 0 }`
- `accelerationIncludingGravity: { x: 0, y: 0, z: 9.81 }`

Temperature, Noise, and Humidity

As you may have noticed in the previous examples, where the sensor supplies a single value, there is a distinct pattern to the way you use the API. In particular, you can update the code in Listing 5-42 to work for light, temperature, noise, or humidity sensor APIs simply by changing the `sensorApiName` variable.

Listing 5-42. The device API pattern

```
import addEvent = require('./AddEvent');

var sensorApiName = 'devicetemperature';

var output = document.getElementById('content');

addEvent(window, sensorApiName, (data) => {
    output.innerHTML = sensorApiName + ' ' + data.value;
});
```

The `sensorApiName` in this example can be changed to any of the following event names and any future event names that follow this implementation pattern.

- `devicehumidity`—the value will be the percentage humidity.
- `devicelight`—the value is the ambient light in lux.
- `devicenoise`—the value is the noise level in dBA.
- `devicetemperature`—the value is the temperature in degrees Celsius.

Sensor Roundup

The device sensor APIs show how the lines between web page, web application, and native device are gradually eroding. The battery status information works almost universally—on laptops, tablets, and smart phones—anywhere a browser supports the API. The other APIs are gaining similar levels of adoption, depending mainly on whether a specific device has the hardware required to obtain a reading.

The pattern used throughout the APIs—listening for a specific event triggered on the window object—means that you don't even need to test the feature before using it. If the API is not available, the event will simply never fire.

Simply put, sensors can be used to supply measurements to the user, but with a little creativity they could be used to provide interesting user interactions, adaptive interfaces, or inventive games. Perhaps you'll choose to change the theme of the page based on the ambient light, control page elements using motion or rotation, or even log the quality of the user's sleep using a combination of light, motion, and noise sensors.

Web Workers

JavaScript was designed to run an event loop on a single thread, and this is the model you should typically follow. If you come across a situation that calls for additional threads, you can use web workers. Web workers allow scripts to run on a background thread, which has a separate global context and can communicate back to the task that spawned the thread using events.

To create a new worker, the code to run on a background thread must be contained in a separate JavaScript file. The code in Listing 5-43 shows the code in worker.ts, which will be compiled into the worker.js file that will be spawned on a background thread.

Listing 5-43. worker.ts

```
declare function postMessage(message: any): void;

var id = 0;

self.setInterval(() => {
    id++;
    var message = {
        'id': id,
        'message': 'Message sent at ' + Date.now()
    };

    postMessage(message);
}, 1000);
```

The setInterval method in this example is not called on window but on self. This reflects the fact that the worker runs in a separate context with its own scope. The postMessage event is the mechanism for sending information back to the main thread from the worker and any object passed to or from a worker is copied not shared.

The code to create the worker and listen for messages is shown in Listing 5-44. The worker is instantiated with the path to the JavaScript file that contains the worker code. The workerMessageReceived function is attached to the message event and is called whenever the worker posts a message.

Listing 5-44. Creating and using a web worker

```
import addEvent = require('./AddEvent');

var worker = new Worker('/Scripts/worker.js');

function workerMessageReceived(event) {
    var response = event.data;

    console.log('(' + response.id + ') ' + response.message);
};

addEvent(worker, 'message', workerMessageReceived);
```

If you run this example enough times, you will encounter a frailty in this implementation: the worker starts to run immediately in the background, which means it may start posting messages before the message event handler has been added. This problem would never occur normally in JavaScript as the main thread is not available to process other items in the event loop until a function completes.

If you need to avoid the race condition that can occur when setting up a worker, you can wrap the code inside of the worker in a function and post a message to tell the worker that you have set up the event listener and are ready for it to begin processing. The updated worker code is shown in Listing 5-45. The original setInterval call is wrapped in a function, which is called when the worker receives a start message.

Listing 5-45. Worker that waits for a start signal

```
declare function postMessage(message: any): void;

var id = 0;

function start() {
    self.setInterval(() => {
        id++;
        var message = {
            'id': id,
            'message': 'Message sent at ' + Date.now()
        };

        postMessage(message);
    }, 1000);
}

self.onmessage = (event) => {
    if (event.data === 'Start') {
        start();
    } else {
        console.log(event.data);
    }
}
```

When the worker is created, it will no longer run the messaging code until it receives the 'Start' message. Passing the start message to the worker uses the same postMessage mechanism that the worker uses to communicate back to the main thread. By placing the start message after adding the event handler, the race condition is prevented.

Listing 5-46. Signalling the worker to start

```
import addEvent = require('./AddEvent');

var worker = new Worker('/Scripts/worker.js');

function workerMessageReceived(event) {
    var response = event.data;

    console.log('(' + response.id + ') ' + response.message);
};

addEvent(worker, 'message', workerMessageReceived);

worker.postMessage('Start');
```

Web workers provide a simple mechanism for processing code on a background thread along with a pattern for safely passing messages between threads. Despite the simplicity, if you find yourself routinely spinning up web workers, you may be using them for the wrong reasons, especially given that long-running operations typically follow the callback pattern without requiring web workers.

If you do find yourself performing a long-running process or calculation, a web worker can allow the event loop to continue processing on the main thread while the number crunching happens in the background.

Packaging Your Program

This section takes a break from the practical examples of interesting APIs to discuss how to package your TypeScript program.

When you switch to TypeScript from JavaScript, it is tempting to transfer your existing packaging strategy to your TypeScript program. It is common to see people switching to TypeScript, using internal modules to organize their program, and adding a build step to combine the code into a single file and minify it before it is included in the final program. This strategy works for programs up to a certain size, but if your program continues to grow, this method of packaging your program cannot scale indefinitely. This is why TypeScript has first-class support for module loading.

If you organize your program using external modules rather than internal modules, you can use a module loader to fetch dependencies as they are needed, loading just the part of the program that you need. This on-demand loading means that, although your program may be hundreds of thousands of lines of code, you can load just the components you need to perform the current operation and load additional modules if (and when) needed.

When you are certain your program will remain small, the bundling and minification strategy may be the right choice, but you can still write your program using external modules and use a tool such as the RequireJS optimizer to combine the output without limiting your future options.

Summary

This chapter has been an epic dash through some diverse but interesting web browser features, from the browser itself to the many APIs that allow you to create interesting and inventive applications. Although there is a lot of information about a large number of features, you can always return to this chapter later to refresh your memory.

Key Points

- By avoiding unnecessary reflows, your program will appear more responsive.

- There are multiple methods for finding elements on a web page. Each of them returns different types, although you can use a type assertion to change that type.

- Constructing a nested set of elements before adding them to the page can be more efficient than adding each in turn.

- AJAX allows asynchronous calls to the server and allows data in many different formats.

- WebSockets offer persistent connections with two-way communication and WebRTC allows real-time audio and video streams.

- You can store data on the local computer using session storage, local storage, or IndexedDB. However, there is no guarantee the data won't be removed.

- You can get the user's location with their permission, and the browser will use the most accurate available method of finding the location.

- There are a number of sensors that you can access, and they all have a similar implementation pattern.

CHAPTER 6

■ ■ ■

Running TypeScript on a Server

If it seems strange to you that Node achieves parallelism by running only one piece of code at a time, that's because it is. It's an example of something I call a backwardism.

—Jim R. Wilson

Running JavaScript on a server is not a new concept—Netscape Enterprise Server offered this feature as long ago as 1994. There are currently a whole host of server-side implementations of JavaScript running on more than six different script engines. As well as these pure JavaScript implementations, JavaScript can also be run within other platforms that supply a script host.

Although the JavaScript language is common to all of these implementations, each one will supply different APIs for performing operations that are not usually available within a JavaScript program. The range of available modules within a server-side implementation is paramount, which is why Node has been such a great success and why it has been selected for this chapter.

Not only does Node have over 70,000 modules available from simple helpers to entire database servers, it is possible to add them to your program with one simple command thanks to the Node Package Manager (NPM). This means you can add a database module such as MongoDB simply by typing `npm install mongodb` into a command window. Node is cross platform and offers installers for Windows, Mac OSX, Linux, and SunOS as well as full access to the source code.

To demonstrate the use of Node within TypeScript, this chapter gradually evolves a simple application into one that uses several modules. This demonstrates the code as well as the process of adding packages and type definitions. Although the examples show screenshots from Visual Studio, NuGet, and Windows Command Prompt, you can easily transfer these to other development tools and operating systems, for example Sublime Text 2 and Terminal on OSX or WebStorm and the terminal on Linux. The combinations are many and varied and several integrated development environments are cross platform if you want a similar experience on different machines (Cloud9, Eclipse, Sublime Text 2, Vim, and WebStorm all run on Windows, OSX, and Linux).

Install Node

You can download the installer for your chosen platform from the NodeJS (`http://nodejs.org`, Joyent, n.d.) website

`http://nodejs.org/download/`

Creating a New Project

The example program will start from a completely empty project. Figure 6-1 shows the starting state of the example project and solution, which contains a single empty `app.ts` file.

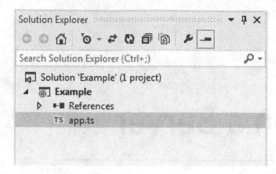

Figure 6-1. *Empty TypeScript project*

If you are using Visual Studio, you can replicate this by creating a new TypeScript HTML application and deleting all of the files except the `app.ts` file. If you are using a different development environment, you can simply start a new project or folder and add an empty `app.ts` file.

To get autocompletion and type checking for Node, you will need a type definition that describes the standard Node API. You can download an existing definition from the Definitely Typed project:

```
http://definitelytyped.org/
```

You also can download the definition using the NuGet package manager in Visual Studio. The Definitely Typed project has definitions for Node and many of the available modules. Figure 6-2 shows the NuGet package manager user interface, with the value `node.TypeScript.DefinitelyTyped` in the search field. Click "Install" to add the type definition to your project.

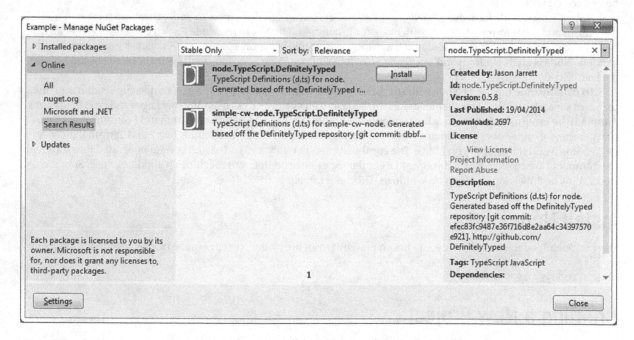

Figure 6-2. *Using NuGet to install Node type definitions*

After installing the Definitely Typed NuGet package for Node, your project will match the image in Figure 6-3. All type definitions are added to the Scripts/typings directory in a folder that matches the library name.

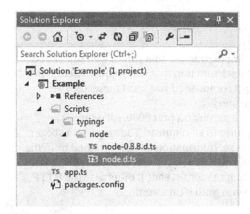

Figure 6-3. *Newly added files*

The final piece of setup to get your project working for Node is to change the project settings to use the CommonJS module system instead of the AMD module system, as shown in Figure 6-4. The AMD module system is for asynchronous module definitions (which is a common pattern to use in web applications) but CommonJS is the module loading pattern used by Node.

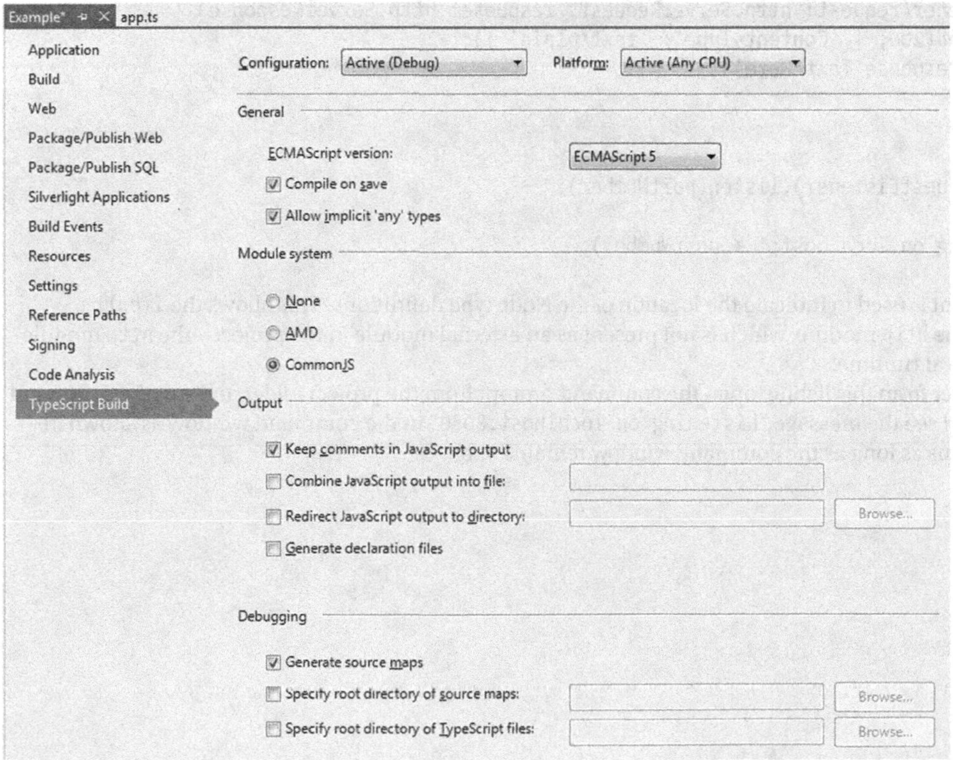

Figure 6-4. *Change project settings to use CommonJS*

This setting is equivalent to passing the `--module commonjs` flag to the TypeScript compiler, as described in Appendix 2.

Simple Node Program

Now that the project is set up, it is possible to demonstrate Node using a simple program that runs a web server and responds to requests. The HTTP server simply passes all requests to a callback function that you supply. There is no built-in facility to handle different requests or routes or to help formatting a response (if you want these, they are available in middleware, such as Express, which is covered later in this chapter).

Listing 6-1 shows the complete program, which creates an http server listening on port 8080. All requests are passed to the requestListener function, which gives a standard text response to all requests. The requestListener function is passed two arguments representing the request and the response. Information can be obtained from the request parameter, such as the method, headers, and body of the request. You can add content to the head and body of the response parameter. You must indicate that you are finished by calling response.end(), otherwise the HTTP server sends no response to the client leaving the client waiting for a response until it times out.

Listing 6-1. A simple Node server

```
/// <reference path="scripts/typings/node/node.d.ts" />

import http = require('http');

var portNumber = 8080;

function requestListener(request: http.ServerRequest, response: http.ServerResponse) {
    response.writeHead(200, { 'Content-Type': 'text/plain' });
    response.write('Response Text Here');
    response.end();
}

http.createServer(requestListener).listen(portNumber);

console.log('Listening on localhost:' + portNumber);
```

A reference comment is used to indicate the location of the Node type definitions. This allows the import statement to reference the http module, which is not present as an external module in the project—the http module will be supplied by Node at runtime.

To run the http server from this listing, open the command prompt from the project folder and run the command node app.js. You should see the message "Listening on localhost:8080" in the command window as shown in Figure 6-5. The server runs as long as the command window remains open.

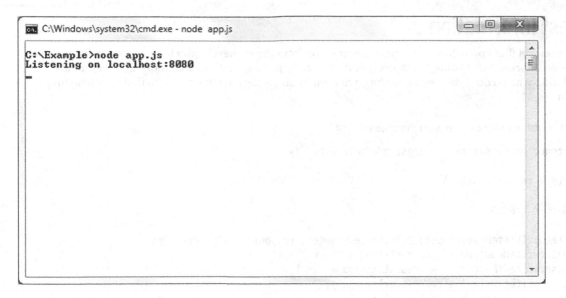

Figure 6-5. Running the program

To make a request to the server, open a web browser and enter localhost:8080 in the address bar. You should receive the "Response Text Here" message shown in Figure 6-6. Because all requests are sent to the same requestListener method, you can enter any address at localhost:8080 and receive the same message, for example localhost:8080/Some/Path/Here/ or localhost:8080/?some=query&string=here.

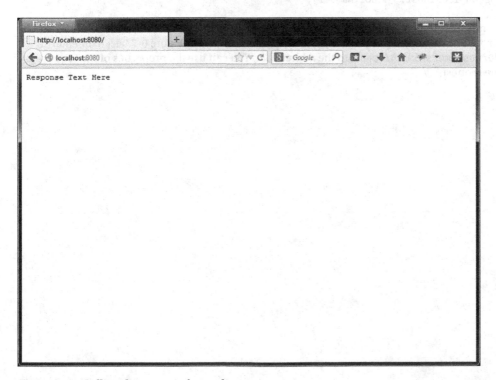

Figure 6-6. Calling the program from a browser

Request Information

It is almost certain that you will want to obtain information from the request to provide a response that matches the requested information. Listing 6-2 shows how to obtain the request method and information about the requested URL, which could be used for routing a request or obtaining data to be used to find data matching the request.

Listing 6-2. Getting more information from the request

```
/// <reference path="scripts/typings/node/node.d.ts" />

import http = require('http');

var portNumber = 8080;

function requestListener(request: http.ServerRequest, response: http.ServerResponse) {
    response.writeHead(200, { 'Content-Type': 'text/plain' });
    response.write('Method: ' + request.method + '\n');
    response.write('Url: ' + request.url + '\n');
    response.write('Response Text Here');
    response.end();
}

http.createServer(requestListener).listen(portNumber);

console.log('Listening on localhost:' + portNumber);
```

In this example the information obtained from the request is simply appended to the response to show you the information in the browser when the request is made. The response is shown in Figure 6-7 based on entering http://localhost:8080/Customers/Smith/John into the address bar. You can use the properties of the request to decide how to handle the request.

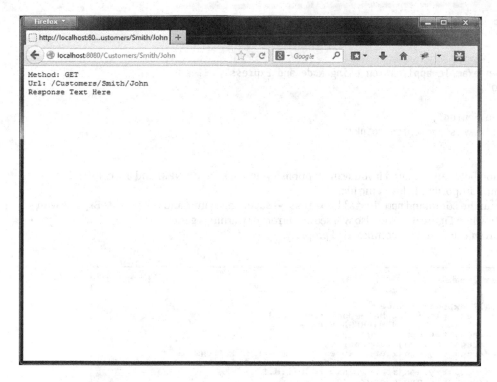

Figure 6-7. *Displaying information about the request*

Although you could use this information to write your own framework for servicing the requests made to your Node server, the work of routing requests and obtaining information from the request has been done elegantly already and is available as a module that you can install with NPM. Unless you want to use the request information to do something unusual, you may find that using an existing module that provides a framework for your program will save time and effort as well as covering scenarios not planned for.

The next section describes how to build an application using the Express module, a lightweight framework for Node applications that doesn't dictate the details of authorization, persistence, or templating.

Using Express to Write Applications

Working with the raw request and response in Node allows access to the low level details of HTTP communication; but in most cases you won't be interested in dealing with all of the details yourself. The Express module provides a framework that allows you to concentrate on your application rather than on routing and HTTP communication. Express is both a quick way to get started and a robust framework for bringing together your program.

Before you install Express, you should create a `package.json` file in your project folder. This file contains metadata for your project and also will be a source of information about your dependencies. An example `package.json` file is shown in Listing 6-3.

Listing 6-3. Example package.json

```json
{
    "name": "Example",
    "description": "An example application using Node and Express",
    "version": "1.0.0",
    "author": {
        "name": "Steve Fenton",
        "url": "http://www.stevefenton.co.uk/"
    }
}
```

The name and version fields are required if you want to publish your package via NPM and are consistently described as being the most important fields in the file.

To install Express, run the command `npm install express --save`. This command downloads Express with all of its dependencies as shown in Figure 6-8. You also will see any errors or warnings generated by your `package.json` file, for example if you haven't supplied a recommended property.

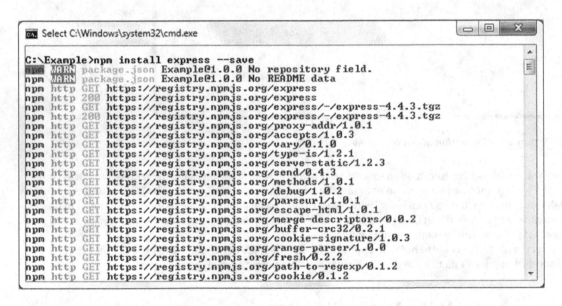

Figure 6-8. *Using Node Package Manager to install Express*

After installing Express using NPM, you will notice that the `package.json` file has been automatically updated to include the dependency on Express, as shown in Listing 6-4. This is only done if you pass the `--save` flag to NPM.

Listing 6-4. Updated package.json

```json
{
    "name": "Example",
    "description": "An example application using Node and Express",
    "version": "1.0.0",
    "author": {
        "name": "Steve Fenton",
        "url": "http://www.stevefenton.co.uk/"
```

```
    },
    "dependencies": {
        "express": "^4.1.1"
    }
}
```

To get autocompletion and type checking for Express, there is a type definition on Definitely Typed. Once again, you can use NuGet to download the type definition in Visual Studio by searching for `express.TypeScript.DefinitelyTyped` (shown in Figure 6-9), or you can download it manually from the Definitely Typed website.

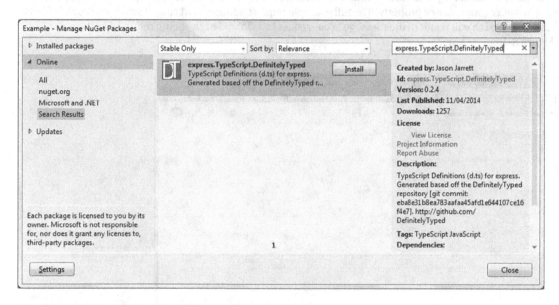

Figure 6-9. *Using NuGet to install the Express type definitions*

Simple Express Program

Listing 6-5 is an updated version of the simple Node program based on Express, rather than on the `http` module. Although the general pattern is similar, the `requestListener` is specifically added to the HTTP GET method at the root address of the application.

Listing 6-5. Using Express

```
/// <reference path="scripts/typings/express/express.d.ts" />

import express = require('express');

var server = express();
var portNumber = 8080;

function requestListener(request: express.Request, response: express.Response) {
    response.send('You requested ' + request.query.firstname + ' ' + request.query.lastname);
}
```

```
server.get('/', requestListener);

server.listen(portNumber, () => {
    console.log('Listening on localhost:' + portNumber);
});
```

This means that the requestListener function will only be called for requests to http://localhost:8080/. Unlike the earlier examples, requests that don't match the route will fail, for example a request to http://localhost:8080/ Customers/Smith/John would receive a 404 response with the message "Cannot GET /Customers/Smith/John".

A correct request to this example should include firstName and lastName query string arguments. Express maps the query string to the request.query property. The full example request address of http://localhost:8080/?first name=John&lastname=Smith will result in the message "You requested John Smith" being returned in the response, as shown in Figure 6-10.

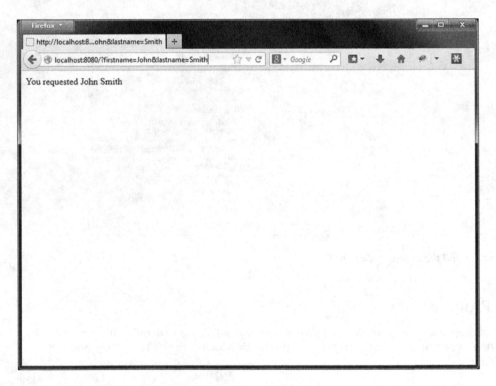

Figure 6-10. *Calling the Express program*

Multiple Routes

You can provide different handlers for different routes in your program, for example the code in Listing 6-6 provides one handler for http://localhost:8080/ and another for http://localhost:8080/Test/. Express handles all of the routing for you and ensures the correct function handles each request.

Listing 6-6. Assigiring handlers to routes

```
function handlerOne(request: express.Request, response: express.Response) {
    response.send('You got handlerOne');
}

function handlerTwo(request: express.Request, response: express.Response) {
    response.send('You got handlerTwo');
}

server.get('/', handlerOne);
server.get('/Test/', handlerTwo);
```

You can test these routes in a browser, just as before, and get the appropriate responses

- `http://localhost:8080/` -> "You got handlerOne"

- `http://localhost:8080/Test/` -> "You got handlerTwo"

Requests to routes that have not been registered will result in a 404 *not found* response.

Handling Errors

You can supply a general error handler for your application by supplying a function that accepts four arguments to the `server.use` method. In Listing 6-7 the `handler` function has been changed to throw a deliberate error. The error handler is set using the `server.use` method and logs errors to the console before returning a 500 response code.

Listing 6-7. General error handler

```
/// <reference path="scripts/typings/express/express.d.ts" />

import express = require('express');

var server = express();
var portNumber = 8080;

function handler(request: express.Request, response: express.Response) {
    throw new Error('Deliberate Error!');
}

server.get('/', handler);

server.use((error, request, response, next) => {
    console.error(error.stack);
    response.send(500, 'An error has occurred.');
});

server.listen(portNumber, () => {
    console.log('Listening on localhost:' + portNumber);
});
```

When you make a request to the application, you should see the error details in the command window as shown in Figure 6-11 and in the browser you will see the message "An error has occurred".

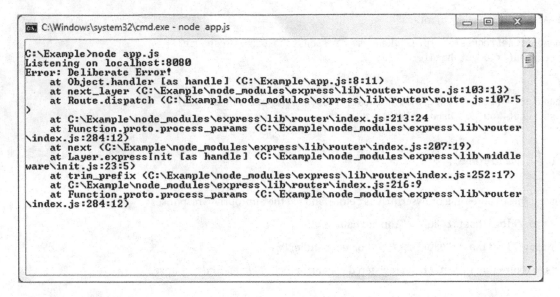

Figure 6-11. *The logged error*

Express Book Project

Now that you have seen the basic elements of an Express application, it is worth looking at a more complete example that accepts requests, serves web pages, and stores data in a database. Although this section won't cover every aspect of Express (a topic that warrants a book in its own right) it will cover what you need to get an application up and running, including accepting input from the user and storing data in a database.

If you are using Visual Studio, you can short-cut the entire process of setting up a new Express application using the NodeJS Tools project on Codeplex (https://nodejstools.codeplex.com, Microsoft, n.d.). The tools add a series of project templates to Visual Studio, including a "TypeScript->Node.js->Basic Express Application" template. You can download the tools from:

https://nodejstools.codeplex.com/

The Basic Express Application template provides a common structure for your Express application, although it is worth bearing in mind that the structure is not a requirement of Express itself, which is incredibly flexible. The template adds Stylus for CSS preprocessing and Jade for templating. If you would prefer to use LESS for CSS preprocessing or EJS for templating, the NodsJS Tools conveniently provide quick access to NPM, which simply replaces NuGet for Node projects; this allows you to download packages to replace the defaults. In particular, both Stylus and Jade provide incredibly terse syntax so you may prefer alternatives that sacrifice brevity for readability. In this section, the defaults have been used in the example project.

To create a new project, select the Basic Express Application template, which is organized under Templates ➤ Other Languages ➤ TypeScript ➤ Node.js shown in Figure 6-12. It is important that you select this version of the template and not the similar template found under the JavaScript language. The TypeScript version comes out of the box with .ts files containing the code and with type definitions for the default components.

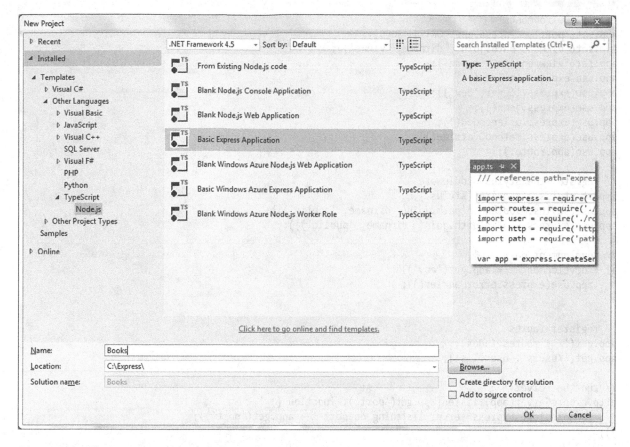

Figure 6-12. *The TypeScript Basic Express Application template*

When the project has been created, you will be prompted to update the NPM packages listed in the packages.json file. Although the project template could have contained all of these files, downloading them at this stage ensures that you have the latest versions of each module.

The app.ts file that comes with the template is a more mature version of the simple Node program from earlier in the chapter. Listing 6-8 shows an example of the code; this sets up the application for logging, routing, and preprocessing.

Listing 6-8. The Express app.ts

```
import express = require('express');
import routes = require('./routes/index');
import user = require('./routes/user');
import http = require('http');
import path = require('path');

var app = express();
```

```
// all environments
app.set('port', process.env.PORT || 3000);
app.set('views', path.join(__dirname, 'views'));
app.set('view engine', 'jade');
app.use(express.favicon());
app.use(express.logger('dev'));
app.use(express.json());
app.use(express.urlencoded());
app.use(express.methodOverride());
app.use(app.router);

// register the stylus middleware
import stylus = require('stylus');
app.use(stylus.middleware(path.join(__dirname, 'public')));
app.use(express.static(path.join(__dirname, 'public')));

// development only
if ('development' == app.get('env')) {
    app.use(express.errorHandler());
}

// register routes
app.get('/', routes.index);
app.get('/users', user.list);

// run the server
http.createServer(app).listen(app.get('port'), function () {
    console.log('Express server listening on port ' + app.get('port'));
});
```

You will need to build the application before you run it to compile the TypeScript. Development environments with strong TypeScript support, such as Visual Studio, will do this automatically when you run the application from the integrated development environment (IDE). When the application runs you will see in the command window that the debugger is attached before the Express server starts and each time a request is made, it is logged to the same window (see Figure 6-13).

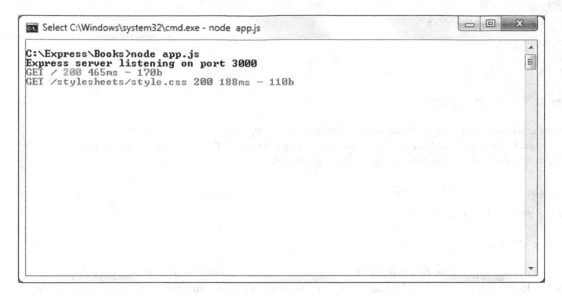

Figure 6-13. The Express server output

Adding the Book Route

To manage a list of books, the application needs to support a /book address. To support a typical address you need to add two files and edit another. You will need to

- Add a TypeScript file to the routes folder
- Add a Jade template to the views folder
- Update the wiring the in app.ts file to register the route

Listing 6-9 shows the book.ts file that will handle requests to the /book address. Like all request handlers, the list function has request and response parameters. The handler calls the response.render method on the result, passing in the view name and the model object that represents the data to be displayed.

Listing 6-9. The routes/book.ts file

```
import express = require('express');

export function list(request: express.Request, response: express.Response) {
    response.render('book', { title: 'Books' });
};
```

For this handler to work there must be a view with the specified name in the views folder. Listing 6-10 shows the book.jade template that will render the data supplied by the request handler. The template re-uses the layout.jade file, which is the default layout for the application and renders the title from the model object.

Listing 6-10. The views/book.jade file

```
extends layout

block content
  h1= title
  p Welcome to the #{title} page.
```

To register this route in your application, you need to amend the app.ts file to add the import statement to reference the book.ts file and to add the route registration. Listing 6-11 shows the two additional lines needed to link the /book address to the book.ts file containing the request handler.

Listing 6-11. The additions to the app.ts file

```
import book = require('./routes/book');

app.get('/book', book.list);
```

When you run your application and visit the /book address in a web browser, you should see a page displaying the message "Welcome to the Books page". If you don't get to the new page, check the command window to view any errors. The most common error is a misspelling, for example accidentally entering 'book**s**' as the view name when it should be 'book'.

Collecting Data

The first step toward storing some data is to supply a form that allows the user to enter information. Listing 6-12 shows the updated book.jade template, which now has a form accepting a title and author as well as an optional ISBN identifier for the book.

Listing 6-12. Adding a form to the Jade view

```
extends layout

block content
  h1= title
  p Welcome to the #{title} page.
  p #{message}
  form(method='post')
    fieldset
        legend Add a Book
        div
            label Title *
                br
                input(type='text', name='book_title', required)
        div
            label Author *
                br
                input(type='text', name='author', required)
        div
            label ISBN
                br
                input(type='text', name='book_isbn', pattern='(?:(?=.{17}$)97[89][ -](?:[0-9]+[ -])
```

```
{2}[0-9]+[ -][0-9]|97[89][0-9]{10}|(?=.{13}$)(?:[0-9]+[ -]){2}[0-9]+[ -][0-9Xx]|[0-9]{9}[0-9Xx])')
     div
          button Save
```

The HTML attributes are added to elements by appending them in parentheses to the element name. Each input's `type` and `name` attributes are added in this way. The notable attribute in the listing is the `pattern` attribute on the ISBN input. The ISBN isn't required, but if it is supplied it must match the pattern supplied in this attribute.

If you are worried about having to write patterns such as the monstrous one above that accepts the various formats of an ISBN, don't worry as this one and many others can be found in the HTML5 Pattern Library at `http://html5pattern.com/`.

To process the form when it is submitted, a function that handles the form post must be added to the `book.ts` file in the routes directory. Listing 6-13 shows the updated file with the `submit` function. At this stage the function simply provides a message to the view to confirm that nothing has been saved because there is no database yet. The database will be added in the next section.

Listing 6-13. Adding a handler to the book.ts file

```
import express = require('express');

export function list(request: express.Request, response: express.Response) {
    response.render('book', { title: 'Books' });
};

export function submit(request: express.Request, response: express.Response) {
    response.render('book', { title: 'Books', message: 'Book not yet saved!' });
}
```

To send the form post to the submit function, the route must be registered in the `app.ts` file. Listing 6-14 shows the updated routes, which has the new post route that will forward matching requests to be handled by the `book.submit` function.

Listing 6-14. The updated routes in the app.ts file

```
// register routes
app.get('/', routes.index);
app.get('/book', book.list);
app.post('/book', book.submit);
```

If you compile and run the updated application and visit the `/book` address, you should see the form that allows books to be added. You will only be able to submit the form in a modern browser if you supply both a title and an author. If you enter any value into the optional ISBN input, it must be a valid format, for example the ten-digit `0-932633-42-0` or the thirteen-digit `9780932633422`.

When you successfully submit the form, you should see the message from the `book.submit` route, which says "Book not yet saved". You will notice that other than this message, the page displayed is same as the `book.list` route; this is because the same view has been used for both at this stage.

Installing Mongoose

There are many options for storing data in your Node application. You can use the file system, a relational database such as MySQL, or a NOSQL database like MongoDB. In this example MongoDB will be combined with Mongoose (http://mongoosejs.com/, LearnBoost, n.d.) to supply the data access for the application. Mongoose can simplify the handling of validation, queries, and type casting among other things.

Before you can follow the code in this section, you will need to set up your database. To download MongoDB for your platform visit http://www.mongodb.org/.

Once you have installed MongoDB, it is best to move it from the installation directory (e.g., Program Files on Windows) into a c:\mongodb directory.

MongoDB stores your data on the file system, so you need to set up a folder to be used for storage. By default, MongoDB looks for a c:\data\db directory, so you should add this directory before you proceed. You can place the data in a different directory if you want to. You will also need to supply the path to MongoDB when you start the database server. For now, just add the default directory.

To start the MongoDB database server, run the code shown in Listing 6-15 in a command window.

Listing 6-15. Running the database server

```
C:\mongodb\bin\mongod
```

You should get a message saying that the server is "waiting for connection on port [number]". The number shown in this message will be needed when you connect to the database from your application. If you get any errors, double-check that you have set up the c:\data\db directory.

You can install Mongoose and MongoDB modules in your application using NPM. In Visual Studio you can right-click on the NPM node in Solution Explorer, search for Mongoose, and press the install button as shown in Figure 6-14. For an alternative, you can manually run npm install mongoose@"*" --save from a command prompt running in your project folder. NPM will download Mongoose and its dependencies, which includes MongoDB.

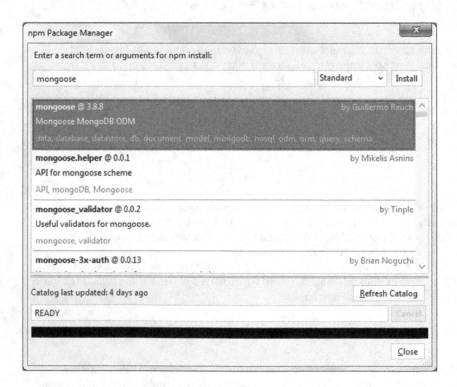

Figure 6-14. *Installing Mongoose and MongoDB*

To get autocompletion and type checking, you should download the `mongoose.d.ts` file from the Definitely Typed project. If you get any errors, you also may need to update your `node.d.ts` definition.

https://github.com/borisyankov/DefinitelyTyped/tree/master/mongoose

You should now have everything you need ready to start saving your data. The next section is a walk-through of the changes to the Express Book Project to store and retrieve the books entered by the user.

Storing Data

To store the data received when the user submits a new book, the `book.ts` file in the `routes` directory must be changed to call the newly installed database.

Listing 6-16 shows the updated handlers, the `list` handler that displays the books from the database, and the `submit` handler that saves new submissions. The code to connect to the database is outside of the functions and is shared between them. A more detailed walkthrough of all the changes is shown below.

Listing 6-16. The updated routes/book.ts file

```
import express = require('express');
import mongoose = require('mongoose');
declare var next: (error: any) => void;

mongoose.connect('mongodb://localhost:27017/books');

var bookSchema = new mongoose.Schema({
    title: String, author: String, isbn: String
});

var Book = mongoose.model<any>('Book', bookSchema);

export function list(request: express.Request, response: express.Response) {
    Book.find({}, (err, res) => {
        if (err) return next(err);
        response.render('book', { 'title': 'Books', 'books': res });
    });
};

export function submit(request: express.Request, response: express.Response) {
    var newBook = new Book({
        title: request.body.book_title,
        author: request.body.author,
        isbn: request.body.book_isbn
    });

    newBook.save(function (err) {
        if (err) return next(err);
        response.redirect('/book');
    });
}
```

The database connection is made using the `mongoose.connect` call. The connection string in the example uses port 27017; you should use the port number that was shown when you started the MongoDB server. When your application connects to the database, each connection will be logged to the mongod command window.

The bookSchema variable is assigned a new Mongoose schema. This schema defines the shape of the documents to be stored in a collection. Mongoose sets up the MongoDB collection for you and can handle default values and validation. The schema for books is set using `title`, `author` and `isbn` properties, which are all assigned the type `String`. The definition of schemas is strikingly similar to TypeScript type annotations. Because of the context of the statement, the TypeScript compiler is intelligent enough to realize that they are not type annotations; therefore it doesn't use type erasure to remove them from the compiled output. The `String` type in question is not the `String` interface that backs the `string` type annotation in TypeScript but a `mongoose.Schema.Types.String`. If you accidentally use the lower-case `string` type, the compiler will give you a warning about your mistake.

The `Book` variable is assigned a model object that Mongoose creates. This saves you having to write your own implementation of a Book class. You can use this model to create new instances of books whenever you need one, just as if you had written your own class.

Although this has taken a few paragraphs of text to explain, it is worth revisiting the code listing to confirm that it is possible to connect to a database and set up the schema for the book data in three lines of code. This setup is used in both of the functions that handle requests.

The `list` function calls the `Book.find` method supplied by Mongoose for retrieving records. You can supply an object to the `find` method to be used to filter the results. The object can be a partial match for the book schema. For example, you could use `{ author: 'Robert C. Martin' }` to retrieve all the books by Uncle Bob. In the example, the empty object indicates that you want all documents in the collection.

Because the query is executed asynchronously, you must also pass in a callback function that will be called once the query has completed. The code to send the response must be nested within the callback, otherwise the response will be sent before the query is finished. You also have the opportunity to handle errors in the callback. The books collection is added to the model object passed to the view.

■ **Note** Although the example uses an empty object to query the collection and retrieve all books, this query will get slower as more and more books are added.

The `submit` function instantiates a new `Book` object with the data submitted by the user and then calls the `save` method that Mongoose provides. Once again the database call is asynchronous and a callback is executed when the action is complete. In the code listing, when the record is saved successfully the response is simply a redirection to the `list` action. Redirecting the request after a submission prevents the user from accidentally resubmitting the same data by refreshing their browser. The pattern of redirecting after a successful submission is named the Post Redirect Get pattern.

Now that the route handler is passing the book data to the view, the view can be updated to show the data. The additional markup to add a table is shown in Listing 6-17.

Listing 6-17. The Jade table template

```
table
    thead
        tr
            th Title
            th Author
            th ISBN
    tbody
        if books
            each book in books
```

```
tr
        td= book.title
        td= book.author
        td= book.isbn
```

The each loop in the Jade template repeats the nested output for each item in the books collection. The table cells are declared using the shorthand syntax (the element name followed by an =). This means that the data variables do not need to be enclosed in the usual #{} delimiters as before.

Jade's each loop will handle an empty array but not an undefined value. The if statement before the each loop in the example prevents undefined values reaching the each loop.

You now have a fully functioning application that will save and display books.

Summary

JavaScript is no stranger to web servers and has gained huge traction thanks to Node and the many thousands of modules available via the Node Package Manager. As bigger programs are written to run on Node, the language features and tooling provided by TypeScript increase quickly in value. A great deal of time can be wasted on simple mistakes such as placing code dependent on an asynchronous call outside of the callback function or using string when you mean to use String, and TypeScript can help to avoid these common errors.

The Express framework is a fast way to get started on Node and will provide some familiarity to programmers that have worked with Sinatra (or Nancy in .NET). Even for those not familiar with this exact style of implementation, the separation of the route handlers, models, and views is likely to be recognizable. Using Express will boost your productivity compared to handling the lower level HTTP requests and responses in Node.

Mongoose fulfils a similar role for the database, providing many shortcuts that will boost your productivity. MongoDB is not particularly tricky if you want to drop down a level and handle the models and validation yourself by calling MongoDB directly to store and retrieve data.

Although this chapter has happily stuck with all of the defaults that ship with Express, you are not limited to using these defaults. If you want to replace a default in your TypeScript program, simply check that your development tools support the alternatives. For example, the Node Tools for Visual Studio ship with Jade support, but you could obtain an extension to add EJS support if you would rather use it for your templates.

Key Points

- JavaScript has been running on web servers for over 20 years.

- Node will happily run on any platform.

- You can get type information for Node and many of the Node modules from the Definitely Typed project.

- Express supplies a lightweight and flexible application framework that is easier to use than the lower level Node HTTP request and response.

- Mongoose and MongoDB supply simple persistence with an asynchronous API.

CHAPTER 7

■ ■ ■

Exceptions, Memory, and Performance

The primary duty of an exception handler is to get the error out of the lap of the programmer and into the surprised face of the user. Provided you keep this cardinal rule in mind, you can't go far wrong.

—Verity Stob

Despite lacking the appeal of language features or runtime environments, understanding exceptions and memory management will help you to write better TypeScript programs. Exceptions in JavaScript and TypeScript may look familiar to programmers who have used C#, Java, PHP, or many other languages, but there are some subtle yet important differences. The topics of exception handling and memory management are inextricably linked because they share a language feature, which is described later in this chapter.

The subject of memory management is often dominated by folklore, falsehoods, and blindly applied best practices. This chapter deals with the facts of memory management and garbage collection and explains how you can take measurements to test optimizations, rather than applying a practice that may make little or no difference (or even perform worse than the original code). This will lead briefly to the subject of performance.

Exceptions

Exceptions are used to indicate that a program or module is unable to continue processing. By their very nature, they should only be raised in truly exceptional circumstances. Often, exceptions are used to indicate that the state of the program is invalid and is not safe to continue.

Although it can be tempting to start issuing exceptions every time a routine is passed a disagreeable value as an argument, it can often be more graceful to handle input that you can anticipate without raising an exception.

When your program encounters an exception, it will be shown in the JavaScript console unless it is handled in code. The console allows programmers to write messages, and it will automatically log any exceptions that occur while running the program.

You can inspect the console for exceptions in all modern web browsers. The shortcut key differs from browser to browser and varies by platform, but if CTRL + SHIFT + I fails to work on your Windows or Linux machine or CMD + OPT + I fails on your Mac, you can usually find the tools in the browser's menu listed under "Developer Tools, Browser Console" or a similar name. For Node, the error and warning output will appear in the command window you use to run the HTTP server.

Throwing Exceptions

To raise an exception in your TypeScript program you use the throw keyword. Although you can follow this keyword with any object, it is best to provide either a string containing an error message, or an instance of the Error object wrapping the error message.

Listing 7-1 shows a typical exception being thrown to prevent an unacceptable input value. When the errorsOnThree function is called with a number, it returns the number, unless it is called with the number three, in which case the exception is raised.

Listing 7-1. Using the throw keyword

```
function errorsOnThree(input: number) {
    if (input === 3) {
        throw new Error('Three is not allowed');
    }

    return input;
}

var result = errorsOnThree(3);
```

The general Error type in this example can be replaced with a custom exception. You can create a custom exception using a class that implements the Error interface as shown in Listing 7-2. The Error interface ensures that your class has a name and message property.

The toString method in Listing 7-2 is not required by the Error interface, but is used in many cases to obtain a string representation of the error. Without this method, the default implementation of toString from Object would be called, which would write "[object Object]" to the console. By adding the toString method to the ApplicationError class you can ensure that an appropriate message is shown when the exception is thrown and logged.

Listing 7-2. Custom error

```
class ApplicationError implements Error {

    public name = 'ApplicationError';

    constructor(public message: string) {
        if (typeof console !== 'undefined') {
            console.log('Creating ' + this.name + ' "' + message + '"');
        }
    }

    toString() {
        return this.name + ': ' + this.message;
    }
}
```

You can use custom exceptions in a throw statement to classify the kind of error that has occurred. It is a common exception pattern to create a general ApplicationError class and inherit from it to create more specific kinds of errors. Any code that handles exceptions is then able to take different actions based on the type of error that has been thrown, as demonstrated in the later section on exception handling.

Listing 7-3 shows a specific `InputError` class that inherits from the `ApplicationError` class. The `errorsOnThree` function uses the `InputError` exception type to highlight that the error has been raised in response to bad input data.

Listing 7-3. Using inheritance to create special exception types

```
class ApplicationError implements Error {

    public name = 'ApplicationError';

    constructor(public message: string) {
    }

    toString() {
        return this.name + ': ' + this.message;
    }
}

class InputError extends ApplicationError {
}

function errorsOnThree(input: number) {
    if (input === 3) {
        throw new InputError('Three is not allowed');
    }

    return input;
}
```

The `InputError` in the example simply extends the `ApplicationError`; it doesn't need to implement any of the properties or methods as it only exists to provide a category of exceptions to use within your program. You can create exception classes to extend `ApplicationError`, or to further specialize a subclass of `ApplicationError`.

■ **Note**   You should treat the native `Error` type as sacred and never throw an exception of this kind. By creating custom exceptions as subclasses of the `ApplicationError` class, you can ensure that the `Error` type is reserved for use outside of your code in truly exceptional cases.

Exception Handling

When an exception is thrown, the program will be terminated unless the exception is handled. To handle an exception you can use a try-catch block, a try-finally block, or even a try-catch-finally block. In any of these cases, the code that may result in an exception being thrown is wrapped within the try block.

Listing 7-4 shows a try-catch block that handles the error from the `errorsOnThree` function in the previous section. The parameter accepted by the `catch` block represents the thrown object, for example, the `Error` instance or the custom `ApplicationError` object, depending on which one you used in the `throw` statement.

Listing 7-4. Unconditional catch block

```
try {
    var result = errorsOnThree(3);
} catch (err) {
    console.log('Error caught, no action taken');
}
```

The err parameter is scoped to the catch block, making it one of the few variables you will encounter that doesn't follow the normal function scoping rules. This parameter behaves as if it was a variable declared with the let keyword, rather than the var keyword, as described in Chapter 4.

It is common in languages that support try-catch blocks to allow specific exception types to be caught. This allows the catch block to only apply to specific types of exceptions and for other types of exceptions to behave as if there were no try-catch block. This technique is recommended to ensure that you only handle exceptions that you know you can recover from, leaving truly unexpected exceptions to terminate the program and prevent further corruption of the state.

There is currently no standards-compliant method of conditionally catching exceptions, which means you catch all or none. If you only wish to handle a specific type of exception, you can check the type within the catch statement and re-throw any errors that do not match the type.

Listing 7-5 shows an exception handling routine that handles ApplicationError custom exceptions, but re-throws any other type.

Listing 7-5. Checking the type of error

```
try {
    var result = errorsOnThree(3);
} catch (err) {
    if (!(err instanceof ApplicationError)) {
        throw err;
    }

    console.log('Error caught, no action taken');
}
```

■ **Note** By handling only custom exceptions, you can ensure that you are only handling the types of exceptions that you know you can recover from. If you use the default catch block with no instanceof check, you are taking responsibility for every type of exception that may occur within your program.

This example will allow the catch block to handle an ApplicationError, or a subclass of ApplicationError such as the InputError described earlier in this chapter. To illustrate the effect of handling exceptions at different levels in the class hierarchy, Figure 7-1 shows a more complex hierarchy that extends the ApplicationError and InputError classes.

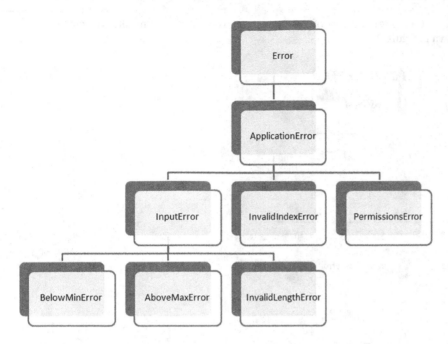

Figure 7-1. *Error class hierarchy*

When you choose to handle the InputError category of exceptions, you will be handling four kinds of exceptions as shown in Figure 7-2: InputError, BelowMinError, AboveMaxError, and InvalidLengthError. All other exceptions will be passed up the call stack as if they were unhandled.

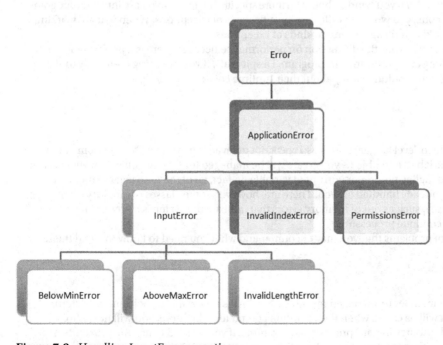

Figure 7-2. *Handling InputError exceptions*

If you were to handle the `ApplicationError` category of exceptions, you would be handling all seven custom exceptions in the hierarchy as shown in Figure 7-3.

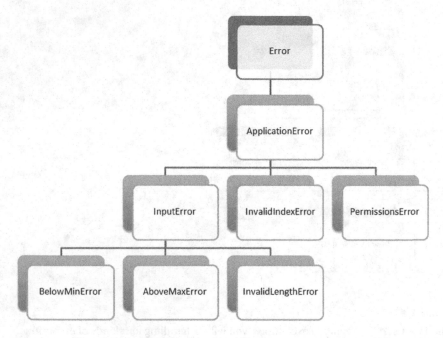

Figure 7-3. *Handling ApplicationError exceptions*

Generally speaking, the exceptions that you handle should be more specific the deeper you are into your program. If you were working near low level code, you would handle very specific types of exceptions. When you are working closer to the user interface, you would handle more general kinds of exceptions.

Exceptions will crop up again shortly with the discussion on performance because there is a performance cost associated with creating and handling exceptions in your program. Despite this, if you are using them only to signal when the routine cannot continue, you shouldn't worry about their runtime cost.

Memory

When you write your program in a high-level language such as TypeScript or JavaScript, you will benefit from automatic memory management. All of the variables and objects you create will be managed for you, so you will never overrun a boundary or have to deal with a dangling pointer or corrupted variable. In fact, all of the manageable memory problems you could encounter are already handled for you. There are, however, some classes of memory safety that cannot be handled automatically, such as out of memory errors that indicate the system's resources have been exhausted and it is not possible to continue processing.

This section covers the types of problems that you may encounter and what you need to know to avoid them.

Releasing Resources

In TypeScript, you are unlikely to encounter unmanaged resources. Most APIs follow the asynchronous pattern, accepting a method argument that will be called when the operation completes. Therefore, you will never hold a direct reference to the unmanaged resource in your program. For example, if you wanted to use the proximity API, which detects when an object is near the sensor, you would use the code in Listing 7-6.

Listing 7-6. Asynchronous pattern

```
var sensorChange = function (reading) {
    var proximity = reading.near ?
        'Near' : 'Far';
    alert(proximity);
}

window.addEventListener('userproximity', sensorChange, true);
```

The asynchronous pattern means that although you can obtain information from the proximity sensor, your program is never responsible for the resource or communication channel. If you happen to encounter a situation where you do hold a reference to a resource that you must manage, you should use a try-finally block to ensure that the resource is released, even if an error occurs.

The example in Listing 7-7 assumes that it is possible to work directly with the proximity sensor to obtain a reading.

Listing 7-7. Imaginary unmanaged proximity sensor

```
var sensorChange = function (reading) {
    var proximity = reading.near ?
        'Near' : 'Far';
    alert(proximity);
}

var readProximity = function () {
    var sensor = new ProximitySensor();
    try {
        sensor.open();

        var reading = sensor.read();

        sensorChange(reading);
    } finally {
        sensor.close();
    }
}

window.setInterval(readProximity, 500);
```

The `finally` block will ensure the sensor's `close` method is called, which performs the cleanup and releases any resources. The `finally` block executes even if there is an error calling the `read` method or the `sensorChange` function.

Garbage Collection

When memory is no longer needed, it needs to be freed for it to be allocated to other objects in your program. The process used to determine whether memory can be freed is called garbage collection. There are several styles of garbage collection that you will encounter depending on the runtime environment.

Older web browsers may use a reference-counting garbage collector, freeing memory when the number of references to an object reaches zero. This is illustrated in Table 7-1. This is a very fast way to collect garbage as the memory can be freed as soon as the reference count reaches zero. However, if a circular reference is created between two or more objects, none of these objects will ever be garbage-collected because their count will never reach zero.

Table 7-1. *Reference counting garbage collection*

Object	Reference Count	Memory De-Allocated
Object A	1	No
Object B	1	No
Object C	1	No
Object D	1	No
Object E	*0*	*Yes*

Modern web browsers solve this problem with a mark-and-sweep algorithm that detects all objects reachable from the root and garbage collects the objects that cannot be reached. Although this style of garbage collection can take longer, it is less likely to result in memory leaks.

The same objects from Table 7-1 are shown in Figure 7-4. Using the reference-counting algorithm both Object A and Object B remain in memory because they reference each other. These circular references are the source of memory leaks in older browsers, but this problem is solved by the mark-and-sweep algorithm. The circular reference between Object A and Object B is not sufficient for the objects to survive garbage collection as only objects that are accessible from the root remain.

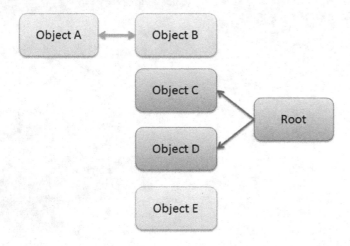

Figure 7-4. *Mark and sweep*

The use of mark-and-sweep garbage collection algorithms means that you rarely need to worry about garbage collection or memory leaks in your TypeScript program.

Performance

There is no doubt that the grail of efficiency leads to abuse. Programmers waste enormous amounts of time thinking about, or worrying about, the speed of noncritical parts of their programs, and these attempts at efficiency actually have a strong negative impact when debugging and maintenance are considered. We should forget about small efficiencies, say about 97% of the time: premature optimization is the root of all evil. Yet we should not pass up our opportunities in that critical 3%.

—Donald Knuth

This is not the first time Donald Knuth ("Structured Programming With go to Statements," *Computing Surveys*, 1974) has been quoted with respect to performance and optimization and it certainly won't be the last. His words, at least in this respect, have stood the test of time (even though they came from a paper defending GOTO statements—a sentiment that has somewhat fallen flat over the course of time).

If the question of performance arises before there is a measurable performance problem, you should avoid optimization. There are many articles that claim that using local variables will be faster than global variables, that you should avoid closures because they are slow, or that object properties are slower than variables. Although these may be generally true, treating them as design rules will lead to a poor program design.

The golden rule of optimization is that you should measure the difference between two or more potential designs and decide if the performance gains are worthy of any design trade-offs you must make to gain them.

■ **Note** When it comes to your TypeScript program, measuring execution time requires running tests on multiple platforms. Otherwise you may be getting faster in one browser, but slower in another.

The code in Listing 7-8 will be used to demonstrate a simple performance test. The lightweight CommunicationLines class will be tested. The class contains a single method that takes in a teamSize and calculates the number of lines of communication between team members using the famous $n(n-1)/2$ algorithm. The function named testCommunicationLines instantiates the class and successfully tests two cases for team sizes of 4 and 10, which have 6 and 45 lines of communication respectively.

Listing 7-8. Calculating lines of communication

```typescript
class CommunicationLines {
    calculate(teamSize: number) {
        return (teamSize * (teamSize - 1)) / 2
    }
}

function testCommunicationLines() {
    var communicationLines = new CommunicationLines();

    var result = communicationLines.calculate(4);

    if (result !== 6) {
        throw new Error('Test failed for team size of 4.');
    }

    result = communicationLines.calculate(10);

    if (result !== 45) {
        throw new Error('Test failed for team size of 10.');
    }
}

testCommunicationLines();
```

The Performance class in Listing 7-9 wraps a callback function in a method that uses the performance.now method to time the operation using the high-fidelity timer discussed in Chapter 4. To get a fair measurement, the Performance class runs the code 10,000 times by default, although this number can be overridden when the run method is called.

The output from the Performance class includes the total time taken to execute the code 10,000 times as well as the average time per iteration.

Listing 7-9. Performance.ts runner

```typescript
class Performance {
    constructor(private func: Function, private iterations: number) {

    }

    private runTest() {
        if (!performance) {
            throw new Error('The performance.now() standard is not supported in this runtime.');
        }

        var errors: number[] = [];

        var testStart = performance.now();

        for (var i = 0; i < this.iterations; i++) {
            try {
                this.func();
            } catch (err) {
                // Limit the number of errors logged
                if (errors.length < 10) {
                    errors.push(i);
                }
            }
        }

        var testTime = performance.now() - testStart;

        return {
            errors: errors,
            totalRunTime: testTime,
            iterationAverageTime: (testTime / this.iterations)
        };
    }

    static run(func: Function, iterations = 10000) {
        var tester = new Performance(func, iterations);
        return tester.runTest();
    }
}

export = Performance;
```

To use the `Performance` class to measure the program, the code must be imported and the call to the `testCommunicationLines` function replaced by passing the function into the `run` method of the `Performance` class, as shown in Listing 7-10.

Listing 7-10. Running the performance test

```
import perf = require('./performance');

class CommunicationLines {
    calculate(teamSize: number) {
        return (teamSize * (teamSize - 1)) / 2
    }
}

function testCommunicationLines() {
    var communicationLines = new CommunicationLines();

    var result = communicationLines.calculate(4);

    if (result !== 6) {
        throw new Error('Test failed for team size of 4.');
    }

    result = communicationLines.calculate(10);

    if (result !== 45) {
        throw new Error('Test failed for team size of 10.');
    }
}

var result = perf.run(testCommunicationLines);

console.log(result.totalRunTime + ' ms');
```

The result of this code is that a total run time of 2.73 ms is logged to the console. This means that the entire run of 10,000 iterations (which is 20,000 calls to the communication lines algorithm) takes less than 3 ms. In most cases, a result such as this is a good indication that you are looking in the wrong place for optimization opportunities.

It is possible to get a very different result by adjusting the code as shown in Listing 7-11. The only change made to the code is to check the call to `communicationLines.calculate` with a team size of four results in seven communication lines. This test will fail and an exception will be raised.

Listing 7-11. Running the performance test with exceptions

```
import perf = require('./performance');

class CommunicationLines {
    calculate(teamSize: number) {
        return (teamSize * (teamSize - 1)) / 2
    }
}
```

```
function testCommunicationLines() {
    var communicationLines = new CommunicationLines();

    var result = communicationLines.calculate(4);

    // This test will now fail
    if (result !== 7) {
        throw new Error('Test failed for team size of 4.');
    }

    result = communicationLines.calculate(10);

    if (result !== 45) {
        throw new Error('Test failed for team size of 10.');
    }
}

var result = perf.run(testCommunicationLines);

console.log(result.totalRunTime + ' ms');
```

Running the code with the failing test and the creation and handling of an exception results in a total run of 214.45 ms—this is 78 times slower than the first test. It is possible to use this data to guide your design decisions. You may want to repeat the tests multiple times or try different iteration sizes to ensure you get consistent results.

Here are some numbers collected using the Performance class from Listing 7-9 to evidence the claims made in respect of optimization at the start of this section. Using a simple, but limited test with a baseline time of 0.74 ms per iteration, the results were as follows (where higher numbers indicate slower execution times):

- Global variables: 0.80 ms (0.06 ms slower per iteration)

- Closures: 1.13 ms (0.39 ms slower per iteration)

- Properties: 1.48 ms (0.74 ms slower per iteration)

Over 10,000 executions you can see small differences in the execution times, but it is important to remember that your program will return different results due to differences such as object complexity, nesting depth, number of object created, and many other factors. Before you make any optimizations, make sure you have taken measurements.

Summary

This chapter has covered three important topics that are likely to be fundamental to any large application written in TypeScript. In most cases, these three areas are likely to be cross-cutting concerns that may be easier to consider before you write a large amount of code that needs to be changed.

Using exceptions to handle truly exceptional states in your program prevents further corruption of the program data. You should create custom exceptions to help manage different kinds of errors and test the types in your catch blocks to only handle errors that you know you can recover from.

Modern runtimes all handle memory using the reliable mark-and-sweep algorithm, which does not fall victim to the circular reference memory leak that older reference-counting garbage collectors suffer from. It is generally accepted that programmers don't need to code with garbage collection in mind, but if you can measure a performance problem and discover that garbage collection is the issue, you may decide to help the garbage collector by creating less objects for it to manage.

Whenever you are working on optimization, you should first measure the performance of your program to prove whether your assumption about optimization is correct when making a change. You should measure your changes in multiple environments to ensure you improve the speed in all of them.

Key Points

- You can use the `throw` keyword with any object, but it is best to use subclasses of a custom error.

- You can handle exceptions with try-catch-finally blocks, where you must specify either a `catch` or `finally` block, or both if you wish.

- You can't reliably catch only custom exceptions, but you can test the exception type within the `catch` block.

- Most APIs you encounter will follow the asynchronous pattern, but if you find you have to manage a resource, use a try-finally block to clean up.

- When it comes to performance, you need before and after measurements to back up any code you change in the name of optimization.

CHAPTER 8

∎ ∎ ∎

Using JavaScript Libraries

I'm not saying that using existing software or libraries is bad. I'm saying that it's always a tradeoff between minimizing effort on one side and minimizing redundant code on the other side. I'm saying that you should consider writing your own code when the percentage of features you need from existing libraries is tiny (let's say less than 20%). It might not be worth carrying the extra 80% forever.

—Lea Verou

The JavaScript community has been one of the busiest when it comes to writing frameworks, toolkits, helpful functions, and useful snippets. If you search for just about any kind of framework or toolkit, you are likely to find a great many options. In fact the number of options is both a blessing and a curse, although you'll have no problem finding behavior driven testing frameworks, unit testing frameworks, model view viewmodel (MVVM) frameworks, networking toolkits, browser polyfills, and more, selecting one out of the myriad options to use is no easy task.

Once you have weighed your choices, you can start using the framework in your TypeScript program right away. At runtime, both your program and the framework will be plain JavaScript, but at design time and compile time you'll be mixing your TypeScript code with the plain JavaScript library. Because the TypeScript compiler has no knowledge of the operations supplied in the JavaScript file, you will need to provide hints in the form of *type definitions* to get the same level of tooling support, as you would get for a TypeScript library.

Type definitions are used by the compiler to check your program and by the language service to provide autocompletion in your development tools. All of the type definitions are erased by the compiler, which means they don't add any weight to your production code. This chapter includes an example application that demonstrates how you can create type definitions for third party JavaScript code, when you need to include it within your TypeScript program.

Creating Type Definitions

To illustrate the creation of type definitions, this chapter uses Knockout as an example of a JavaScript library. Knockout is an MVVM framework that simplifies dynamic user interfaces by mapping a model to a view, keeping the two in sync as changes occur. Although Knockout is used to illustrate the process of creating a type definition from scratch, this technique can be used to describe any JavaScript code in a way that TypeScript will understand even your own legacy libraries.

Of course, if you are adding a popular library such as Knockout to your program, the chances are that someone has already undertaken the work of creating a type definition. Therefore, before you spend time making one of your own, check the listings on the Definitely Typed project

```
https://github.com/borisyankov/DefinitelyTyped/
```

If you are using an open-source library that isn't listed, after you have created a type definition submit it to the Definitely Typed project to help other programmers in the future.

Creating a TypeScript Application with Knockout

The application in this chapter allows passengers to reserve seats on an airline along with an in-flight meal. The application consists of an HTML page and an `app.ts` file containing the Knockout code that binds the data to the view. The HTML page shown in Listing 8-1 provides the view for the application and comes from one of the Knockout tutorials available at

`http://learn.knockoutjs.com/`

The interesting parts of this example are the `data-bind` attributes used by Knockout to bind the view model to your HTML page. Each `data-bind` attribute takes an expression that describes where on the element the data should be bound, for example, the `value` attribute or the inner text, and which data should be displayed.

Listing 8-1. The HTML page

```
<!DOCTYPE html>
<html lang="en">
<head>
    <meta charset="utf-8" />
    <title>Knockout App</title>
    <link rel="stylesheet" href="app.css" type="text/css" />
</head>
<body>
    <h1>Your seat reservations (<span data-bind="text: seats().length"></span>)</h1>

    <table>
        <thead>
            <tr>
                <th>Passenger name</th>
                <th>Meal</th>
                <th>Surcharge</th>
                <th></th>
            </tr>
        </thead>
        <tbody data-bind="foreach: seats">
            <tr>
                <td><input data-bind="value: name" /></td>
                <td><select data-bind="options: $root.availableMeals, value: meal, optionsText:
                'mealName'"></select></td>
                <td data-bind="text: formattedPrice"></td>
                <td><a href="#" data-bind="click: $root.removeSeat">Remove</a></td>
            </tr>
        </tbody>
    </table>

    <button data-bind="click: addSeat, enable: seats().length < 5">Reserve another seat</button>

    <h2 data-bind="visible: totalSurcharge() > 0">
        Total surcharge: $<span data-bind="text: totalSurcharge().toFixed(2)"></span>
    </h2>
```

```
        <script src="knockout.js"></script>
        <script src="app.js"></script>
    </body>
</html>
```

The app.ts file contains the code that binds the data to the view using Knockout, as shown in Listing 8-2. This file will not be changed throughout this section, but it will instead be used to drive out the type definitions that are needed to get past the compiler errors and provide quality autocompletion and type checking for Knockout.

Listing 8-2. The program in app.ts

```
// Class to represent a row in the seat reservations grid
function SeatReservation(name, initialMeal) {
    var self = this;
    self.name = name;
    self.meal = ko.observable(initialMeal);

    self.formattedPrice = ko.computed(function () {
        var price = self.meal().price;
        return price ? "$" + price.toFixed(2) : "None";
    });
}

// Overall viewmodel for this screen, along with initial state
function ReservationsViewModel() {
    var self = this;

    // Non-editable catalog data - would come from the server
    self.availableMeals = [
        { mealName: "Standard (sandwich)", price: 0 },
        { mealName: "Premium (lobster)", price: 34.95 },
        { mealName: "Ultimate (whole zebra)", price: 290 }
    ];

    // Editable data
    self.seats = ko.observableArray([
        new SeatReservation("Steve", self.availableMeals[0]),
        new SeatReservation("Bert", self.availableMeals[0])
    ]);

    // Computed data
    self.totalSurcharge = ko.computed(function () {
        var total = 0;
        for (var i = 0; i < self.seats().length; i++)
            total += self.seats()[i].meal().price;
        return total;
    });
```

```
    // Operations
    self.addSeat = function () {
        self.seats.push(new SeatReservation("", self.availableMeals[0]));
    }
    self.removeSeat = function (seat) { self.seats.remove(seat) }
}

ko.applyBindings(new ReservationsViewModel(), document.body);
```

If you place these files into your development environment, you will receive ten errors from the TypeScript compiler due to Knockout's ko variable being unknown. An example of these errors is shown in Figure 8-1.

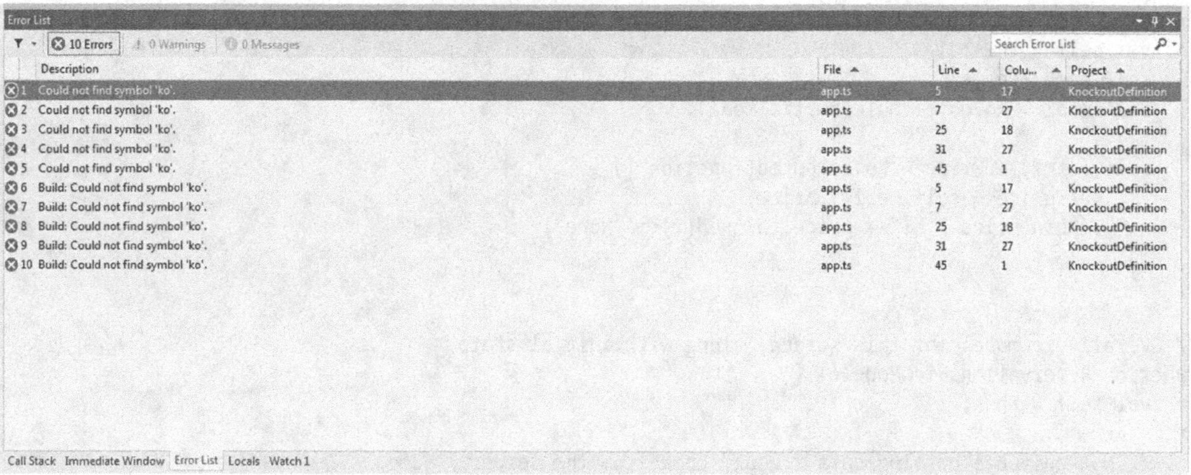

Figure 8-1. *The compiler errors*

Silencing the Compiler

If you are just interested in silencing the compiler, you simply need to provide a quick hint that tells the compiler you will take responsibility for all of the code that uses the ko variable causing all of the errors. The type definition that provides this hint is shown in Listing 8-3.

The type definition would normally be placed in a file named knockout.d.ts and referenced in your app.ts using a reference comment or import statement.

Listing 8-3. The quick type definition fix

```
declare var ko: any;
```

When you use this kind of type definition, you turn down the compiler's offer of checking your program and you will not get autocompletion. So although this is a quick fix, it is likely that you will want to write a more comprehensive type definition.

Iteratively Improving Type Definitions

One of the great things about writing type definitions is that you can write them in small increments. This means you can decide how much effort you want to invest in the type definition in return for the benefits of type checking and autocompletion that each increment provides.

Listing 8-4 shows a small incremental improvement in the type definition for Knockout. The Knockout interface supplies type information for all of the first-level properties that are used in the application: applyBindings, computed, observable, and observableArray. The specific details of these four properties are not given; they are simply assigned the any type.

The declared ko variable is updated to use the new Knockout interface, rather than the any type that was used to silence the compiler.

Listing 8-4. First-level type definition

```
interface Knockout {
    applyBindings: any;
    computed: any;
    observable: any;
    observableArray: any;
}

declare var ko: Knockout;
```

Despite the simplicity of this updated definition, it can prevent many common errors that would otherwise go undetected until the incorrect behavior was noticed in the application. Listing 8-5 shows two example errors that would be caught by the compiler based on this first-level type definition.

Listing 8-5. Compiler errors for incorrect code

```
// Spelling error caught by the compiler
self.meal = ko.observabel(initialMeal);

// Non-existent method caught by compiler
ko.apply(new ReservationsViewModel(), document.body);
```

The misspelling of observabel where observable should have been used and the nonexistent apply call where applyBindings should have been used will both result in compiler errors. This is as far as the compiler can go because only the names have been specified in the interface, not the method signatures.

To increase the detail in the type definition, it is worth referring to the official documentation for the library. In the case of applyBindings, the documentation states that the method can accept one or two of the following arguments:

- viewModel—the view model object you want to use with the declarative bindings it activates.

- rootNode (optional)—the part of the document you want to search in for data-bind attributes.

In other words, the viewModel is an object and must be supplied, whereas the rootNode is an HTMLElement and is optional. The updated Knockout interface with this additional type information is shown in Listing 8-6.

Listing 8-6. 'applyBindings' definition

```
interface Knockout {
    applyBindings(viewModel: {}, rootNode?: HTMLElement): void;
    computed: any;
    observable: any;
    observableArray: any;
}

declare var ko: Knockout;
```

■ **Note**   Even if you don't yet know the exact signature of a function or object in a library, restricting the type to a general `Function` or `Object` type will prevent a number of possible errors, such as the passing of a simple type.

This updated type definition provides more comprehensive type checking, ensuring that at least one argument is passed to `applyBindings` and that all arguments passed are the correct type. It also allows development tools to provide useful type hints and autocompletion as shown in Figure 8-2.

```
ko.applyBindings(|
```
```
applyBindings(viewModel: {}, rootNode?: HTMLElement): void
```

Figure 8-2. *Autocompletion for the `applyBindings` method*

Another technique for expanding type information is to supply a signature that you infer from your own usage of the library. Both instances of `ko.computed` in the application are passed a function that performs the computation. You can update the type definition to show that the `computed` method expects a function to be supplied as shown in Listing 8-7.

If the return type of the evaluator was fixed, you could specify this in the type definition inside the parentheses. Likewise, if you need to use the value returned from the `computed` method, you could update the return type outside the parentheses to supply details of the return type.

Listing 8-7. 'computed' definition

```
interface Knockout {
    applyBindings(viewModel: any, rootNode?: any): void;
    computed: (evaluator: () => any) => any;
    observable: any;
    observableArray: any;
}

declare var ko: Knockout;
```

You can continue expanding the definition using the official documentation or by inferring the types based on examples to create the Knockout interface shown in Listing 8-8. This has both first- and second-level type information.

Listing 8-8. Complete second-level definition

```
interface Knockout {
    applyBindings(viewModel: {}, rootNode?: HTMLElement): void;
    computed: (evaluator: () => any) => any;
    observable: (value: any) => any;
    observableArray: (value: any[]) => any;
}

declare var ko: Knockout;
```

To complete the type definition, you repeat the process of transforming each use of any into a more detailed type until you no longer rely on hiding details with dynamic types. Each time a definition expands to an unmanageable size, you can divide it using an additional interface to help limit the complexity of any particular part of your definition.

Listing 8-9 demonstrates the "divide and conquer" technique by moving the details of the applyBindings method into a separate KnockoutApplyBindings interface. This is then used in the Knockout interface to bind the type information to the method.

Listing 8-9. Dividing type definitions into interfaces

```
interface KnockoutApplyBindings {
    (viewModel: {}, rootNode?: HTMLElement): void;
}

interface Knockout {
    applyBindings: KnockoutApplyBindings;
    computed: (evaluator: () => any) => any;
    observable: (value: any) => any;
    observableArray: (value: any[]) => any;
}

declare var ko: Knockout;
```

Although this type definition for Knockout is far from complete, it covers all of the features of Knockout needed to run the example application. You can add more type information as needed, investing only when you get a reasonable payback.

Converting a JavaScript Application

If you have an existing JavaScript application and are switching to TypeScript, there are two potential strategies for handling your old code. You could create type definitions for your existing code, effectively treating it as a third-party library. However, if you are going to go to the trouble of defining type information, you could just paste your existing JavaScript into a TypeScript file and add any required type annotations directly onto the code rather than in a separate file. By upgrading your existing JavaScript, you will save time, as the compiler can infer many types, and that means you won't need to supply explicit type annotations.

The process for converting your JavaScript to TypeScript is similar to the process for writing a type definition. Once you have pasted your JavaScript into a .ts file, you can silence errors by annotating variables and parameters with the any keyword, first introduced in Chapter 1. You can then replace these temporary annotations with more specific type information. As you turn up the dial on the type annotations, you may find genuine errors in your program such as misspellings or incorrect method calls that you can fix as you find them (or disguise with the any keyword if you don't want to affect behavior at this stage).

If you have a large number of JavaScript files to upgrade, you can upgrade low level dependencies to TypeScript, while the higher level JavaScript files continue to reference the compiled output from your TypeScript files. At runtime, it makes no difference whether the file was originally written in TypeScript or JavaScript as long as you add only type annotations and don't restructure the program.

It is best to save any restructuring work until your entire program is written in TypeScript as the refactoring support for TypeScript is more intelligent.

Summary

Almost every popular JavaScript library will already have a type definition listed on Definitely Typed, but if you do come across a more exotic library or a brand new one that isn't listed you can create your own type definitions. Using an incremental approach to writing type definitions allows you to get the best payback for the amount of time and effort you invest, and you can use the library's documentation to find the type information or infer it by reading examples.

You can re-use your own JavaScript code using the same technique of creating type definitions, but it is likely to be less time consuming to simply move your JavaScript into a TypeScript file and adding any type annotations that the compiler is unable to infer for you.

Whether you are writing type definitions or upgrading your JavaScript to TypeScript, the compiler may find mistakes caused by JavaScript's lack of type checking—you may be surprised what had been missed before.

Key Points

- Type definitions are usually placed inside a file with a .d.ts file extension.

- You can create new type definitions incrementally—you don't need to invest the time in generating type information for an entire library in one go.

- It is usually easier to upgrade a file from JavaScript to TypeScript than it is to create a type definition file.

- Because JavaScript is entirely dynamic, you will probably discover and fix bugs that you didn't know existed when you upgrade to TypeScript.

CHAPTER 9

■ ■ ■

Automated Testing

My definition of an expert in any field is a person who knows enough about what's really going on to be scared.

—P. J. Plauger

Automated testing is an essential topic for anyone writing the kind of large-scale applications TypeScript was invented for. By automating the testing of the program, developers are able to spend more time on new features and less time fixing defects. No single method of testing provides a high enough defect detection rate and that means a combination of several kinds of testing is needed to detect a reasonable number of problems before the software is released.

It may be surprising, but the empirical evidence suggests that you will achieve the following defect detection rates for different kinds of testing, as documented by Steve McConnell in *Code Complete* (Microsoft Press, 2004):

- Unit testing detects up to 50% of defects.

- Integration testing detects up to 40% of defects.

- Regression testing detects up to 30% of defects.

These numbers suggest that as testing is performed later in the software development life cycle, more defects escape through the net. It is also well known that defects cost more if they are detected later. With this in mind, perhaps test first programming provides one of the most effective methods of reducing bugs (as pair programming, as collaborative working methods have been found to detect even more defects than any kind of testing). Proponents of test-driven design (TDD) also will be quick to point out that tests are an added bonus, not the primary purpose of TDD, a tool that aids the design of cohesive units of code.

The purpose of this chapter isn't to convert you to test-driven design. The information in this chapter will be useful whether you choose to write tests before you code, write unit tests after you have written part of a program, or wish to automate tests rather than perform them manually.

■ **Note** The acronym TDD was originally coined for test-driven development, but the revised description of test-driven design pays tribute to the role this practice plays in helping to shape the design of your program.

Framework Choices

There are a number of high-quality testing frameworks written in JavaScript that you can use to test your program. A select few are listed here, but there are many more not listed and you don't even need to use a framework, as testing is possible in plain TypeScript code too.

- Jasmine
- Mocha
- QUnit

All of the examples in this chapter are written using Jasmine, a simple and elegant framework that will test your TypeScript program whether it is designed to run in a browser or server. The code shown in the examples covers the first few steps of the FizzBuzz coding kata. A coding kata is a method of practice that involves solving a simple problem that gradually adapts to challenge your design. Coding katas are explained in Appendix 4. The FizzBuzz kata is based on a children's game consisting of a series of counting rules. As you perform the kata, your aim is to pass only the next rule in the game; avoiding the temptation to read or think ahead. As you write more code, the design will emerge and you can refactor your program (safe in the knowledge that if your tests pass, you haven't changed the behavior by accident).

Testing with Jasmine

Jasmine is a testing framework designed to be used for behavior driven development, but it can be adapted to any kind of testing you may wish to perform. Jasmine does not depend on any other framework and can run without a web page.

The Jasmine syntax is easy to pick up and if used as intended, the tests create a natural kind of documentation that explains the behaviors in your program.

Installing Jasmine

Because Jasmine 2.0 is a recent and substantial upgrade to the framework, the NuGet package is not as yet up to date. Until the package catches up, you can download Jasmine 2.0 (or higher) from

```
https://github.com/pivotal/jasmine/tree/master/dist
```

The type definitions for Jasmine can be downloaded from the Definitely Typed project or via the NuGet package manager as shown in Figure 9-1.

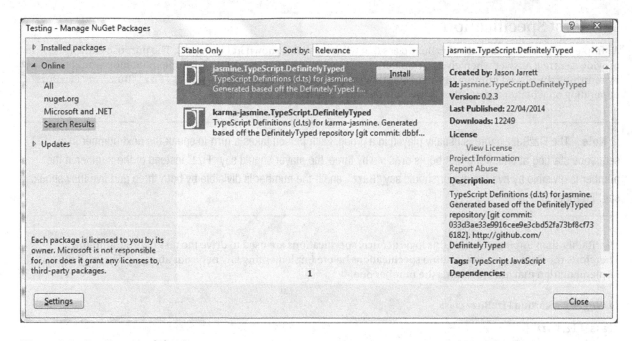

Figure 9-1. *Jasmine type definitions*

Jasmine can run your tests anywhere that JavaScript can run, including inside of Node or in a web browser. The web page in Listing 9-1 is a simple host for your Jasmine specifications. It includes the standard Jasmine CSS file, three Jasmine JavaScript files, and any JavaScript files that have been output by your program.

Listing 9-1. Specification runner

```html
<!DOCTYPE html>
<html lang="en">
    <head>
        <meta charset="utf-8" />
        <title>FizzBuzz Tests</title>

        <!-- Required by Jasmine -->
        <link href="css/jasmine.css" rel="stylesheet" />
        <script src="Scripts/jasmine.js"></script>
        <script src="Scripts/jasmine-html.js"></script>
        <script src="Scripts/boot.js"></script>

        <!-- Your code and specifications -->
        <script src="fizzbuzz.js"></script>
        <script src="specifications.js"></script>
    </head>
    <body>
    </body>
</html>
```

The two files that you own are the `fizzbuzz.js` file, which is the output of a `fizzbuzz.ts` TypeScript file and the `specifications.js` file, which is the output from `specifications.ts`.

The First Specification

A simple implementation of the FizzBuzz class that will be tested is shown in Listing 9-2. The purpose of the class is to provide a correct answer when given a number played in the FizzBuzz game. The full implementation would respond by returning the played number or by substituting the number with a game word such as "Fizz", "Buzz", or "FizzBuzz" depending on whether the number is divisible by three, five, or both three and five

---

■ **Note** The FizzBuzz game is usually played in a group. Each person takes a turn to speak the next number in a sequence starting at one. If the number is divisible by three, the player should say "Fizz" instead of the number. If the number is divisible by five the player should say "Buzz", and if the number is divisible by both three and five they should say "FizzBuzz".

Rather than implement all of this logic at once, specifications are used to drive the task of programming. Therefore, the class awaits the Jasmine specifications before implementing any behavior above and beyond the initial implementation that always returns the number one.

Listing 9-2. Starting FizzBuzz class

```
class FizzBuzz {
    generate(input: number) {
        return 1;
    }
}
```

The Jasmine specification that matches this behavior is shown in Listing 9-3. The specification represents the first sentence in a conversation you may have with someone to whom you were explaining the rules of FizzBuzz for the first time. For example, "You should say '1' when the number 1 is played."

Listing 9-3. Jasimine specification.

```
describe('A FizzBuzz generator', () => {
    it('should return the number 1 when 1 is played', () => {
        var fizzBuzz = new FizzBuzz();

        var result = fizzBuzz.generate(1);

        expect(result).toBe(1);
    });
});
```

The describe method accepts the name for a suite of specifications and a function that will test each one. The it method represents a single specification. The language used in the suite and the specification is intended to by human readable. In this case, combining the suite description with the specification text reads,

A FizzBuzz generator should return the number 1 when 1 is played.

By choosing the language in your specification carefully, you can get free documentation from your test suite. You may even think of a better way of phrasing this description that describes the behavior in even more human terms. If that is the case, you should change the description to match your improved phrasing. It is worth agonizing a little over these details as it makes the specifications more valuable in the long run.

The function passed into the specification matches this claim by instantiating the FizzBuzz class, playing the number one and checking that the result is one. If you run this specification by opening the FizzBuzz Tests web page, you should see the following results:

```
1 spec, 0 failures
    A FizzBuzz generator
        should return the number 1 when 1 is played
```

Driving the Implementation

Now the test automation is in place, it is possible to drive the implementation using new specifications. Listing 9-4 shows a second specification for the behavior that is expected when the number two is played in a game of FizzBuzz.

Listing 9-4. Extending the specification

```
describe('A FizzBuzz generator', () => {
    it('should return the number 1 when 1 is played', () => {
        var fizzBuzz = new FizzBuzz();

        var result = fizzBuzz.generate(1);

        expect(result).toBe(1);
    });

    it('should return the number 2 when 2 is played', () => {
        var fizzBuzz = new FizzBuzz();

        var result = fizzBuzz.generate(2);

        expect(result).toBe(2);
    });
});
```

The second specification actually will fail because the FizzBuzz class returns a one no matter which value is played. The result of running the test page will now be

```
2 specs, 1 failureSpec List | Failures
A FizzBuzz generator should return the number 2 when 2 is played
Expected 1 to be 2.
```

The failure message states that the test "Expected 1 to be 2", this means that Jasmine failed the test because a one was returned, when a two should have been returned.

To pass the test, the FizzBuzz class must be updated as shown in Listing 9-5. Returning whichever number is input will pass both of the existing specifications. Although you may know that you will soon be adding more specifications that will not be covered by this implementation, waiting for a failing test before writing more code ensures that tests for each different specification are written and fail before you write the code that causes them to pass. Knowing your tests will fail if the behavior is incorrect will give you confidence when you later refactor your program.

189

Listing 9-5. Updated FizzBuzz class

```
class FizzBuzz {
    generate(input: number) {
        return input;
    }
}
```

When you rerun the specifications after this change, all specifications will now pass. The results are shown in the following:

```
2 specs, 0 failures
    A FizzBuzz generator
        should return the number 1 when 1 is played
        should return the number 2 when 2 is played
```

Listing 9-6 shows the next specification that drives the implementation of the FizzBuzz class. This specification requires that when the number three is played, it should be substituted for the word "Fizz".

Listing 9-6. The Fizz specification

```
it('should return "Fizz" when 3 is played', () => {
    var fizzBuzz = new FizzBuzz();

    var result = fizzBuzz.generate(3);

    expect(result).toBe('Fizz');
});
```

After checking first that the specification fails, you can update the implementation shown in Listing 9-7. This update again is the simplest code that will pass the test.

Listing 9-7. The updated FizzBuzz class

```
class FizzBuzz {
    generate(input: number) : any {
        if (input === 3) {
            return 'Fizz';
        }

        return input;
    }
}
```

The results of running the specifications at this stage are shown in the following:

```
3 specs, 0 failures
    A FizzBuzz generator
        should return the number 1 when 1 is played
        should return the number 2 when 2 is played
        should return "Fizz" when 3 is played
```

Refactoring

Now that a number of specifications have been written and the code to pass them implemented, it is worth refactoring the program. Refactoring code involves changing the structure and design of a program without changing the behavior. The easiest way to know that you really are refactoring (and not inadvertently changing the actual function of the program) is to have automated tests that will highlight any incidental changes.

It also is worth highlighting the fact that your test code deserves to be as well written and maintainable as your production code. For this reason, Listing 9-8 shows the refactored specifications, where the duplicated instantiation of the FizzBuzz class has been moved into a beforeEach method, which Jasmine will automatically run before every specification.

Listing 9-8. Refactored specifications

```
describe('A FizzBuzz generator', () => {
    beforeEach(() => {
        this.fizzBuzz = new FizzBuzz();
    });

    it('should return the number 1 when 1 is played', () => {
        var result = this.fizzBuzz.generate(1);

        expect(result).toBe(1);
    });

    it('should return the number 2 when 2 is played', () => {
        var result = this.fizzBuzz.generate(2);

        expect(result).toBe(2);
    });

    it('should return "Fizz" when 3 is played', () => {
        var result = this.fizzBuzz.generate(3);

        expect(result).toBe('Fizz');
    });
});
```

If you didn't notice the use of arrow functions before, it is important to take a look at them now. As you may remember from Chapter 1, arrow functions are not just shorthand function declarations; they also alter the scope of the function to preserve the lexical scope of the this keyword.

If you use arrow functions for your specifications, you also must use an arrow function for the beforeEach function. If you don't keep your entire suite consistent, either by always using arrow functions or by never using them, you won't be able to access the instantiated class.

Whenever you refactor your code, you should rerun all of your tests to ensure that you haven't changed the behavior of your program.

Listing 9-9. A working FizzBuzz class using conditional statements

```
class FizzBuzz {
    generate(input: number): any {
        var output = '';
```

```
        if (input % 3 === 0) {
            output += 'Fizz';
        }

        if (input % 5 === 0) {
            output += 'Buzz';
        }

        return output === '' ? input : output;
    }
}
```

The code in Listing 9-9 shows a working version of the FizzBuzz class that covers the default rule of returning a number as well as the three variations for Fizz, Buzz, and FizzBuzz. At this point, although the generate method is still quite short, it is possible to see alternate designs emerging from the code. In particular, as new rules are added (perhaps numbers containing the digit '7' should return 'Bazz') you may decide to use a design pattern to capture specific rules.

■ **Note** The FizzBuzz coding kata is often solved with a design pattern called a *chain of responsibility*, although there are other possible solutions.

The specifications that were created to drive this implementation are shown in Listing 9-10. There are now eight specifications in total to cover the four possible kinds of response.

Listing 9-10. The specifications for the working FizzBuzz class

```
describe('A FizzBuzz generator', () => {
    beforeEach(() => {
        this.fizzBuzz = new FizzBuzz();
        this.FIZZ = 'Fizz';
        this.BUZZ = 'Buzz'
        this.FIZZ_BUZZ = 'FizzBuzz';
    });

    it('should return the number 1 when 1 is played', () => {
        var result = this.fizzBuzz.generate(1);

        expect(result).toBe(1);
    });

    it('should return the number 2 when 2 is played', () => {
        var result = this.fizzBuzz.generate(2);

        expect(result).toBe(2);
    });

    it('should return "Fizz" when 3 is played', () => {
        var result = this.fizzBuzz.generate(3);
```

```
            expect(result).toBe(this.FIZZ);
    });

    it('should return "Fizz" when 6 is played', () => {
        var result = this.fizzBuzz.generate(6);

        expect(result).toBe(this.FIZZ);
    });

    it('should return "Buzz" when 5 is played', () => {
        var result = this.fizzBuzz.generate(5);

        expect(result).toBe(this.BUZZ);
    });

    it('should return "Buzz" when 10 is played', () => {
        var result = this.fizzBuzz.generate(10);

        expect(result).toBe(this.BUZZ);
    });

    it('should return "FizzBuzz" when 15 is played', () => {
        var result = this.fizzBuzz.generate(15);

        expect(result).toBe(this.FIZZ_BUZZ);
    });

    it('should return "FizzBuzz" when 30 is played', () => {
        var result = this.fizzBuzz.generate(30);

        expect(result).toBe(this.FIZZ_BUZZ);
    });
});
```

As well as testing the FizzBuzz class, these specifications supply accurate documentation for the program. The output reads

```
A FizzBuzz generator
    should return the number 1 when 1 is played
    should return the number 2 when 2 is played
    should return "Fizz" when 3 is played
    should return "Fizz" when 6 is played
    should return "Buzz" when 5 is played
    should return "Buzz" when 10 is played
    should return "FizzBuzz" when 15 is played
    should return "FizzBuzz" when 30 is played
```

These tests are clearly a form of executable specification—a living form of documentation that also proves your program performs the documented behaviors.

Isolating Dependencies

There may come a time when you need to test a part of your code that depends on a resource, which makes your tests brittle. For example, it may depend on a third-party API or on a database in a particular state. If you need to test code without relying on these dependencies, you can isolate them when testing using the techniques described in this section.

In many programming languages, it has become natural to reach for a mocking framework whenever you need to supply a test double. In TypeScript though, creation of test doubles is so easy you may never need to search for a framework.

Listing 9-11 shows a modified version of the FizzBuzz class that relies on localStorage, which in TypeScript implements the Storage interface. The constructor takes in the storage object and the generate function uses it to get the display message to be shown in the case of "Fizz".

Listing 9-11. A FizzBuzz class that relies on storage

```
class FizzBuzz {
    constructor(private storage: Storage) {

    }

    generate(input: number): any {
        if (input === 3) {
            return this.storage.getItem('FizzText');
        }

        return input;
    }
}
```

You can satisfy this dependency with a simple object as shown in Listing 9-12. The storage variable matches just enough of the Storage interface to pass the test. Unlike other programming languages, this solution to the test double issue is so easy; you hardly need to consider using a framework to solve the problem.

Listing 9-12. Using an object

```
describe('A FizzBuzz generator', () => {
    it('should return "FakeFizz" when 3 is played', () => {
        // Create a test double for storage
        var storage: any = {
            getItem: () => 'FakeFizz'
        };

        var fizzBuzz = new FizzBuzz(storage);

        var result = fizzBuzz.generate(3);

        expect(result).toBe('FakeFizz');
    });
});
```

Jasmine does supply some additional methods for creating something called a *test spy* that not only returns the fake value, but also keeps tabs on any calls to the property being spied on. Listing 9-13 shows the `jasmine.createSpy` method in action recording all calls to the `getItem` method and returning the fake return value specified when the spy is created.

Listing 9-13. Using a Jasmine spy

```
describe('A FizzBuzz generator', () => {
    it('should return "FakeFizz" when 3 is played', () => {
        // Create a test double for storage
        var storage: any = {
            // Use a spy to lisen to calls to getItem and return a fake value
            getItem: jasmine.createSpy('getItem').and.returnValue('FakeFizz')
        };

        var fizzBuzz = new FizzBuzz(storage);

        var result = fizzBuzz.generate(3);

        expect(result).toBe('FakeFizz');

        // Check a call was made... almost never do this!
        expect(storage.getItem).toHaveBeenCalledWith('FizzText');
    });
});
```

The final expectation in this example checks whether the `getItem` method was called with a particular value. Although this demonstrates one use of a Jasmine spy, testing whether a dependency has been called with a specific value is a surefire way to couple your tests to implementation details. This means you are no longer testing behavior but specific calls.

On the whole, you should stick with simple objects as test doubles, and your tests should check, not specific implementation details, but outcomes. Knowing that you get "Fizz" when you play three is a strong behavioral test, but checking that a `storage` object has been called to supply a value matching a specific key is not a good test at all.

Summary

Hopefully the value of automated testing has been demonstrated in this chapter. However, if you are still skeptic you can try running coding katas both with and without tests to see if it helps to make up your mind. You can read more in Appendix 4.

Although this chapter has used Jasmine for all of the examples, using Mocha or QUnit is just as easy and both provide an equally simple syntax. Jasmine's usefulness as a library of documentation that can also be executed to test your program makes it a strong contender for both executable specifications and test-driven design.

Key Points

- Unit tests are more effective than integration testing or regression testing (although a good strategy is to use many different kinds of testing to get the best possible defect detection rate).

- There are a lot of frameworks for JavaScript and TypeScript, but you can look at Jasmine, Mocha, and QUnit if you want to narrow things down a bit.

- You can use Jasmine to write specifications that act as tests and documentation.

- Driving the implementation with specifications ensures tests fail if the behavior is not correct. Writing tests after the implementation doesn't guarantee the tests will ever fail.

- You should refactor both production code and test code.

- You can isolate your dependencies using simple objects and these are preferable to clever tools that may bind your test too tightly to the implementation.

APPENDIX 1

JavaScript Quick Reference

If you aren't already familiar with JavaScript, this quick reference is intended to provide an overview of the basic core features of JavaScript you'll be using within a TypeScript program.

Variables

Variables are used to store the application's state in JavaScript and can contain data of any type from strings to numbers to objects to functions.

Listing A1-1 shows a selection of variables with simple types. Variables can be assigned at the same time as they are declared, in a single statement, or they can be declared and assigned separately. A variable will have the type corresponding to the value that was most recently assigned to it. If no value has been assigned, the value of the variable will be undefined.

Listing A1-1. Variables

```
// Variable declaration

var variable;

// Variable assignment

variable = 'A string is assigned';

// Dynamic assignment (changes variable's type to a number)

variable = 10;
```

You can store arrays in a variable. You can use the empty literal [ ] to create a new empty array and add items using array.push. You can also create and fill an array in a single step by placing the value inside the array literal, as shown in Listing A1-2.

Listing A1-2. Arrays

```
// Creating an empty array and adding values

var myArray = [];

myArray.push(1);
myArray.push(3);
myArray.push(5);
```

```
// Adding values using an array literal

var myLiteralArray = [1, 3, 5];
```

An *object* can be used to represent data in complex structures. Objects can contain properties that each are like a variable and can contain strings, numbers, arrays, functions, and other objects. Just as with arrays, you can create an empty object using an empty object literal { }, or create and fill an object in a single step by placing the properties within the object literal. Both styles are shown in Listing A1-3.

Listing A1-3. Objects

```
// Objects

var myObject = {};

myObject.title = 'Example Object';
myObject.value = 5;

// Object literals

var myLiteralObject = {
    title: 'Example Object',
    value: 5
};
```

In all of the examples, literal assignments have been made, rather than instantiating values using the new keyword. It is possible to create arrays using new Array(), objects using new Object(), and even strings using new String()—but in JavaScript the literal syntax is preferred.

Functions

Functions can be used to create re-usable blocks of code in your program. You can create a function using either a function declaration or a function expression as shown in Listing A1-4.

Listing A1-4. Functions

```
// Function declaration

function myFunction(name) {
    return 'Hello ' + name;
}

// 'Hello Steve'
var greeting = myFunction('Steve');

// Function expression

var myFunctionExpression = function (name) {
    return 'Hi ' + name;
};

// 'Hi Steve'
var greeting = myFunctionExpression('Steve');
```

When you declare a function using a function declaration it is created at parse time, which means it is available throughout your program wherever its scope is available. Using a function expression means the function is evaluated at runtime and it can only be called where both its scope is available and the calling code appears *after* the function expression.

Conditional Statements

Conditional statements can be used to branch logic in your program. You can use conditional statements to execute code only if a certain condition is met.

If statements allow code to be branched based on a custom condition that evaluates to either true or false. The if statements shown in Listing A1-5 execute different code depending on the value in the age variable, for example.

Listing A1-5. If statement

```
// If statements

var age = 21;

if (age > 18) {
    // Code to execute if age is greater than 18
}

if (age > 40) {
    // Code to execute if age is greater than 40
} else if (age > 18) {
    // Code to execute if age is greater than 18
    // but less than 41
} else {
    // Code to execute in all other cases
}
```

A *switch statement* is useful for controlling multiple branches based on a single variable and where only specific values will cause branching. Listing A1-6 shows a typical switch statement that can execute different code based on the value of the style variable. The default condition will execute if no other condition has been executed.

Listing A1-6. Switch statement

```
// Switch statements

var styles = {
    tranditional: 1,
    modern: 2,
    postModern: 3,
    futuristic: 4
};

var style = styles.tranditional;

switch (style) {
    case styles.tranditional:
        // Code to execute for traditional style
        break;
```

```
    case styles.modern:
        // Code to execute for modern style
        break;
    case styles.postModern:
        // Code to execute for post modern style
        break;
    case styles.futuristic:
        // Code to execute for futuristic style
        break;
    default:
        throw new Error('Style not known: ' + style);
}
```

■ **Note**   Switch statements work even better with TypeScript enumerations, which are described in Chapter 1.

Loops

Loops are used to repeat a section of code in your program. The most common loop in JavaScript is the *for loop*, which can be used to repeat an action for every item in an array as shown in Listing A1-7.

Listing A1-7. For loop

```
var names = ['Lily', 'Rebecca', 'Debbye', 'Ann'];

for (var i = 0; i < names.length; i++) {
    console.log(names[i]);
}
```

A *while loop* allows a section of code to be repeated until a condition is met, as shown in listing A1-8. A common use of this would be to add a character to a string and repeat the process until the string matched a certain length.

Listing A1-8. While loop

```
var counter = 10;

while (counter > 0) {
    counter--;
    console.log(counter);
}
```

A *do-while loop* is almost identical to a while loop, except it will run the code at least one time, even if the condition doesn't match.

Listing A1-9 is similar to the while loop shown previously, except the counter variable already matches the exit condition because it is not greater than zero. Despite this, the code runs one time before the condition is evaluated, causing the loop to exit.

Listing A1-9. Do-while loop

```
var counter = 0;

do {
    counter--;
    console.log(counter);
} while (counter > 0);
```

Summary

Although this Appendix is a fast dash through some very basic features of JavaScript, they are the essential parts that you need to know to get started with TypeScript. There is much more to learn in JavaScript and in the different environments it executes in.

Having read this quick start, you should be able to read this book without coming across anything too surprising as all of the TypeScript language features are described in detail.

APPENDIX 2

TypeScript Compiler

The TypeScript compiler may well be hidden behind your development tools, but it is worth familiarizing yourself with the various compiler options. The compiler itself is optimized for compiling entire projects, rather than individual files. Running the compiler against the whole project means that you are only loading the standard library once, rather than many times. You may find that running compilation for a single file takes nearly as long as compiling the entire project.

The compiler is called `tsc.exe` and is usually found in one of the following directories on Windows:

- C:\Program Files (x86)\Microsoft SDKs\TypeScript

- C:\Program Files\Microsoft SDKs\TypeScript

To run the compiler, simply call `tsc` from the command line passing in your starting file name, as demonstrated below. You may need to enter the full address of the `tsc.exe` file. If you get bored of entering the full path, you can add the path to the TypeScript folder to your environment variables.

```
tsc app.ts
```

You can also run the TypeScript compiler using NodeJS on any operating system, as the compiler is written in TypeScript and compiled to JavaScript, as shown here. You will need to enter the full path to the `tsc.js` file (not to the `.ts` file).

```
node tsc.js app.ts
```

Getting Help

If you ever have trouble remembering all of the options for the compiler, you can get help using one of the following commands, which will display a list of all the available compiler flags you can set. Each compiler flag exposes a setting that allows you to change how the compiler behaves.

```
tsc --help
node tsc.js
```

Common Flags

There are a few compiler flags that are so common you are almost certain to use them at some point. These flags are described in the following sections.

Module Kind

The module compiler flag is used to generate code that loads external modules using either CommonJS or AMD module patterns. The valid values for the module kind are commonjs and amd.

```
tsc --module amd app.ts
```

ECMAScript Target Version

The target flag allows you to set the target ECMAScript version. Currently you can target versions 3 and 5 of the ECMAScript specification, but version 6 will be available once the ECMAScript 6 specification is stable. You currently specify the version using ES3 or ES5.

If you are targeting ECMAScript 3, you can't use properties in your TypeScript program as they rely on an ECMAScript 5 feature. When the ECMAScript 6 option is added, it will perform fewer transformations during compilation. This is because ECMAScript 6 supports many of the basic TypeScript features, such as modules, classes, arrow functions, and special parameter types. The ECMAScript 6 support should also allow the new JavaScript features such as let, generators, and destructors.

```
tsc --target ES5 app.ts
```

Generate Declarations

The declaration flag will generate an additional file with the suffix .d.ts, which will contain ambient declarations for your code.

```
tsc --declaration app.ts
```

Remove Comments

The removeComments flag erases all comments from the output, which will make it smaller if you have a lot of comments in your source code.

```
tsc --removeComments app.ts
```

Combined Output

You can combine your entire TypeScript program into a single output file using the out compiler flag. When you use the out flag you must also supply a name for the combined file.

```
tsc --out final.js app.ts
```

No Implicit Any

The noImplicitAny flag disallows the compiler from inferring the any type. You can still explicitly annotate items with the any type, but if the compiler attempts to infer a type and can't, it will generate an error. The beauty of this flag is that it lets you write less cluttered code because you can leave out type annotations except where the compiler warns you it can't infer the type.

```
tsc --module noImplicitAny app.ts
```

APPENDIX 3

■ ■ ■

Bitwise Flags

As described in Chapter 1, you can use an enumeration to define bit flags. Bit flags allow a series of items to be selected or deselected by switching individual bits in a sequence on and off. To ensure that each value in an enumeration relates to a single bit, the numbering must follow the binary sequence whereby each value is a power of two, for example

```
1, 2, 4, 8, 16, 32, 64, 128, 256, 512, 1024, 2048, 4096, and so on
```

Listing A3-1 is a copy of the example from Chapter 1 and shows bit flags in action. Appendix 3 describes bit flags and bitwise operations in more detail.

Listing A3-1. Flags

```
enum DiscFlags {
        None = 0,
        Drive = 1,
        Influence = 2,
        Steadiness = 4,
        Conscientiousness = 8
}

// Using flags
var personality = DiscFlags.Drive | DiscFlags.Conscientiousness;

// Testing flags

// true
var hasD = (personality & DiscFlags.Drive) == DiscFlags.Drive;

// false
var hasI = (personality & DiscFlags.Influence) == DiscFlags.Influence;

// false
var hasS = (personality & DiscFlags.Steadiness) == DiscFlags.Steadiness;

// true
var hasC = (personality & DiscFlags.Conscientiousness) == DiscFlags.Conscientiousness;
```

Bit Flags Explained

The flags in Listing A3-1 are illustrated in Table A3-1. Because the bit flags are represented as 32-bit integers in big-endian order, the bit representing the greatest value appears on the left. To show the values in the order they are represented, "Conscientiousness" is shown on the left, because it is represented by the bit with the greatest value in the example: 8.

Table A3-1. *Bit flags illustrated*

Conscientiousness (8)	Steadiness (4)	Influence (2)	Drive (1)	Binary	Decimal
0	0	0	1	0001	1
0	0	1	0	0010	2
0	1	0	0	0100	4
1	0	0	0	1000	8
0	0	1	1	0011	3
1	1	1	1	1111	15

If the flag is switched on, the column shows a 1. If the flag is switched off the column shows a 0. The binary value shows that each digit in the binary representation corresponds to a value in the enumeration; whenever "Drive" is switched on, the right-most column will contain a 1. This is the reason the value of an enumeration being used for flags must use the binary sequence as it is the only sequence that means each flag will only affect a single bit in the set.

Bitwise Operations

Using bit flags also means you can use bitwise operators to manipulate the bits representing the items in the enumeration. Listing A3-2 uses a bitwise AND operator (&) to find matching traits in two sets of flags. Only items that are switched on in both sets of flags are switched on in the result of the bitwise AND operation, this is why a bitwise AND is used to see if an individual value is switched on.

Listing A3-2. Finding matches with a bitwise AND

```
// Both personalityA and personalityB include DiscFlags.Influence
var personalityA = DiscFlags.Drive | DiscFlags.Influence | DiscFlags.Conscientiousness;
var personalityB = DiscFlags.Influence | DiscFlags.Steadiness;

// The result of a bitwise AND contains only matching flags

// DiscFlags.Influence
var matchingTraits = personalityA & personalityB;
```

The results of various bitwise operations are illustrated in Table A3-2. They produce the following results:

- AND results in bits being switched on if both sets have the bit switched on.

- OR results in bits being switched on if either, or both, of the sets have the bit switched on.

- XOR results in bits being switched on if one of the sets has the bit switched on. The bit is switched off if neither of the sources has the bit switched on or if both of the sources has the bit switched on.

- NOT inverts a set, switching off all of the "on" bits and switching on all of the "off" bits.

Table A3-2. Bitwise operations

First set	Second set	Bitwise operation	Result
1011	1101	& (AND)	1001
1001	0011	| (OR)	1011
1011	1101	^ (XOR)	0110
1011	n/a	~ (NOT)	0100

APPENDIX 4

■ ■ ■

Coding Katas

Coding katas have become increasingly popular since their invention in 1999. If you want to improve your programming chops, coding katas are like a sharpening block you can use to hone your skills. This appendix will explain what coding katas are and how to get the most out of them. There are some links to coding kata collections that you can use to practice your TypeScript programming.

A coding kata is method of practicing programming techniques and many katas are designed to exercise your design skills and give you mastery of your tools and workflow. The instructions for a kata describe a problem, gradually increasing the complexity throughout the kata. It is possible to repeat a kata by adding constraints, for example, limiting the language features that can be used.

Because a coding kata is just practice, you can try out ideas safely because you can always delete the code and start from scratch. Something you may opt to do several times even if your first attempt goes well. You can even use a kata to try out a new programming language or a new integrated development environment.

You can perform a coding kata individually, but there is even more value in pairing up with another programmer to work on a kata. Not only will you be working on your programming skills, you'll be sharing and learning with your partner. Group kata workshops supply opportunities to pair with plenty of other programmers. The more diverse you make your practice, the more experience you bring to your real work. Some of the benefits of coding katas are

- Learning features of your development environment, such as keyboard shortcuts.

- Practicing test-first development.

- Designing object-oriented solutions to the kata problem.

- Refactoring and design pattern practice.

You can make katas even more interesting by changing the way you approach them. One valuable technique you can employ when undertaking a coding kata with a partner is to play ping-pong. You write a failing test to represent a single behavior and your partner must write the simplest code possible to make the test pass. Then your partner writes a test and you in turn must make it pass in the simplest way. You pass the problem back and forth, alternately writing a test or making it pass. You may even find that this practice makes its way into your daily working methods.

Another challenge you can set yourself during a coding kata is to use only the keyboard to complete the task. By discarding all other input devices, you will find interesting and helpful keyboard shortcuts to perform the operations you normally undertake using point, click, and touch.

■ **Note**   The term *coding kata* was coined by "Pragmatic" Dave Thomas. He also maintains a library of kata ideas at `http://codekata.com/`.

Performing a Kata

All you need to perform a coding kata is the following:

- A development environment
- A unit testing framework or library (see Chapter 9)
- The kata instructions

A coding kata often relies on creating an increasingly complex problem, which is designed to cause your first design to break. You are forced to rework your code just as you must when writing a real program. Because of this, you'll get more from a kata if you resist the temptation to read ahead. (Likewise, if you run a coding kata workshop, you should reveal the problem gradually to make the practice more effective.)

The rules of the kata should reflect the aspirations of the team; this usually means following practices such as test-first programming, pairing, and refactoring. With TypeScript in particular, you should aim to exercise the object-oriented programming practices described in Chapter 3.

The Fizz Buzz Kata

This coding kata originated as a job interview test created by Imran Ghory (http://imranontech.com/2007/01/24/using-fizzbuzz-to-find-developers-who-grok-coding/, *Using FizzBuzz to Find Developers who Grok Coding*, 2007) based on the children's game Fizz Buzz. The original game can be summed up in just a few simple rules, but as the program increases in size to satisfy the rules it should be just complex enough to give rise to one of many possible design solutions.

Remember, try not to read ahead, implement just one requirement in its entirety before reading the next one. This makes the practice as life like as possible.

Requirement 1

Write a program that outputs numbers from 1 to 100.

Requirement 2

For any number that is divisible by three, replace the number in the output with the word *Fizz*.

Requirement 3

For any number that is divisible by five, replace the number in the output with the word *Buzz*.

Requirement 4

For any number that is divisible by both three and five, replace the number in the output with the words *Fizz Buzz*.

Requirement 5

For any number that is divisible by seven, replace the number in the output with the word *Bazz*. If the number is divisible by three and seven, the output should be *Fizz Bazz*. If the number is divisible by five and seven, the output should be *Buzz Bazz*. If the number is divisible by three, five, and seven, the output should be *Fizz Buzz Bazz*.

Fizz Buzz Summary

These requirements are typically enough to stretch the first design for the program. Requirement 5 is actually based on a variation of the original Fizz Buzz game—there is nothing wrong with adapting this kata based on some of the variations of the game or by adding a new rule of your own invention. Known alternative versions of Fizz Buzz are based on whether the number contains a digit, rather than being divisible by a number.

Summary

Once you have practiced the Fizz Buzz kata, there are many more available online (for example, `http://codekata.com`). Don't be limited by existing lists of coding katas though; invent your own based on games or problems that you have encountered. The original coding kata was actually an experiment with different solutions to a real problem in a production system; so if you are about to add a feature to your program, run a kata to generate and evaluate potential solutions.

Index

Get the eBook for only $10!

Now you can take the weightless companion with you anywhere, anytime. Your purchase of this book entitles you to 3 electronic versions for only $10.

This Apress title will prove so indispensible that you'll want to carry it with you everywhere, which is why we are offering the eBook in 3 formats for only $10 if you have already purchased the print book.

Convenient and fully searchable, the PDF version enables you to easily find and copy code—or perform examples by quickly toggling between instructions and applications. The MOBI format is ideal for your Kindle, while the ePUB can be utilized on a variety of mobile devices.

Go to www.apress.com/promo/tendollars to purchase your companion eBook.